The Oxfordshire Light Infantry In South Africa: A Narrative Of The Boer War From The Letters And Journals Of Officers Of The Regiment And From Other Sources

Anonymous

THE

OXFORDSHIRE LIGHT INFANTRY

IN

SOUTH AFRICA.

A Narrative of the Boer War

From the Letters and Journals of Officers of the Regiment, and
from other Sources.

EDITED BY

LIEUT.-COLONEL A. F. MOCKLER-FERRYMAN.

London:

EYRE AND SPOTTISWOODE,

Government and General Publishers,

EAST HARDING STREET, E.C.

1901.

PREFACE.

A CONSIDERABLE part of this book has already appeared
in the OXFORDSHIRE LIGHT INFANTRY CHRONICLE for
1899 and 1900; but inasmuch as the CHRONICLE is
a somewhat expensive publication, and the number
of copies limited, it has been thought that a re-print
of the information relating to the doings of the Officers
and men of the Regiment in South Africa, supplemented with news up to the spring of 1901, will
be of considerable interest to the relatives and friends
of the soldiers of the Oxfordshire Light Infantry.

The book does not pretend to be a literary work, but
rather a plain straightforward tale told by those at
the seat of war; neither is it intended to be, in any
sense, a history of the Boer War, but, as its title implies,
the record of the part played by one Regiment in the
war—the work of a " fly on the wheel," perhaps,
though none the less worthy of being handed down
to posterity.   The general plan adopted has been to form
a foundation of extracts from the diaries of various
Officers, and on this to build up the narrative, with the

aid of portions of Officers' letters, and cuttings from the newspapers; while in some of the chapters are given the personal experiences of certain Officers of the Regiment who have returned from South Africa and have had time to write up their journals.

The scenes in South Africa are all from photographs taken by Regimental Officers, and we are indebted to Mr. J. Easden (formerly a Sergeant in the Regiment) for most of the portraits of the killed and wounded soldiers.

May 1901.

CONTENTS.

LIST OF ILLUSTRATIONS.

———

LIST OF ILLUSTRATIONS.

LIST OF ILLUSTRATIONS.

MAPS.

CHAPTER I.

INTRODUCTION.

THE causes which led up to the Boer War, the ultimatum sent to the British Government, and the eventual declaration of war by the Boer Governments, as well as the opening events of the campaign in the autumn of 1899, are too well known to require any notice at our hands. Suffice it to say that the mobilization of the 1st Army Corps commenced in the latter part of September, and the proclamation calling up the 1st Class Army Reserve was issued on the 7th October. The 1st Battalion of the Regiment, recently arrived at Devonport from Ireland, belonged (on paper) to the 1st Army Corps, and it was a bitter disappointment to all ranks to find that it was not mentioned in the mobilization order. The reason was, however, soon made known. Each Battalion required a certain number of Reserve men to bring it up to war strength, and (unlike what took place in 1882) Reserve men were only to be called up for duty with their own Regiments; consequently it was found that, owing to the weak state of our Regimental Reserve, it was impossible to complete the numbers of the Battalion. The reason why our Reserve mustered only some 360 men may be accounted for by tracing back the movements of the two Battalions for the previous fourteen years. In 1885 both Battalions were serving abroad—the one in India, and the other in Egypt. In 1886 the 2nd Battalion moved to India, and as the 1st Battalion was under orders for home early in

1887, reinforcements were not sent abroad for either Battalion, it being decided that the 1st Battalion should transfer to the 2nd, before leaving India, all men with a certain number of years' Army service to complete. The 1st Battalion came home at the beginning of 1887, transferring 310 men to the 2nd Battalion, and landing in England only 395 strong. The home authorities, aware that the Battalion would arrive in a weak state, formed a Provisional Battalion, which supplied the 1st Battalion on arrival at Shorncliffe with about 400 recruits, who had enlisted principally in 1885–86. Both Battalions were now well up to strength, and recruiting was therefore for some time checked. Under the existing system a man enlists for 12 years, 7 of which is supposed to be with the colours, and 5 in A, B, or C Sections of the Reserve, though from time to time this has been modified, so that (for instance) a man might be allowed to serve 5 years with the colours, and 7 in the Reserve. After completing his full Reserve period, the soldier has the option of being transferred to D Section of the Reserve for 4 years, this section not being liable for mobilization until all other sections have been called up.

From this statement of facts it will be seen that it was impossible to avoid a period when the Reserve would be below strength, because of the few men enlisted between 1887 and 1891; and this period of a weak Reserve unfortunately came at the most inopportune moment. By 1898 all the 400 men of the Provisional Battalion had completed their 12 years, and, except for a comparatively few transfers to D Section, had disappeared altogether; what Reserve remained therefore in 1899 consisted of men who enlisted in more recent years. The following shows the state of the 1st class Army Reserve of all ranks on the

Lt. Hon. G. W. F. S. Foljambe.   Lt. C. E. Forrest.   2nd Lt. H. L. Wood.   Lt. C. F. Henley.   Capt. G. N. Colvile.   Lt. A. G. Bayley.
2nd Lt. R. R. M. Brooke.   Capt. F. J. Henley.   2nd Lt. J. F. C. Fuller.   Lt. J. A. Ballard.   Lt. P. H. Stapleton.   2nd Lt. V. A. Ball-Acton.

Capt. E. A. E. Lethbridge.   Capt. and Adjt. C. H. Cobb.   Major R. W. Porter.   Major C. R. Day.
        Major G. F. Mockler.   Lt.-Col. Hon. A. E. Dalzell.   Capt. F. G. L. Lamotte.

30th September of each year since 1893 :—1893, 1015 ; 1894, 865 ; 1895, 663 ; 1896, 614; 1897, 567 ; 1898, 560. After 1898 came the decline, and when eventually the Reserve was called upon, in December 1899, it was only able to furnish a total of 361 men (excluding the few members of D Section).

All hope of going on active service was abandoned, and in November the Battalion moved to Aldershot, where it commenced to settle down to ordinary garrison duty, but within a week it became known that another Division was to be sent to South Africa, and on the 2nd December, to the satisfaction of everyone, there appeared a Special Army Order relating to the mobilization of the 6th Infantry Division, and calling out the Reserve men of A, B, and C Sections of the Regiments of the Division.

6TH DIVISION.

Lieutenant-General . .	Major - General (*local Lieut.-General*) T. Kelly-Kenny, C.B.
Aides-de-Camp . . .	Major H. I. W. Hamilton, D.S.O., Royal West Surrey Regiment.
	Captain W. H. Booth, East Kent Regt.
Assistant Adjutant-General	Colonel A. E. W. Goldsmid.
D.A.A.G.	Major C. C. Monro, Royal West Surrey Regiment.
	Major J. E. Caunter, Lancashire Fus.
Assistant Provost-Marshal .	Major M. G. Wilkinson, King's Own Scottish Borderers.
Principal Medical Officer .	Lieut.-Colonel W. L. Gubbins, Royal Army Medical Corps.
Divisional Signalling Officer	Lieut. J. T. Burnett-Stuart, Rifle Brig.

12TH BRIGADE.

Major-General .	Colonel (*local Major-General*) R. A. P. Clements, D.S.O., A.D.C.
Aide-de-Camp .	Captain H. de C. Moody, South Wales Borderers.
Brigade-Major .	Captain R. S. Oxley, King's Royal Rifles Corps.

Troops.

2nd Bedfordshire Regiment.   1st Royal Irish Regiment.
2nd Wiltshire Regiment.

13TH BRIGADE.

Major-General	.	Colonel (*local Major-General*) C. E. Knox.
Aide-de-Camp	.	Captain O. H. E. Marescaux, Shropshire Light Inf.
Brigade-Major	.	Captain R. W. Thompson, North Lancashire Regt.

Troops.

2nd The Buffs (East Kent Regiment).   1st West Riding Regiment.
1st Oxfordshire Light Infantry.

At a meeting of Commanding Officers held at the Brigade Office on the 6th December, Major-General C. E. Knox presiding, it was decided : —

1. *Dress.* - Khaki uniform of Officers to have the " stand and fall " collar, as it is not considered that it would make the coat at all conspicuously distinguishable from that worn by the men ; colour to be as nearly as possible identical with the men's.   No metal badges of rank to be worn, but Officers to have them in their possession.   The exact order as to distinguishing marks of rank to be awaited.   In the Mounted Infantry Companies, the Officers to wear putties of the same colour as the men's, and a bandolier.

2. *Equipment.*—Sam Browne belt ; it is considered somewhat difficult to make it less conspicuous than it is, but wearing the double brace would do so to a certain extent, as also staining it if new.   It is hoped that swords will not be carried further than the base, and that carbines will be substituted for them for dismounted Officers.   Experiments are now being carried out in the several Battalions as to the mode of carrying great coats by dismounted Officers, and the best pattern will be adopted.

3. *Horse Furniture.*—Regimental bit to be discarded, and a plain hunting (single or double) bridle to be worn, with the headstall. White head-rope to be discarded, its place being taken by ordinary knee-haltering gear made of raw hide, which had better be procured at Cape Town.   The ordinary hunting saddle is too large for colonial horses, and it is recommended that the panel saddle be taken.   Felt numnahs or blankets will be found most useful.   Saddle-bags may be carried.

4. *Warrant Officers.*—To be equipped as the Officers.

5. *Staff Sergeants.*—No alteration in regulation considered necessary.

6. *N.C.O.'s and Men.*—Belts and straps to have the pipeclay scraped off (which the G.O.C. considers sufficient).   The staining of haversacks will be at once proceeded with.   It has been noticed that the great coat,

when taken into action on the man's back, forms an excellent target when the man is lying down. Khaki covers to be provided regimentally for coats and mess tins.

7. *Distinguishing Badges for Battalions.*—For Officers and men, to be the shoulder-strap of the red serge, tacked over the pugaree on the left-hand side of the helmet (except in the case of the 2nd Gloucester Regiment, who will wear it behind). · Shapes to be as follows :—

  2nd East Kent Regiment (the Buffs) □

  1st West Riding Regiment ..   .. ◯

  1st Oxfordshire Light Infantry .. ◇

8. *Baggage.*—Must be distinctly labelled "To be left at base" or "Required on arrival," as the case may be.

It is important that if the Brigade is ordered to entrain directly for the front, the absolutely-necessary baggage to accompany each Battalion should be ready.

The order detailing the Battalion to form part of the 6th Division had no sooner been promulgated than telegrams and letters of congratulation poured in from all sides. Amongst the former we may mention three :—

"Good luck to you and a safe return.—4TH RIFLE BRIGADE."

"Best congratulations on departure for South Africa ; hope Regiment will have many opportunities of increasing brilliant record, and all return safe and well.—PAYNE, 15, Alva Street, Edinburgh."

"Hope you will kindly inform me when Regiment starts for seat of war, as I should like to send the men pipes and tobacco. I wish the Regiment every success in South Africa.—ROTHSCHILD, New Court."

The letters received by the Commanding Officer were innumerable. Field-Marshal Lord Roberts wrote as follows :—

"Allow me to congratulate you most heartily on getting command of the Battalion at such an opportune time, and please let all ranks know how glad I am that they have been selected for service. I feel sure they will worthily uphold the glorious traditions of the Old 43rd Light Infantry."

Then came offers of assistance in the way of warm caps and clothing for the men, and sums of money to

THE COLOURS OF THE BATTALION IN CHRIST CHURCH
CATHEDRAL, OXFORD.

purchase comforts for them in South Africa. An old 43rd Officer sent a cheque for £50, others sent smaller sums, but the most remarkable gift was one of twenty guineas from Mr. H. C. Lea, "late No. $\frac{Ox.}{2912}$ B Co.," who, in forwarding a cheque for the amount, wrote :— " It affords me great satisfaction to think that I am able to give my old Regiment something before it leaves for South Africa." The money received in this manner amounted to nearly £200, with which it was decided to form a Commanding Officer's Fund, for the purpose of assisting the men during the campaign.

Mobilization commenced on the 4th December, and during the week correspondence passed between the Officer Commanding and the Dean of Christ Church Cathedral, Oxford, relative to depositing the colours in the Cathedral during the absence of the Regiment. Dr. Paget most willingly accepted the trust, and on the 9th December the colours were duly escorted to Oxford. The following account of their reception is taken from the *Times* of the 11th December :—

THE OXFORDSHIRE LIGHT INFANTRY COLOURS.

An impressive service was held in Christ Church Cathedral, Oxford, on Saturday afternoon, on the occasion of depositing the Regimental colours of the Oxfordshire Light Infantry within the Cathedral, where they will remain whilst the Regiment is upon active service in South Africa. The colours were conveyed from Aldershot by an escort con- sisting of Captain Watt and Lieutenants the Hon. G. W. Foljambe and A. G. Bayley, three Colour-Sergeants, and about twenty rank and file. At Oxford Railway Station the Non-Commissioned Officers and men fixed bayonets, and, with the colours flying, borne by the two Lieu- tenants, they marched to the Cathedral, the men being greeted with repeated cheering throughout the route by the crowds which lined the streets. The Cathedral was thronged. Amongst those present were the Vice-Chancellor (the President of Corpus Christi) and many dis- tinguished members of the University, Lord Valentia, M.P., Mr. G. H. Morrell, M.P., Sir Henry Acland, the Bishop of Reading, the Rev. Canons Ince, Bright, Moberly, Sanday, and Driver. The Mayor and members of the Corporation, attired in their scarlet robes, walked in procession to the Cathedral. The Colour-bearers advanced to the chancel steps with the Colour-Sergeants, and the rank and file of the escort marched up the aisle and stood with fixed bayonets two deep behind the colours. The service commenced with the singing of the Old Hundredth hymn. The Colours were received by the Dean of Christ Church (Dr. Paget), who, standing on the chancel steps and holding a colour in each hand, said he accepted thankfully the trust with which the Regiment had honoured them. The Colours should be kept in the Cathedral with honour and reverence until they returned, please God, in safety—and God grant it might be ere long—to reclaim them. Meanwhile the colours would not be idle or without meaning, for they would know that they were there and guarded in this house of God and reverenced by them as by the Regiment. And they would be a constant help, helping them to make their prayers for the men very constant and very earnest, and helping also to keep before them the standard of duty and obedience and courage and soldierly loyalty, which was the secret of an honourable life, whether it be for soldiers or for civilians. He bade the men present and those they represented good-bye and God-speed. They were going to serve a Queen who loved her people and had never failed to do her utmost for their welfare and happiness. They were going to serve a country dear, most dear, to them, and of which they were all proud—a country that had ever held high the standard of honour and liberty and justice. God grant to them all to live day by day that they might not be afraid, if it be His will, to die, or to live that the fear of death might, please God, seem as nothing to them in comparison with the sense of duty. God be with them now and always. They all were in His hands, and might He in His love and mercy help them all according to their several callings to do His will. The short service was brought to a conclusion with the singing of the National Anthem, in which the large congregation very heartily joined.

After this interesting ceremony, Dr. Paget entertained the escort at the Deanery, and it is, perhaps, needless to say that his kindness and courtesy were much appreciated. In a letter addressed to the Commanding Officer on the following day, he wrote :—

Christ Church, Oxford,
December 10th, 1899.

DEAR COLONEL DALZELL,

I am grateful with all my heart for the very great kindness with which you have written to me. The trust with which you and

S 1300.   B those under your command have honoured us has stirred up a deep feeling here : many of us, I think, will bear in mind and heart a fresh sense of the link which binds us to the Regiment : and we shall be longing to hear of its welfare, and looking forward to its safe return, please God, with one more honour added to the long list already on its colours. And I hope that the trust which you have bidden us to keep for you till you come back will help us all, both young and old, to do our work with more of that high sense of duty which the Army sets before us.

I cannot tell you how greatly I have valued the privilege of bearing any part in the reception of the Colours, or how much I have been touched by the kindness which has attended their coming here.

Believe me to be, dear Colonel Dalzell,

With great respect and with all good wishes,

Very truly yours,

FRANCIS PAGET.

The 11th was the last day for the joining of the Reserve men (A, B, and C Sections), and up to midnight the Depôt presented a busy scene. Batches of men came in from the country towns, in all cases having received an enthusiastic " send-off " from their fellow townsmen.

DEPARTING RESERVE MEN.

A remarkable scene of enthusiasm was witnessed at High Wycombe yesterday, when a large number of men left to join the 1st Oxfordshire Light Infantry, which is the territorial Regiment of Buckinghamshire.. They were entertained at luncheon in the Town Hall, the Mayor presiding, and among those present was Earl Carrington, who, addressing the Reservists as a Buckinghamshire man, wished them good luck, God speed, a successful campaign, and a safe return. The troops, who were the recipients of many gifts, were played to the railway station by the volunteer band, the streets being crowded to an extent unequalled since the funeral of Lord Beaconsfield.[1]

The 12th at the Depôt was spent in clothing and equipping the men, and on the 13th the party left the barracks for Aldershot, under the command of Major G. F. Mockler (who had been ordered to proceed with the Regiment on active service). Oxford rose to the

---

[1] From the *Daily Graphic*, December 12th, 1899.

occasion, and all honour was done to the departing troops; the whole route from Cowley to the railway station was decorated with flags, and a dense crowd lined the streets and accompanied the men; while at the station a scene of the wildest excitement followed. The police were quite unable to cope with the surging crowd, who invaded the platform and bore the soldiers off their legs. In the course of time,. however, something like order was restored, and the men were entrained, when the Mayor, in his full robes, delivered a parting address, which was replied to by Colonel Strachan, commanding the Regimental District. A deputation from the ladies of Oxford then presented the Reservists with pipes and tobacco, and the train eventually steamed away amidst deafening cheers.

The date of embarkation was now fixed for the 22nd instant, and the intervening time was devoted to preparations, such as fitting the Battalion with khaki clothing, and equipping them for active service. A course of musketry was also commenced, but, owing to frost and snow, it had to be considerably curtailed. Captain K. R. Hamilton and Lieut. S. F. Hammick joined the Battalion from the Depôt. One Company of the Battalion (G), made up to a strength of 120 rank and file, under the command of Captain G. N. Colvile, was detailed for Mounted Infantry duty, and with similar Companies from the other Battalions of the 6th Division was temporarily formed into a separate command under Major F. J. Evelegh, to follow the Division when fully equipped and horsed. The officers' mess was broken up, the furniture stored in Aldershot, the plate and other valuables lodged with the Bank, official records sent to the Depôt, and all made ready for departure.

CHAPTER II.

ALDERSHOT TO CAPETOWN.

ON the 22nd December the Details, consisting of some 270 men under 20 years of age, or otherwise unfit for active service, proceeded to Limerick, under the command of Captain C. J. Wilkie, who was still suffering from the effects of illness contracted in the Tirah Campaign. On the same day the Battalion (660 of all ranks)[1] marched out of Aldershot, and leaving Farnborough by special troop train at 10.40 a.m., reached Southampton Docks before 1 p.m., when the men were at once embarked on the Union S.S. Company's twin screw, R.M.S. *Gaika*. The Southampton correspondent of the *Times* thus describes the departure of the troops :—

The business of to-day, which has been carried on in nasty and sloppy weather, has been confined to one vessel, the Union Company's *Gaika*. She is one of the Company's intermediate boats, and she carries passengers as well as troops. Moreover, she carried the troops as passengers and she is a comfortable boat. The sight of her as she left the old extension dock was distinctly inspiriting. A week ago I confess that the aspect of the rank and file of one particular Battalion left upon me the impression that we were getting to something like the dregs of the cup. But the look of the Royal Horse Artillerymen and of the Northumberlands yesterday went a long way to remove that impression, and the appearance of the two Battalions, which formed the main body of the passengers in the *Gaika* to-day, has caused it to vanish altogether. These Battalions were the 2nd Battalion East Kent Regiment (the Buffs), 881 strong, and the 1st Battalion Oxford Light Infantry. Both were in fine fettle and in good spirits, and to see and hear the ship move off with the band of the Buffs playing amidships was a noble experience.

[1] Major F. J. Evelegh, Captain G. N. Colvile, Lieut. C. E. Forrest, 2nd Lieut. R. R. M. Brooke, and 131 N.C.O's and men of the Mounted Infantry Company (G) to embark later.

Apart from officers, there left on board the *Gaika*, besides the two Battalions already named, four men of the 13th Brigade Staff, four of Post Office Corps, ten Military Foot Police, and 57 men of No. 7 Company R.A.M.C.; also three Warrant Officers, one to each of the principal Battalions and one to the Company of the R.A.M.C., and in all nine horses.

The officers were as follows:—1st Battalion Oxfordshire Light Infantry.—Lieut.-Colonel Hon. A. E. Dalzell; Majors R. W. Porter, G. F. Mockler, and C. R. Day; Captains F. G. L. Lamotte, E. A. E. Lethbridge, R. E. Watt, F. J. Henley, and K. R. Hamilton; Lieuts. S. F. Hammick, F. H. Stapleton, J. A. Ballard, Hon. G. W. F. S. Foljambe, C. F. Henley, and A. G. Bayley; 2nd Lieuts. H. L. Wood, J. F. C. Fuller, V. A. Ball-Acton, and G. A. Sullivan; Captain and Adjutant C. H. Cobb; Lieut. and Quartermaster W. Ross, 2nd Battalion East Kent Regiment.—Colonel R. A. Hickson; Major J. B. Backhouse; Captains A. R. Eustace, R. G. Marriott, F. W. B. Dynem, W. H. Trevor, and F. Godfrey-Faussett; Lieuts. E. H. Finch-Hatton, C. D. K. Greenway, C. A. Worthington, G. B. McRonald, H. H. C. Baird, and F. S. Firth; 2nd Lieuts. Greatwood and Houblom; Captain and Adjutant A. D. Geddes; Lieut. and Quartermaster G. Boon. Royal Garrison Artillery.—Captains Thomas and Pendergast. Royal Army Medical Corps.—Majors Pike, Geddes, and Fayle; Captain Chambers; Lieut. Rattray.

More important were the three officers of the 13th Infantry Brigade Staff — Major-General Knox, commanding; Captain R. Thompson, Brigade-Major; and Captain O. H. E. Marescaux, Aide-de-Camp.

Southampton had witnessed so many similar scenes during the previous weeks that enthusiasm on any great scale was hardly to be expected from the townspeople; moreover, the weather was wet, and the day cheerless; but old officers and non-commissioned officers came down in force to bid farewell to the corps, and the appearance of the Regiment drawn up in quarter-column for embarkation was commented on most favourably. Many of the officers and men were wearing the ribbon for the Tirah Campaign, and though numerically weak, there was a business-like look about each Company, which drew forth from an old embarking official the remark that in his opinion we were keeping back our best material till the last. At about 3.30 the *Gaika* got under weigh, and hearty cheers from those on shore followed her until the strains of the band died out and the vessel disappeared in the gloom. Of the past and present officers of the Regiment who assembled to bid farewell to the old corps, we may mention the following:—Lieut.-General F. Green-Wilkinson (Colonel of the Regiment); Lieut.-General F. M. Colvile, C.B.; Colonels Livesay, Money, Sir St. V. A. Hammick, Strachan, Johnstone, Powys, Cunliffe, and Williamson (four of whom had previously commanded the Battalion); Majors H. C. Talbot, F. A. B. Talbot, and H. Terry; Captains Parr, Luard, Darell - Brown, W. Owen, Sir C. Cuyler, Fairtlough, and Marriott-Dodington; besides Colour-Sergeant Lakin, and several old Non-Commissioned Officers and men.

Gifts of woollen caps and other warm clothing had been sent on board for the men by Mrs. Postlethwaite, the Regimental ladies, the ladies of Oxfordshire and Buckinghamshire, and many others; while Lord Rothschild and his brothers sent pipes and an ample supply of tobacco for the whole Battalion. Numerous farewell telegrams also were received by the Battalion before leaving, and it was felt by all that, if good wishes count for anything, the old 43rd should be crowned with good fortune.

EMBARKATION RETURN OF THE 1st OXFORDSHIRE LIGHT INFANTRY.

Embarked at Southampton in Hired Transport Gaika, and sailed for South Africa, 22nd December, 1899.

Letter of Company.	Officers.					Warrant Officers.	N. C. O.'s and Men.						Total embarked.	Officers' chargers.	Remarks.
	Field Officers.	Captains.	Subalterns.	Staff.	Medical Officer (attached).		N. C. O's, Class 16.	N. C. O.'s, Classes 17, 18, 19.	Buglers.	Corporals.	Privates.	Army Ordnance Corps.			
A	1	—	2	—	—	—	1‡	6	2	8	80	—	100		G., or the Mounted
B	—	1	2	—	—	—	—	5	2	8	76	—	94		Inf. Company
C	—	1	1	—	—	1†	—	6	2	6	72	—	89		(strength, 1 F.
D	—	1	2	—	—	—	—	7	2	6	72	—	90		O., 1 capt., 2 sub-
E	1	—	1	—	—	—	—	6	2	6	76	—	92		alterns, 4 sergts.,
F	—	1	1	—	—	—	—	7	2	7	71	—	89		2 buglers, 6 cor-
H	1	—	1	—	—	—	—	7	2	7	82	—	100		porals and 120
Staff	1	1	—	2	1*	—	—	—	—	—	—	1§	6	3	pvts.), remained at Aldershot to embark later.
Total	4	5	10	2	1	1	1	44	14	48	529	1	660	3	

* Major W. W. Pike † Sergeant-Major T. Pears.
‡ Qr.-Mas. Sergeant T. Ivey. § Sergeant T. Lewis.

1st OXFORDSHIRE LIGHT INFANTRY.

Increase and Decrease between the 1st and 22nd December, 1899.

(Excluding Officers and Warrant Officers.)

Increase.

Joined as recruit	1
From Army Reserve on mobilization	361
Tranfers from other Corps	1[1]
From Depôt	23
From 2nd Battalion	4
Promoted	16
Total increase	**406**

Decrease.

Deserted	1
To Depôt	24
To details (unfit for active service)	270
Promoted	16
Total decrease	**311**

Total effectives, 1st December	673
Total effectives, 22nd December	768
Embarked 22nd December	637
Awaiting embarkation (Mounted Infantry)	131
Wanting to complete Establishment	311[2]

[1] Master Tailor, from Hampshire Regiment.
[2] To be made up from D section Army Reserve Militia Reserve, and Details.

AT DUTY'S CALL.[1]

GOOD-BYE, ye Oxford redcoats !
   You're wanted far away ;
And may your bearing ever be
   As gallant as to-day.

You know we wouldn't lose you—
   We bid you to be gone
Because Old England needs your arms ;
   So onward, Oxford ! on !

May health and safety cheer you
   While riding on the waves,
And land you safe in Table Bay
   Among good Buller's braves.

May fortune's star attend you
   And guide you in the fight—
We know you'll stand up gallantly
   And battle for the right.

Although the snow is falling,
   And wintry is the scene,
Your hearts are warmly beating for
   Your country and your Queen.

They say you're " absent-minded "—
   But, be it false or true,
Old Oxford will remember, and
   Her heart will be with you.

And now away, ye redcoats,
   To Afric's sunny shores—
From Oxford to Pretoria,
   To tame the boasting Boers.

They're coming, " Uncle " Kruger !
   You'll soon be hearing from
The men who left their battle-flag
   Beneath Old Oxford Tom.

[1] From the *Oxford Times.*

DIARY OF THE VOYAGE.

December 23rd.—Fine morning, with bright sunshine. Sea smooth, though the boat rolling slightly. A few heads hanging over the side, but the majority of the men smoking hard at Lord Rothschild's much appreciated tobacco. Parade at 10.30 a.m.; men told off to fire stations. Food for all hands so far very good. Saloon accommodation for officers cramped, but otherwise good. Several civilian passengers on board—mostly for Teneriffe or St. Helena. Position of *Gaika* at noon, Lat. 48° 26', Long. 5° 29'. Run, 222 miles.

December 24th.—Fine morning. Parade at 10 a.m., and Church Parade at 11 a.m., at which Lieut.-Colonel Dalzell officiated. Position at noon, Lat. 44° 39', Long. 9° 46'. Run, 287 miles.

December 25th.—Parade at 10 a.m. The Commanding Officer went round the dinners at 1 p.m. The Christmas fare provided by the ship

BOARDSHIP DRILL.

for the men was excellent, consisting of roast beef, stewed rabbits, vegetables, and plum pudding, and there were no absentees at the mess tables, as the weather was bright and fine. At 6.30 p.m. the officers and passengers sat down to their Christmas dinner, which was of the best, with champagne at the expense of the Union S.S. Company. The toasts, after "The Queen," were "Sweethearts and Wives," given by Captain Strong (the commander of the ship), and responded to by General Knox, who then proposed the health of the officers and crew of the ship, for which the 4th Officer returned thanks. Dr. Bell (a passenger on his way to the Cape as a volunteer surgeon) next proposed the health of the General, Colonel Hickson (The Buffs), Colonel Dalzell, and the officers and men of both Regiments, General Knox again replying. After dinner our band played on deck, and the men danced and sang songs until 10 p.m., when "lights-out" was sounded. Position at noon, Lat. 40° 6', Long. 11° 50'. Run, 289 miles.

December 26th.—Another lovely day. Commenced physical drill. A concert on deck after dinner. Position at noon, Lat. 35° 23', Long. 13°. 35'. Run, 294 miles.

December 27th.—Half the officers and about fifty men in bed, having been inoculated against enteric fever ; others to be done in small parties every day. Position at noon, Lat 30° 37', Long. 15° 24'. Run, 300 miles.

December 28th.—Reached Teneriffe at 7 a.m. Landed about a dozen passengers, mostly invalids going to spend the winter at Orotava. The town of Santa Cruz, off which we anchored, was a dirty-looking place, and made dirtier by three or four days' rain before we arrived. There are two small forts close to the sea, mounting about ten guns each, with a small detachment of Spanish troops (Infantry and Artillery). A German training ship (the *Charlotte*) was in the roadstead, and a great many of her boats rowed round us during the day, but there was no cheering, or anything of that sort on either side. There was also a small French man-of-war in the port. Most of the officers went on shore, and, after coaling, we left again at 4 p.m.

December 29th.—Weather considerably warmer as we get south, necessitating a change of clothing. Parades and physical drill—first one Regiment, then the other—all day. Position at noon, Lat. 24° 23' N., Long. 17° 10' W. Run, 251 miles from Teneriffe.

December 30th.—Usual parades, fire alarm, etc. Position at noon, Lat. 19° 40' N., Long. 15° 50' W. Run, 300 miles.

December 31st.—Church Parade at 10.30 a.m., Lieut.-Colonel Dalzell taking the service. Passed the Union Company's S.S. *Gaul* at 4 p.m. ; she signalled no news, but as she must have left Cape Town before we sailed from England we did not expect any from her. Position at noon, Lat. 14° 29' N., Long. 18° 6' W. Run, 296 miles. So ends 1899, if not the century ; we hope to reach St. Helena this day week, and the one thought even now, is what news we shall hear—will Ladysmith have been relieved.

January 1st, 1900.—Weather fine but very hot ; troops went into khaki clothing. An outbreak of influenza on board, 30 men of the Regiment and 50 of the Buffs in hospital. Position at noon, lat. 93° 2' N. ; long. 17° 1' W. Run 305 miles.

January 2nd.—Influenza increasing. Very hot day ; rain in afternoon. Position at noon, lat. 4° 37' N. ; long. 15° 4' W. Run, 317 miles.

January 3rd.—Revolver match, Officers Oxfordshire Light Infantry *v.* Officers of the Buffs. Target : bottles hung at the end of a pole over

A GAME OF CRICKET.

the ship's side ; firing point, the gangway ; range, about 60 feet ; conditions, six a-side, six shots each. The result was a tie, each side securing six hits. The tie was then shot off, and resulted in a win for the Oxfordshire Light Infantry by one hit. Crossed the line about 2 p.m.—the furthest south that the Battalion has been since its return from New Zealand in 1866. Position at noon, lat. 0° 27' N., long. 12° 59' W. Run, 280 miles.

January 4th.—S.E. trade winds encountered ; much cooler. Influenza increasing, two serious cases. Position at noon, lat. 3° 46' S., long. 11° 18' W. Run, 272 miles.

January 5th.—Corporal Baxter dangerously ill with influenza. Position at noon, lat. 8° 10′ S. ; long. 9° 23′ W. Run, 288 miles.

January 6th.—Quoit handicap ; Musketry practice by Reserve men continued. Much cooler ; in serge clothing again.

January 7th.—Reached St. Helena at 9 a.m. Many of the officers went on shore, and visited the various points of interest connected with Napoleon's exile. Left the same evening.

January 8th.—Major Pike's charger died.

January 9th.—General Knox's charger died.

January 13th.—The *Gaika* arrived at Table Bay at midnight, the voyage from St. Helena having been without incident.

NEARING CAPE TOWN.

CHAPTER III.

THEBUS AND MODDER RIVER.

THE military situation in South Africa on the arrival at Cape Town of the Battalion may be summed up as follows :—

In Natal, Ladysmith was still besieged; General Buller's relief force, having met with a reverse at Colenso, had crossed the Tugela higher up at Potgieter's Drift, and was attempting to relieve Ladysmith from that direction. In Cape Colony, south of the Orange River, the British troops were on the defensive; the Boers, holding the river crossings, had invaded the Colony in considerable numbers, and had gained some minor successes. Kimberley was invested by the Boers, and Lord Methuen's force was held in check by the enemy in position about Magersfontein. Mafeking was still holding out, but with little prospect of being relieved; while a small force under Colonel Plumer was operating in Northern Rhodesia. The new plan of campaign had, however, been already worked out by Lord Roberts, who had arrived in South Africa a few days before the Battalion. Up to this, practically no head had been made against the Boers in any part of South Africa; they had invaded British territory on all sides, and so far we had been powerless to eject them. It was a great stroke of luck for the Battalion that it arrived at Cape

Town in the nick of time, and was enabled to take part in Lord Roberts' first successes—the most decisive operations of the whole campaign.

Diary continued :—

January 14th.—The *Gaika* entered the harbour at 9 a.m., and the troops disembarked at once, with orders to entrain for Naauwpoort forthwith. Several hours were spent on the quay sorting the baggage, which had been hopelessly mixed up by the ship's people, and eventually the troops had to go on without their baggage, which followed by a later train. The Headquarters of the Brigade and the Headquarters of the Buffs left Cape Town at 4 p.m., Headquarters Oxfordshire Light Infantry at 5 p.m., and the remainder at 10 p.m.

January 16th.—By 2.30 p.m. the whole of the Battalion had reached Naauwpoort.[1]

Extract from letter, dated January 17th, Naauwpoort :—

On arrival here we were told that General French (with his Cavalry Brigade and two Batteries R.H.A.) was out near Colesberg, and that General Clements (with three Battalions of his Infantry Brigade) had gone out to join him. Constant fighting on a small scale is going on, but it is too far away for us to see or hear anything of it. The country round this place is a stony desert, with rugged hills (kopjes) rising out of it—much more open than that to the south, through which we have passed. From what we can gather, the idea is that two Divisions will concentrate here, and an advance made *viâ* Norval's Pont, into the Free State. But one cannot say what will happen, as we get much less news here than you do in England. Anyhow I fancy, however things go, our Division will be well in it. We are likely to remain here a day or two, as we have not yet got our transport ; but, as soon as that arrives, we may be off any day, the first object of the concentration here being to drive the Boers out of our territory and over the Orange River. Then we shall have to get across, which I fancy will be a stiff job, as the river is rising daily, and is already quite unfordable. Our swords have been exchanged for carbines, and we are being equipped with buff belts, so that we may resemble the men as much as possible. Ruck Keene is at Colesberg, his Mounted Infantry Battalion being attached to French's force. Fanshawe is also

---

[1] *Vide* General Map, *Frontispiece.*

here in charge of a section of the railway line, and is constantly up and down seeing that the Volunteers guarding the various bridges and stations are at their posts and on the alert. It is very hot here, but of course nothing like the Punjab in the hot weather. Officers' kits have been cut down to 35 lbs., including bedding.

Extract from letter, dated Thebus, 26th January :—

We left Naauwpoort on the 24th January, and railed, *via* Rosmead Junction, to this place, the object of the movement being to repair the line from Rosmead to Steynsberg, and eventually (when

NAAUWPOORT STATION.

Gatacre has it) to Stormberg. Another reason for our visit to this part of the country is, that it is a hotbed of disloyalty (especially the Dutch farmers), and our Intelligence people are busy finding out who are absent from their farms, with a view to settling up with them later on. Our force here consists of ourselves, the Buffs, two field guns, and a Railway Company, R.E., the latter strengthened by a good many refugee railway men from the Free State and the Transvaal. We also have 150 of the 1st City (Cape Town) Mounted Infantry —a very fine lot. The journey from Naauwpoort to Rosmead was an ordinary one ; but soon after leaving the latter place, we picked up the

Mounted Infantry, who scouted on ahead of the train, while our Engineer Officers examined the bridges and culverts before we crossed. On arriving at this place, it was found that an iron girder bridge (span about 100 feet) was a good deal damaged; so we halted and pitched camp, and the Engineers are now repairing it. The work will take two or three days, as the occasional heavy rains bring down flushes from the hills, and the *donga* becomes a torrent, thus delaying the work. I believe that the gentleman who did the damage is known, as the head ganger, who was forced to bore the holes in the piers for the explosive, has split on him. He is a local farmer, and he and his family are away from home at present.

We saw a most revolting sight at one of the farms here yesterday—a deaf and dumb idiot chained up to a post in front of the house. The poor creature was filthily dirty, and apparently treated like a dog. From all accounts idiots are very numerous in the country, and they are always treated in this way; they are supposed to be the result of the in-breeding among the Dutch farmers.

AT THEBUS.

We officers have discarded Sam Browne belts, and badges of all sorts, and we now parade in exactly the same kit as the men, except that we carry a carbine instead of a rifle. The men still get excellent food, fresh provisions most days, including bread. Water is rather scarce, so there is not much washing done.

Our next move will be about eight miles further on, to a spot where another bridge has been destroyed; there we have a hope that we may

THE ADJUTANT AND OFFICERS' CHARGERS.

meet our first Boers, as it is more than probable that they will push forward a force from Stormberg to check our advance.

On the 30th January, while the Regiment was still at Thebus, sudden orders were received to strike camp and entrain. No destination was mentioned, but the trains conveyed the Regiment and the rest of General Knox's Brigade to Naauwpoort, De Aar, and eventually to Modder River. Each time the train stopped everyone imagined that the journey was at an end, but as it turned out, the troops did not leave the train for a day and a half.   The following is extracted from an officer's letter :—

We had a jolly journey, as you may imagine. No carriages were available, so we went in the ordinary open trucks, and ours (to make matters more pleasant) had carried coal on its last trip. What with the heat, the dust from the permanent way, and the coal dust, we were a nice-looking lot at the end of our thirty-two hours' journey ; anyhow it brought matters to a crisis, and I *had* to have a tub yesterday—the first for twelve days. (*N.B.* Water was a bit scarce at Thebus.) We are encamped here (Modder River) on the ground over which the Guards advanced during the fight. No wonder they lost heavily, for the country is perfectly flat and absolutely destitute of cover of any kind. The river flows about 800 yards to our north, and both banks still show traces of the Boer trenches, though most of them have been filled in, and the ground levelled for camping on. Across the river to the north is our Artillery position, and shells are fired into the Magersfontein position at frequent intervals, but the Boers do not reply now. At the present moment the balloon is up, and giving information as to aiming to our gunners. Our camp, being on the extreme south, is well out of the range of the Boer guns. Our Brigade should be complete this evening, when the West Riding Regiment comes in, and General Kelly-Kenny arrives to-morrow. Report also says that Lord Roberts is to be here very shortly ; if so, it looks like an advance into the Free State at once. The Kimberley searchlight was hard at work signalling all last night, but as everything was in cypher, of course we could read nothing. Hamilton has had to go into hospital with dysentery, and young Henley (C.F.) is still in hospital at Naauwpoort, so we are getting short-handed already, before seeing a shot fired. The usual daily dust-storm is just coming on.

Extract from letter, dated Modder River Camp, 8th February :—

We have had a week of inaction, though we have just got an order to be ready to move at a moment's notice, which way we have no idea, but we imagine it will be backwards. Lords Roberts and Kitchener are actually here now, and they rode round the outposts to-day. The Highland Brigade have been out for the last few days to the west (Koodoosberg), and apparently they have had a fight, as a convoy of wounded (about eighty) passed through our camp this afternoon. Dust, dirt, and picquet duty are the only excitements in camp, with an occasional shell from the naval guns into the enemy's camp, just to let them know that we are still here. The Regiment is wretchedly weak, under 600, and we shall be glad to get the draft which we hear is coming out. Hamilton is fit for duty again, and has been appointed Adjutant of Mounted Infantry. Private Turner was drowned while bathing in the river on the 4th, his body not being recovered until the next day.

AT NAAUWPOORT.

CHAPTER IV.

THE INVASION OF THE ORANGE FREE STATE.[1]

The presence of Lord Roberts and Lord Kitchener in Modder River Camp was at once taken as an indication that some movement of considerable importance was about to take place; nor was much time given for speculation, for on the 10th February the machinery was set in motion, and the great advance commenced. So secret was everything kept, that even when the troops had started, nothing had transpired as to the immediate objective.

Certain changes had taken place in the 6th Division, the 18th Brigade having been substituted for the 12th Brigade (Major-General Clements), which it had been found necessary to leave in the neighbourhood of Colesberg. The strength and composition of the Division was as follows :—

6TH DIVISION.

In Command . . .	Lieut.-General T. Kelly-Kenny, C.B.
Aides-de-Camp . . .	Captain Booth, The Buffs; Captain Maurice, Derbyshire Regiment.
Assistant Adjutant-General and Chief Staff Officer .	Colonel A. E. W. Goldsmid.
D.A.A.G.'s . . .	Major C. C. Monro, The Queen's, Major J. E. Caunter, Lancashire Fusiliers; and Major Webb, Army Service Corps.

---

[1] *Vide* Map, page 86.

Commanding Royal Engineers	Lieut.-Colonel Buston.
Commanding Royal Artillery	Lieut.-Colonel McDonnell.
Principal Medical Officer .	Lieut.-Colonel W. L. Gubbins, Royal Army Medical Corps.
Medical Officer . . .	Major Skinner.
Assistant Provost-Marshal.	Major M. G. Wilkinson, King's Own Scottish Borderers.
Signalling Officer . .	Captain J. T. Burnett-Stuart, Rifle Brigade.
Chaplains . . .	Rev. F. Norman-Lee, and Rev. J. Blackburn.

13TH BRIGADE.

In Command . . .	Major-General C. E. Knox.
Aide-de-Camp . . .	Captain O. H. E. Marescaux, Shropshire Light Infantry.
Brigade-Major . . .	Captain R. W. Thompson, Loyal North Lancashire Regiment.

Troops.

2nd The Buffs (East Kent Regiment) .	Lieut.-Colonel Hickson, 18 officers, 786 N.C.O's and men.
2nd Gloucestershire Regiment . .	Lieut.-Colonel Lindsell, 23 officers, 716 N.C.O's and men.
1st West Riding Regiment . . .	Lieut.-Colonel Lloyd, D.S.O., 23 officers, 789 N.C.O's and men.
1st Oxfordshire Light Infantry .	Lieut.-Colonel the Hon. A. E. Dalzell, 20 officers,[1] and 598 N.C.O's and men.

---

[1] Names of the Officers :—Lieut.-Colonel. Hon. A. E. Dalzell (commanding) ; Major R. W. Porter (2nd in command); Capt. C. H. Cobb (Adjutant); Lieut. W. Ross (Quartermaster); Lieut. A. G. Bayley (Transport Officer); Major W. Pike, R.A.M.C. (Medical Officer). A Company : Lieut. Hon. G. W. F. S. Foljambe, 2nd Lieut. G. A. Sullivan. B Company : Capt. F. J. Henley, Lieut. C. F. Henley. C Company : Capt. E. A. E. Lethbridge, Lieut. S. F. Hammick, Lieut. F. H. Stapleton. D Company : Capt. R. E. Watt, Lieut. H. L. Wood. E Company : Major G. F. Mockler, Lieut. L. F. Scott. F Company : Capt. F. G. Lamotte, 2nd Lieut. V. A. Ball-Acton, H Company : Major C. R. Day. Lieut. J. F. C. Fuller commenced the march, but was invalided on Feb. 11th.

18TH BRIGADE.

In Command .	.	Major-General T. E. Stephenson.
Aide-de-Camp .	.	Lieut. Howard, Essex Regiment.
Brigade-Major .	.	Lieut. Pratt, Essex Regiment.

Troops.

1st P.W.O. Yorkshire Regiment	Lieut.-Colonel H. Bowles, 21 officers, 953 N.C.O's and men.
1st Welch Regiment . .	Lieut.-Colonel Banfield, 23 officers, 875 N.C.O's and men.
1st Essex Regiment . . .	Major F. Brown, 23 officers, 936 N.C.O's and men.

BRIGADE DIVISION, R.A.

76th Battery	Major Harrison.
81st „	Major Chapman.
82nd „	Major Pratt.

ROYAL ENGINEERS.

38th Field Company . . .	Major Roper.

Although we are only concerned with the movements of the 6th Division, a better understanding of these will be arrived at by knowing something of Lord Roberts' general plan, which can best be described by quoting at length from a valuable article that appeared some months afterwards in the *Times* :—[1]

It was obvious that Bloemfontein would be the object of the Field-Marshal's move. There were three lines open for an advance upon this objective, each of which had railway communication, at least as far as the frontiers of the Orange Free State. A meaner strategist than Lord Roberts might have chosen the more direct line. An advance to either Norval's Pont or Bethulie would have had the advantage of clearing Cape Colony of the enemy before the counter-invasion was undertaken. Such an advance would doubtless have raised the siege of Kimberley and have lessened the pressure in Natal. But the enemy, destroying his railway, would have had a very strong line of defence in the Orange River, and even when driven from it, no doubt at heavy cost, would have fallen back, unbroken in *moral*, to gather again to oppose in strength the subsequent advance. Lord Roberts's strategy was more

---

[1] See also extracts from *Lord Roberts' Despatches*, Chapter XIX. of this book.

comprehensive and far-reaching. Rather than clear Cape Colony, he purposely weakened his line in front of Colesberg and gathered his strength for the decisive blow which, with one stroke, would relieve Kimberley, place the British forces in command of a direct road in favourable country upon the Free State capital, scatter the enemy, and automatically influence the pressure in Cape Colony and Natal. That the scheme necessarily included the capture of Cronje and his force is perhaps giving it too comprehensive a standard. But Lord Roberts was at least justified in expecting from it the capture of some of the guns

AN UPSET ON MODDER PONTOON BRIDGE.

and other *impedimenta* of the force investing Kimberley as the latter broke away to the north or west. Besides, when Lord Roberts decided upon his line of advance, he could not have known that Cronje would select the line of the Modder River for his retreat. If this had been certain the Cavalry would never have been sent into Kimberley. The Field-Marshal's first object was to maintain as many as possible of the enemy in Cape Colony and to keep Cronje at Magersfontein. With great secrecy the Cavalry Division was withdrawn from the neighbourhood of Colesberg, to join the army of 40,000 men which was concentrating between the Modder and Orange rivers.   Then a demonstration was made to Koodoosberg against Cronje's right, and by February 11, one month after his arrival in South Africa, Lord Roberts was able to set in motion the great strategical mvement which was to prove the turning-point in the war.   It must have been an anxious moment when the mounted force, under General French, was launched into the arid plains of the Western Free State.   Its duty was to cut the communication with Bloemfontein of the force investing Kimberley, and to hold the drifts over the Modder and Riet rivers until the Infantry, which had concentrated at Ramdam and was following the mounted men by forced marches, could establish themselves in the positions which the Cavalry had won.   The move was successful ; the Modder River drifts were captured on February 13, and Kimberley was entered two days

CROSSING THE MODDER.

later.   Cronje had been hoodwinked by the simple strategy of the demonstration against his right and by his conviction that British Infantry could never march away from the line of the railway.

PAARDEBERG AND BLOEMFONTEIN.

The characteristic of Boer strategy has been that they have always done the unexpected. Instead of retreating to the north with the whole of his force, Cronje, when on February 15 he raised the siege of Kimberley, sent part of his force north, and with the remainder made a dash for Bloemfontein, stealing a passage between the British Cavalry and the advancing Infantry. General Kelly-Kenny, commanding the Sixth Division, was the senior officer at Klip Drift, but Lord Roberts had relegated the control of operations in this part of the field to Lord Kitchener. With admirable promptitude Lord Kitchener stopped the movement on Kimberley and made the whole force wheel to the right after Cronje, simultaneously advising the Cavalry by the field telegraph. Luck was with the British arms, for though Cronje managed, by skilfully set rearguards, to ward off the attacks of the Mounted Infantry with the Sixth Division, yet the Cavalry, by a forced march from Kimberley, succeeded on February 17, only by a few minutes, in seizing the Koodoosrand Drift by which Cronje had intended to cross the Modder, and in heading him back on Wolveskraal Drift, three miles further down. The next morning he prepared to cross, but the Sixth and Ninth Divisions, under Lord Kitchener, had already come up on the south bank, and at once attacked. The attack was only partially successful, and the price of the attempt to reduce Cronje before he was intrenched was a heavy list of casualties. This action has been much criticised ; but it should be remembered that when it was made it was not known how far French's Cavalry had rendered escape for the Boers impossible—the situation of the baggage caught in the act of crossing the drift offered an opportunity of striking a heavy blow under conditions considered favourable for British attack. Moreover, everything pointed to the presence of Boer reinforcements in the vicinity. The exact whereabouts and strength of these reinforcements was unknown, consequently as a military precaution it was expedient to effect the reduction of Cronje's position in case the outside force should be in a position to succour him before the British cordon was complete. Although the action was not so well developed tactically as it might have been, it had the effect of so crippling Cronje that he was unable to effect a further movement. Lord Roberts arrived in person at Paardeberg on the day following the unsuccessful attack. This attack and the loss of a valuable convoy at the Riet River on February 15 were the only incidents which marred the complete success of Lord Roberts's first move. Cronje surrendered unconditionally on February 27. As a strategical move, the advance against Cronje's communications had been fraught with even more success than Lord Roberts could have anticipated. The automatic reduction of pressure in Natal and Cape Colony, which it was designed to effect, was complete. General Buller, after some of the severest fighting in the war, was able to drive back, on the same day that Cronje surrendered, the force with which Louis Botha held the Tugela, and the siege of Ladysmith was raised on the following day. Grobler and Olivier fell back, under telegraphic orders from President Steyn, from their positions in Cape Colony almost without an effort on the part of Generals Gatacre and Clements to dislodge them. And such was the haste with which these withdrawals were effected, that very little damage was done to the direct railway communication between the Free State Capital and the Colony.

Extract from letter, dated Klip Drift, Orange Free State, 15th February, 1900 :—

We left Modder River Camp at 10 p.m., 10th February, and railed to Enslin, where we slept the night in bivouac near the railway station. We have left all our tents at Modder, and have little in the way of kit—officers 50 lbs. On the 11th we halted at Enslin, waiting for the rest of the troops, and early on the morning of the 12th we marched to Ramdam, about eight miles. The Regiment was on rearguard, and no incident whatever occurred. The country was open and level. Reached Ramdam about 11 a.m., the 18th Brigade marching in from Graspan Station at about the same time. From the look of things every one now thought that we were bound for Bloemfontein, but we were told nothing. Lethbridge and Henley went on with their companies as escort to a large convoy, and marched all night to Riet River.

On the 13th we started at 5 a.m. for Waterval, on the Riet River, about 11 miles. Flat country, which had been recently burnt ; put up any number of hares and koran. The whole Division marched together, consequently it was a long and trying march, with constant halts and checks. We halted for an hour or so, some four or five miles after starting, at the only water to be got during the day. Arrived at Riet Camp at 1 p.m., the whole Division done to a turn (from heat and want of water), and the men made for the water and drank from any stagnant pool. No baggage reached the drift until quite late in the afternoon, and it had hardly arrived before we received orders to continue the march at 1.30 a.m. next morning to a camp near Jacobsdal, about 12 miles. Bright joined us to-day, and Foljambe was sent back sick.

On the 14th we marched at 1 a.m., and after going five miles halted till daybreak, as there were dangerous hills on either side of the route,

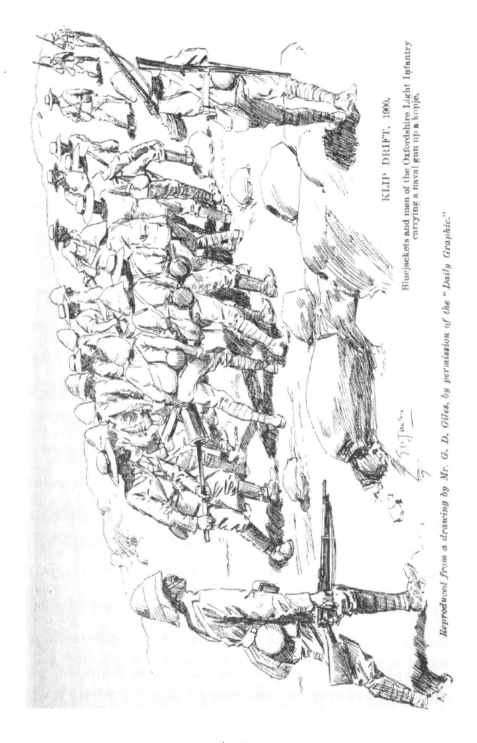

KLIP DRIFT, 1900.

Bluejackets and men of the Oxfordshire Light Infantry
carrying a naval gun up a kopje.

Reproduced from a drawing by Mr. G. D. Giles, by permission of the "Daily Graphic."

necessitating careful reconnoitring by the Mounted Infantry. Resumed the march at 6 a.m.; but progress was slow, and the men took advantage of the frequent halts to get a nap. Reached Wegdraai Drift at about 10 a.m., and at noon the outposts were suddenly attacked by a party of Boers from Jacobsdal. We all stood to our arms, but nothing much happened, and the enemy was driven off by the picquets. We now imagined that we were to have a rest, but at 2 p.m. we got orders to be ready for a start at 5.30 p.m., and at that hour we were off again for a drift on the Modder. We were told that we had to go eight or ten miles and that we should be in by 10 p.m., but it was not until 1 a.m. this morning (15th February) that we halted. It was a wretched march, made worse by two drenching showers, and as we heard that the Boers were in possession of the drift that we were making for, we changed our direction during the night. We had covered nearly 30 miles in the 24 hours; the men were wet through, had marched in intense heat during the daytime, and practically without water, but they stuck to it to the end, when they dropped to the ground and slept like logs. The Battalion had only ten men out of the ranks when it halted. Want of water is, and must always be, our greatest trouble; we are only allowed one 100-gallon cart for the Battalion, and those of us who have served in India long for the good old *bheestie*, who never failed us.

Lord Kitchener has been with us during the last two marches, and the object of the forced march was to relieve French (who had seized two drifts at Rondeval and this place) and allow him to push on to the relief of Kimberley. We crossed the river soon after daylight and bivouacked, and when French knew that we had done so and were in possession of the drift, he moved ahead. Mockler and two companies went as escort to two long 12-pounder naval guns, and had a tough bit of work helping to get the guns in position on a rocky kopje. Eventually the sailors pulled their guns to pieces (in the good old Military Tournament way), and then the sailors and soldiers carried them bodily up to the top, receiving considerable praise from Lord Kitchener, who was present. The guns were soon in action and making excellent practice, shell after shell being pitched into the retreating Boers as they were galloping full tilt towards Magersfontein. We could hear French hard at it about a couple of miles away, his 42 R.H.A. guns and our three Field Batteries shelling the 3,000 or 4,000 Boers out of their laager. Mockler's two Companies remained with the naval guns until about 1 p.m., by which time French had got clear, and we hope he is now well on the way to Kimberley. I expect we shall be on the move again to-morrow early. Lots of mutton and beef here, as this move of ours has been a bit of a surprise to the Boers, and they went

off in a hurry, leaving their stock behind on the farms. No meat is
issued, but we send out parties, take what we want, and slaughter it
ourselves, so, as you can imagine, the regulation one pound is not
weighed very carefully.

FIELD BAKERY.

CHAPTER V.

THE FIGHT AT KLIP KRAAL.

General French, with his Cavalry Division, had successfully forced his way through the Boers, who had been in two laagers—about four miles and ten miles respectively from our outposts. Early on the 16th, it was discovered that, during the night, the laagers had been evacuated, and that Cronje was in full retreat towards Bloemfontein. The pursuit was at once taken up by the 6th Division, the 13th Brigade, 81st Battery, and a portion of the Mounted Infantry marching along the north bank of the river, the remainder of the Mounted Infantry along the south bank; while the 18th Brigade held the drift and furnished the outposts north of the Modder. Commandant Roos commanded the Boer rearguard throughout the day, and so ably that he succeeded in checking General Knox's advance, though only (as it afterwards turned out) at the sacrifice of the main body of Cronje's force. Roos held his own until darkness set in, and played considerable havoc with Knox's Brigade, but the delay proved fatal to Cronje's chance of escape.

Diary :—

16th February, Friday.—The Brigade paraded at 3 a.m., with orders to reinforce the outpost line, as a large force of Mounted Infantry were to go ahead to Kimberley, and we were if necessary to protect their flank or await orders. The Mounted Infantry were fired on as soon as they moved out on to the veldt. The Brigade advanced to the right flank, in extended order. The Boers had taken up a position on some kopjes [1] overlooking the river. We (43rd) were on the right flank and river bank ; the Buffs, on our left, moved up towards the kopjes, where there was a good deal of firing. We (43rd) then forded the river, and marched along the other bank, two Companies on the bank itself, the remainder across the open. Boer fire pretty heavy. After we had got across the open, we hit off the bend of the river again, crossed it at a drift, and found that the Boers had cleared off the kopjes. They left two or three wagons, which were looted and then burnt.

The Brigade re-formed in extended order, and commenced the advance to a big kopje (Klip Kraal), on to which the Boers had retired. We (43rd) were on the right, and moved round under cover of a ridge to the right of the kopje. Lethbridge's and Bright's Companies (C and A) were on the extreme right, keeping well away to that flank, but, as they had not a blade of cover, they had eight or nine casualties before going far, and were soon obliged to halt. D Company was on the left of the firing line, and Mockler's Company (E) and half F (in support) halted in echelon, a little to the left rear of A and C, and by lying flat managed to keep fairly under cover behind a low ridge, but any man who moved was immediately blazed at. E and half F fired fifty or sixty rounds from where they were at the Boers on the kopje, about 1,000 to 1,200 yards away. The Boers continued firing the whole day, in spite of the two guns that we had shelling them. The other half of F Company was escort to the guns, and H Company was in reserve.

By 3.30 p.m. it seemed evident that our frontal attack was not likely to succeed, and men were dropping fast. E Company had already lost Private Yerby killed and three wounded, but the men were so done up for want of water and lying in the broiling sun that one or two at a time were sent back to the river (about half a mile in rear) to fill water bottles. They drew a heavy fire, but fortunately there were no casualties. At 4 p.m. Lethbridge and Bright decided to retire to the river, as their men had run out of ammunition and had no water, moreover their position was so exposed that they were suffering severely. E and half F followed A and C to the river, several of the wounded having to be left behind for the time being, as the stretcher bearers could not be brought up. The retirement was the signal for a fierce Boer fusillade, but no one was hit (why, heaven only knows). We had been lying under fire from 8 a.m. to 4 p.m., and the men, when they reached the river, were completely fagged out.

The remainder of our Companies worked round towards the left with the Buffs and West Riding Regiment, but the Boers were not *turned*

---

[1] North of Drieputs.

out of their position (which was practically impregnable), though they evacuated it after dark. We imagined at first that the kopje was only held by a few of the enemy, but we found out afterwards that we were opposed to the whole of Cronje's rear-guard.

The Brigade bivouacked for the night behind a low ridge facing the kopje.

Result as far as we were concerned :—Stapleton (in charge of the Maxim) wounded in the thigh, 10 men killed and 39 wounded ; while the Colonel had a bullet through his helmet, and Day had his field-glasses smashed.[1] The Battalion fired 16,645 rounds.

Another Account :—

Extract from a letter from Lieut.-Colonel the Hon. A. E. Dalzell :— Much, of course, is not mentioned by the press, and it is a pity that no correspondents were present at Klip Kraal, which was by far the hottest affair we have yet had. The men behaved very well here, and it was practically our own little show, for the other Regiments of the Brigade took but a minor part in the action. It was quite early in the morning when we advanced against the Boers, composed of from 2,000 to 3,000 of Cronje's men, and we were the right Regiment of the Brigade, having the river on our right. Lord Kitchener was very anxious to get some men across the river, but it was supposed to be impassable, as the enemy held a very strong position along its bank (at the bend which ran across our right flank, about a mile in front), from which they were already peppering us ; Knox, our Brigadier, came up to me, and said, " I'm afraid it's no good, but if you could get over the river anyhow we might best them." I ran along the bank, searching keenly for some possible place, and had at last determined to try and swim the Regiment over. Porter tried at one place, sank up to his armpits in the muddy bottom, and convulsed me with laughter. Suddenly, I saw a rock protruding from our bank, which I argued, probably pointed to a bit of rocky bed, and so it proved, enabling us all to wade across, up to our middles only. I sent word back to Lord Kitchener that we were across, and that I should advance at once unless he ordered otherwise. When we were all over (Stapleton got his Maxim across very cleverly), I extended two Companies across the open country, as a blind, whilst I

---

[1] As an instance of *esprit de corps*, the following incident, recorded by Major Caunter, D.A.A.G., 6th Division, is worth quoting:—" After the Klip Kraal fight I came across a wounded man of the Oxfordshire Light Infantry, and inquired about his wounds and condition. His reply was in the form of a question as to *how the Regiment had behaved in action*—showing that the uppermost thought in the soldier's mind was the well-being of his corps."—ED.

sent three Companies up the river bank amongst the trees and bushes, Porter and I running backwards and forwards to encourage the men, the fire by this time having become fast and furious. Porter and I both very nearly got bagged here, and I felt quite sorry for Porter on one occasion when a bullet missed me by a hair, throwing up all the dirt into my mouth as we lay side by side in the open. Porter said, " Hullo, Colonel ! " as if he had almost felt the promotion in his grasp ! Well, we crept up successfully, and regularly turned the Boer's right, so that they bolted, leaving some wagons, horses, and other loot in our hands. Meanwhile the West Riding had been working along our left, on the other side of the river, and when we crossed at the weir, we met their advanced Company.

We continued our pursuit, and the Boers retired to a very strong position on a kopje, from which we tried (aided by some guns) to turn them out. The fight went on until dark, and was certainly the warmest entertainment at which I ever wish to assist. Some of our Companies crept right up to the foot of the kopje, and were within 150 yards of the enemy. With two other Companies I tried to work round and turn their flank ; but there was no flank to turn, for a flank attack upon a kopje becomes of necessity a direct or frontal attack. The men behaved capitally, and so did the officers. I look back now with wonder at how anyone escaped. Personally I had advanced with Bright, who was in command of A Company, and we were right up in the firing line at the foot of the kopje. He *would* sit up and keep looking at the Boers (though he was not more than 150 yards from them), and I kept telling him to lie down. When I found that the firing line could not advance any further, the fire being simply deadly, I told him to remain where he was, and that I would go back to the support and see if I could not make a diversion. The thing was *how* to get back to the support across a perfectly open fire-swept zone. However, it was no use looking at it, and the Regiment was waiting for further orders, so I said good-bye to Bright, and just turned round and bolted for the support (about two hundred yards back, behind a small rise). I had not gone six yards before a regular deluge of lead came down upon me, one bullet going through my helmet, and another carrying away my right shoulder strap. But I bested them, and got back—*only*, I am sure, by the goodness of Providence, and then sent Henley to work up the river bank and draw off the fire from the firing line, which he did very well.

In the meantime, Watt managed to get back with his Company and direct the Major of the Battery where to concentrate his fire. We were the only Regiment engaged until quite late in the afternoon, when the West Riding and Buffs managed to get up. Poor Stapleton was shot

S 1300. D

through the thigh as he sat by my side, lamenting that he could not get his Maxim into action. After dark we searched for our dead, and found ten, besides many wounded. The Boers all bolted in the night, and made off for Paardeberg.

Diary continued :—

February 17th.—Marched early morning ; after four miles halted to cook some food, the men being given live sheep and goats. Crossed the river, moved on another three miles, halted for an hour, and then did another seven miles (which we had been told would be three). Halted and bivouacked a little after midnight.

OFFICER IN FIGHTING KIT.

CHAPTER VI.

PAARDEBERG.

Telegrams from Lord Roberts :—

Jacobsdal, Feb. 16.

I have good reason for belief that the Magersfontein trenches have been abandoned, and that the Boers are endeavouring to escape.

French is scouring the country to the north of Kimberley.

One of Kenny's Brigades of Infantry is in pursuit of a very large Boer convoy moving towards Bloemfontein.

Jacobsdal, Feb. 17, 5.50 a.m.

Kelly-Kenny's Brigade captured yesterday 78 wagons laden with stores, two wagons with Mauser rifles, eight boxes full of shells, ten barrels explosives, and large quantity of stores, all belonging to Cronje's laager, which was still being shelled by our Artillery when Lord Kitchener despatched the messenger.

Telegrams through Reuter's Agency :—

Riet River, Feb. 14.

General French left Modder River on Sunday morning for Ramdam, 12 miles to the east of Enslin, where the whole Division concentrated next day. He made a rapid march to the Riet River, where a party of Boers contested his passage at the Dekiel and Waterval Drifts. General French shelled the enemy for some hours, and drove them away; and, crossing the river yesterday, continued his march to the Klip and Rondeval Drifts on the Modder.

Here again there was a short engagement. The enemy were again vigorously shelled and forced to retire precipitately, leaving five laagers in our hands, together with a great quantity of cattle and 2,000 sheep.

The rapidity of his march, and the overwhelming nature of his force enabled General French, in spite of the difficulties of water and transport, thoroughly to outwit and surprise the enemy.

During General French's movement the enemy were watching the Orange River, from which a Brigade of Mounted Infantry under Colonel Hannay was marching towards Ramdam. This force met on Sunday a body of 500 Boers with two guns, and were obliged to engage them in order to allow of the passage of our convoy. The Boers held a kopje which practically commanded a short valley along which the convoy was bound to pass. The fighting lasted the whole day, the Boers bringing up two guns in the afternoon. There appears to have been hard fighting. Our men approached within 200 yards of the Boers.

During the fight an unpleasant incident occurred. Our extreme left lay under cover unperceived, but the enemy suspected its presence. According to a description which I have received from an officer who was present, the Boers sent out an ambulance practically for the purpose of discovering our whereabouts. The officer commanding parleyed with the Boer doctor, and, according to my informant, an agreement was made that half a Company of our men should be allowed to go and get water from a farmhouse in the neighbourhood. The ambulance then retired, but had no sooner done so than the enemy rushed down and cut off the water party, of whom the officer in charge and about ten men were made prisoners.

During the night our convoy continued its journey in safety, the Boers having disappeared after nightfall.

We now hold both the Modder and Riet rivers between the Boers intrenched at Magersfontein and their base at Bloemfontein.

Everywhere the farms of the Free Staters have been respected, but the owners in almost every case had fled, taking their effects with them.

The health of our troops is excellent, and their spirits buoyant. Sickness prevails among our horses.

Outside Jacobsdal, Feb. 15.

Yesterday a small Cavalry patrol entered Jacobsdal, which they found full of wounded, including several of ours from Rensburg. The Boers sent back a patrol and occupied the town in small force. A series of skirmishes ensued. To-day a Battery of Artillery shelled the environs and drove out the Boers. The enemy, in order to escape, were obliged to pass over a ridge, where they afforded a splendid mark for our guns, which poured a shower of accurately directed shrapnel upon them in rapid succession.

Jacobsdal is now in our possession.

The Boers have left Alexandersfontein, which is now occupied by the garrison.

Lord Roberts is in excellent health and spirits. Rapid marching and the unavoidable hardships of the advance appear to agree with the whole Army, which is in splendid spirits, and is greatly cheered and encouraged by the presence and leadership of its Commander-in-Chief.

Jacobsdal, Feb. 15.

To-day Lord Roberts, at the head of the troops, entered Jacobsdal, which has been in our possession since yesterday.

The utmost order prevails. Military police patrol the streets, and nothing has been taken. At each store a sentry is placed, and soldiers are allowed to enter and purchase what they want. The inhabitants express the utmost surprise at this, for they had been told that the British, when they entered a town, always looted the place. As soon as the impression produced by these reports had been removed, the towns-people welcomed us as friends and not as enemies. The Landdrost offered to retire, but was not allowed to do so.

From conversations I have had with different inhabitants, there can be no doubt that the Free State burghers are heartily sick of the war. They freely declare that President Steyn betrayed them.

The town since the battle of Modder River has been empty of troops, and has been regarded strictly as a hospital. The large German hospital remains in beautiful order, and is clean and sweet. Here the wounded of both sides receive equally careful attention from the doctors. Colonel Henry, who was taken prisoner on the 14th, was found slightly wounded in the hospital with several others.

I have had many talks with the Boer wounded. They confess that they were nonplussed by our movements. Even now they are under the impression that the sole object of our march was the capture of Jacobsdal, and when informed that Kimberley had been relieved they were taken aback.

News has been received that the Boers are leaving Magersfontein. The strategic movements of Lord Roberts have puzzled and scared the enemy, who are stated to be returning in disorganized masses to their farms. In any case the invasion of the Free State has struck a tremendous blow at the enemy, and one which, without too much optimism, may be regarded as likely to result in the defection of a considerable proportion if not of all of the Free State burghers.

February 16.

The troops of General French's Division were received at Kimberley with extraordinary enthusiasm. The officers dined last night at the Kimberley Club.

As the result of yesterday's fighting on the Riet River the Boers captured the convoy, which was a large one. Our casualties, in view of the tremendous bombardment, were very slight. Fewer than 30 men were wounded, and only one man was killed.

The news of General French's entry into Kimberley has greatly cheered the troops, who are working splendidly.

The Boers are reported to be leaving Spytfontein in a north-westerly direction.

Cronje, with 10,000 men, is in full retreat towards Bloemfontein. General Kelly-Kenny is fighting a rear-guard action, and is harassing his retreat.

9.45 p.m.

Owing to the fatigue of his oxen, General Cronje was obliged to outspan and form a laager with his uncaptured wagons. When the report was despatched, at a quarter to seven this evening, our Artillery was vigorously shelling Cronje's laager.

Later.

Now that Lord Roberts's great strategic movement has been crowned with success, it is possible to give some details of the achievement.

The Mounted Troops and Horse Artillery in four days covered a distance of 90 miles, fought two small engagements, and finished by relieving Kimberley. The rapidity of their movements helped to solve one of the problems of the war, and will enable us now to disregard Boer intrenched positions wherever the country permits of Cavalry movement.

The movement began on Sunday morning at three o'clock by the concentration of General French's Division at Ramdam. As the Infantry appeared in sight early next morning, General French moved forward and seized two drifts on the Riet River. General Tucker's Division followed, and close behind came General Kelly-Kenny's Division. The drift was almost impassable for the transport, which was obliged to park on the south side of the river ; but energy and perseverance overcame all obstacles. It was found impossible for a team of mules to draw its load up the steep north bank, and it therefore became necessary to run relays of oxen, which were hitched on in addition to the mules, and thus the loads were dragged over. At four o'clock next morning most of the transport was on the north side of the river.

Lord Kitchener accompanied General Tucker's Division, which marched to within three miles of Jacobsdal, being obliged to keep to the river on account of the water. Here the Division stayed till the arrival of General Kelly-Kenny, who then moved straight towards Klip Drift on the Modder. General French, who was awaiting the Infantry there, left for Kimberley immediately on the arrival of the Division.

Thursday night saw the completion of the movement.

Lord Methuen was opposite Magersfontein, and General Tucker held Jacobsdal, with General Colvile's Division close at hand, ready to move wherever required, and General Kelly-Kenny's holding the Klip and

Rondeval Drifts on the Modder. General French had meanwhile arrived at Kimberley.

General Cronje had thus been completely outflanked, and the position of the Boer army at Spytfontein was untenable. Starvation or retreat was the only alternative. The Boer commander chose the latter, and at the moment of writing we are uncertain whether it is his whole force which is retreating *via* the Modder to Bloemfontein or only a portion of it, while the rest is going away to the north of Kimberley. According to the latest reports, General Kelly-Kenny is pressing hard on Cronje's rearguard, following him and harassing his retreat.

There are three points to be noted in connection with the movement—viz., General French's mobility, the efficiency of the transport arrangements, and the splendid marching of the Infantry.

1. It has been proved that a large mobile force is able to move on exterior lines with sufficient rapidity to completely outflank the Boers, although they are themselves so wonderfully mobile. The effect of General French's march upon the enemy has been sufficient to move them out of a strong, indeed, almost impregnable position which they had been preparing for two months. So far, the relief of Kimberley has not cost us 50 men.

2. The transport arrangements have been beyond praise. The long marches were made across a veldt of deep sand, without water. Progress was necessarily slow, and four Divisions had to be fed while they were purposely cut off from their base. It is hardly possible to adequately appreciate the marvellous work accomplished by the transport department under such conditions. Added to all the work of the day was the duty of issuing stores during the night, so that the Transport Officers toiled continuously. This they did with the utmost cheerfulness, and without the slightest fuss they everywhere evolved order out of chaos.

3. The marching of the Infantry, considering the great heat and the absence of water, once more proves that the British soldier is willing and ready to respond to any call. The men never faltered. Some fell out of the ranks from sheer exhaustion ; but these, as soon as they had sufficiently recovered, seized the first opportunity to rejoin their Companies. It was, perhaps, a finer sight than any battle to see the Battalions moving through the heavy sand under a broiling sun, every man determined, persevering, and cheerful. Not a murmur was heard, and the whole force was animated by a grand faith in their Commander. It is no exaggeration to say that nearly the whole of the troops, horse, foot, and artillery, and especially the transport service men, had not more than three hours' sleep on any of the last three nights. Yet there is no

sign of any falling off in their health or strength. All are willing and cheerful, and ready and anxious to do all that men can do.

February 17.

General Kelly-Kenny is still pursuing General Cronje's army. He has captured over 100 wagons and a German ambulance. The prisoners state that if the pursuit is continued, the whole force will probably surrender.

The Highland Brigade last night made a forced march from here, and, arriving to-day at General Kelly-Kenny's headquarters, joined in the pursuit. General French left Kimberley, moving rapidly in order to complete the interception of the Boers, who are in full retreat. He is harassing them terribly.

According to Dutch reports received here, General French twice charged home through the retreating Boers to the north-west of Kimberley.

General Pole-Carew and the Guards Brigade occupy Magersfontein, the Boer former position.

The Boer laagers have been deserted everywhere, and a great quantity of stores, tents, &c., has been taken.

The repairing of the railway is proceeding.

Later.

.The enemy are fighting a good rearguard action. They are occupying successive kopjes in order to allow the moving of the convoy, which, however, is forced to go at a slow pace, as apparently the animals are dead beat. The last reports show that the Boers are in the neighbourhood of Klipkraal's Drift, and that they are undoubtedly disheartened.

The shelling of the Boers is still proceeding vigorously.

Telegram from the *Times* Special Correspondent :—

Modder River, Feb. 18, 11.40 a.m.

The following is a summary of the movements of the army since Monday.

The Cavalry Brigade, under General French, left Honeynest Kloof on Monday, crossed Dekiel's Drift on Tuesday, and captured Klip Drift and Drieput Drift on the Modder River. On Thursday he moved on Kimberley, 10,000 strong, and fought two engagements at points distant 18 miles and four miles from Kimberley.

The Sixth Division left the Modder on Monday, Enslin on Tuesday, Waterval on Wednesday, and Klip Drift on Saturday morning for Klip Kraal. The Seventh Division came through Dekiel's Drift. The Ninth Division arrived at Klip Kraal on Friday.

The rearguard of General Cronje's force, with 1,000 wagons, in full retreat, was attacked at Klip Drift and Drieput, where the kopjes were held, the battle lasting all day. General Knox's Brigade distinguished itself under the direction of Lord Kitchener. This is probably the beginning of a rearguard fight all the way to Bloemfontein. Our casualties are few.

Two of the enemy's laagers have been captured, both having been evacuated with the utmost haste. A telegram from the Boer commandant was found complaining that the Boers were completely caught.

One day's delay in relieving Kimberley would probably have meant surrounding the whole Boer force.

We are at present harassing the rear with all the Infantry and with the Cavalry, which have returned from Kimberley.

Jacobsdal was captured after a short fight on Wednesday afternoon.

Magersfontein and Spytfontein were evacuated on Thursday evening.

At Kimberley the greatest enthusiasm prevails. Provisions are being pushed forward.

The whole conception of Lord Roberts's scheme was excellent. The block at Dekiel's Drift, which was almost impassable to wagons, delayed the operation a day, otherwise all the movements were carried out exactly to time.

No Boers remain west of Drieput kopje, where the whole of the Sixth Division is still fighting the retreating Boers. The naval guns pushed forward to-day outrange the Boer gun used to cover the retreat. The great exertions of the Boers are hampered because their ox wagons are overworked.

The well-known mobility of the Boers has now vanished.

The City of London Imperial Volunteers came into Klip Drift camp to-day. The troops are eager to move forward.

It is doubtful when I shall be able to send my next message, as I shall have to rely on the field telegraph.

Telegrams through Reuter's Agency :—

Paardeberg Drift, Feb. 20.

On Sunday the British forces fought one of the most costly actions of the war near here. General Kelly-Kenny's Division, which was advancing in pursuit of the retreating Boers under General Cronje, caught up the enemy's rearguard at Klip Drift and followed up the Boers to where they were in laager at Koodoosrand Drift.

The action began at daybreak, when the Mounted Infantry drove the rearguard up the river towards the main body, while another detachment of the Mounted Infantry manœuvred on the right front and flank of the enemy. Our main body, which was on the north bank of the river, advanced to outflank the Boers. Their laager was likewise on the north bank.

General Kelly-Kenny, having seized the two drifts, found the enemy, who was enclosed, and ordered his men to attack. In the advance to attack the Highland Brigade was on the left, and the Brigade under General Knox in the centre and on the right, while General Smith-Dorrien's Brigade crossed the river and moved along the north bank.

Both on the north and south banks the ground was level, and the advance across it was deadly. Our losses were heavy.

The battle was an almost exact replica of Lord Methuen's action on the Modder. The soldiers were under fire for the whole day, but all the fighting left the position unchanged. The Boers were enclosed and remained enclosed.

Our guns shelled the laager vigorously, and the Boers confessed to a loss of over 800.

On Monday the shelling—the combined fire of 50 guns—was resumed with increased energy, and to-day General Cronje has written to the British Commander asking for an armistice.

Later.

Cronje's magnificent night march from Magersfontein, though successful at the beginning, now appears likely to end in disaster.

The main body of the enemy are enclosed in a veritable death-trap. They are hiding in the bed of the Modder, commanded by our Artillery and enclosed on east and west by our Infantry.

Sunday witnessed a gallant stand by the retreating enemy, who, tired, weary, and harassed, still showed a bold front to the British force.

It is somewhat difficult to explain Sunday's action, in which all our force was engaged, and in which Cronje, although in difficult circumstances, managed to hold his own.

On Saturday night the Mounted Infantry came in touch with Cronje's rearguard, driving back the main body.

On Sunday morning our men renewed the action, but the Boers had intrenched themselves in the bed of the river during the night, and prevented the further advance of the Mounted Infantry in this direction.

Meantime the Highland Brigade, comprising the Seaforths, Black Watch, and Argyll and Sutherland Highlanders, advanced from the south bank, while the Essex, Welch, and Yorkshire Regiments closed in in a long line, the left of which rested on the river, the Welch Regiment occupying the extreme right.

The whole line was ordered to envelop the enemy, who lined both banks of the river. Firing soon became heavy. The Boers, holding a splendid position, commanded the left of the Highland Brigade, which advanced partly up the river bed and partly in the open. While the other Regiments swung round to the front, the Highland Brigade, on level ground destitute of cover, were exposed to a terrible fire, which obliged the men to lie prone. This they did for the rest of the day. The fighting began at 7.30 in the morning, and through dreadful heat and a terrible thunderstorm, the men hung on to their position, answering the enemy's fire and shooting steadily.

Meanwhile, the rest of the Infantry performed their enveloping movement, the Welch Regiment succeeding in seizing the drift, and thus completing the envelopment of the enemy, who fought throughout with splendid courage.

Cronje's laager, full of carts, wagons, ammunition, and stores, could be plainly seen near the north bank.

General Smith-Dorrien collected a large body of men, including the Canadians, crossed the river by Paardeberg Drift, and advanced towards the laager, which shelled them vigorously. Here the body made a gallant attempt to charge into the laager, but failed. The enemy, before seizing the western drifts, had occupied a kopje on the south bank of the river, and running down to its edge. Our force was, therefore, cut in two. The enemy holding the kopje possessed one Vickers-Maxim, and probably one or two other guns.

Towards evening the battery on the south side opened fire, co-operating with the battery on the north side. A wonderful sight was then to be seen. The shells fell with remarkable precision along the river bed, forcing the enemy back until they reached the bed of the river opposite the laager, which was shelled thoroughly, everything it contained being damaged. One shell set fire to a small ammunition wagon, and many other wagons were burnt. The Infantry kept up a terrible fire, which was answered vigorously. The whole scene towards nightfall was terribly picturesque, wagons were blazing, and the roar of artillery was mingled with the crackle of the Infantry fire.

Paardeberg, Feb. 20.

With the fall of night on Sunday the fire suddenly ceased. Both sides were thoroughly tired and glad of a rest. The men slept where they had fought all day, while the bearer parties scoured the field, collecting the dead and wounded. The action was one of the most fiercely contested in the history of the war, the Boers fighting desperately for their lives, while the British slowly and doggedly pressed their attack.

Our Mounted Infantry did good work throughout the day. The Highland Brigade fought steadily and sternly, though the men were much worn out. The behaviour of the whole force was excellent. By evening the cordon round the enemy had been completed, and every outlet had been closed. After nightfall almost perfect silence prevailed.

A few of the enemy came in during the night. They all confessed that they were sick of fighting, and had been urging Cronje to surrender.

During the battle the 81st Field Battery, which was engaged on the north side of the river, was exposed to a heavy rifle fire. Four horses were wounded, and the pole of one of the wagons was broken. The struggling, terrified horses inextricably mixed the trace ropes, and the position looked serious. The Gordons, however, who formed the escort, silenced the enemy's fire, and enabled the wagon to be withdrawn.

The men suffered terribly from thirst, and it was impossible to supply them with water. A heavy thunderstorm which broke over the battle-field in the afternoon considerably relieved their sufferings.

Lord Kitchener was present with the force during Sunday's fighting. General MacDonald, of the Highland Brigade, was wounded in the foot, but not severely.   Later.

Monday morning broke, finding the enemy in the same place. During the night they had constructed intrenchments round the laager, which was still threatened by General Smith-Dorrien's force. The Infantry rested after their terribly hard day's work yesterday, but the Mounted Infantry and a Battery of Artillery started to observe the enemy's position on a kopje. As they were riding round the southern side of the hill a heavy fusillade was directed against them by the Boers on the kopje, and they were obliged to move further out. There were no casualties, thus affording another proof of the enemy's bad marksmanship.

Pushing on they found that the kopje extended a considerable way to the west, and sloped gradually to the plain. A good defensive position was seized and garrisoned. The remainder of the force continued the movement, and completely turned the enemy's position, on the extreme left of which a farmhouse was strongly held. The battery vigorously shelled this, and the force returned to camp at nightfall, leaving the garrison on the ridge. Meanwhile a desultory bombardment of the Boer position had been proceeding, and there had been a good deal of rifle fire at one point where the Essex Regiment attempted to push up the river.

About midday a cry of " French has arrived " passed down the ranks, but the Cavalry Division operated out of sight of our force. Lord

Roberts arrived later, and addressed several Regiments. He was vigorously cheered.

Early in the day Cronje asked for a twenty-four hours' armistice in order to bury his dead. Lord Kitchener refused to comply. A little later came another message to the effect that if the British were inhuman enough to refuse an armistice for the purpose of allowing the Boers to bury their dead, General Cronje saw no other course but to surrender. Upon this Lord Kitchener proceeded to the Boer laager, in order to arrange for a capitulation, but he was met by a messenger who stated that the whole thing was a mistake. General Cronje had not the slightest intention of surrendering, but would fight until he died.

Lord Kitchener therefore returned to camp and ordered a bombardment of the enemy's position. The 18th, 62nd, and 75th Field Batteries and the 65th (Howitzer) Battery took up a position directly in front of the laager, and began a terribly accurate fire, the howitzers using lyddite freely. The Boers were seen retiring to their trenches in the river bed to seek cover, but no cover could protect them from such fire. The howitzers especially dropped lyddite shell with marvellous precision in the very bed of the river, and the trenches were soon filled with the green fumes from the explosive.

During the night deserters again arrived in camp. They were frightened and terribly shaken. They stated that the Boers had water in abundance, but only very scanty supplies could be drawn from the laager during the night.

To-day (Tuesday) is the third day of Cronje's imprisonment and stubborn resistance. Early in the morning the Infantry engaged the enemy in the bed of the river, driving them back a short distance. The morning sun disclosed the Boers working like ants on their intrenchments round the laager. A few shells were fired to prevent this. Most of the day passed quietly. We heard General French's artillery to the east, presumably engaging the Boer reinforcements.

Every opportunity was given to the enemy to surrender, but when, towards the afternoon, they still gave no sign of doing so, Lord Roberts determined to crush Cronje's resistance once for all. On the south bank he placed in position at a range of 2,000 yards the 18th, 62nd, and 75th Field Batteries, and two naval 12-pounders; and on the north bank, enfilading the whole of the river bed, the 65th (Howitzer), 76th, 81st, and 82nd Field Batteries and three naval 4·7 in. guns.

Then followed the most wonderful scene it has ever been my lot to witness. Once before, in Thessaly, I have seen 110 guns in action, but never such a number of powerful guns concentrating their fire on a spot about a mile square. The lyddite shells raised great clouds of green smoke, which filled the bed of the river, while shrapnel burst along the edge of each bank, except for a small space where the proximity of our Infantry would have made the Artillery fire dangerous to them. Our shells searched every bush and every ravine on the river banks. The enfilading guns must have done terrible execution ; yet in a spirit of desperate madness now and again a Boer would attempt a "sniping" shot at one of the naval guns, which were firing at a range of only 1,000 yards.

On each side of the river lay two Battalions, the whirring of whose Maxim fire sounded pretty by the side of the deafening roar of the big guns. What loss the Boers suffered is not yet known.

I am writing in the middle of the sleeping camp. Not a sound disturbs the heavy slumber of the tired soldiers. Down in the river bed not a fire is to be seen nor a cry heard.

February 21.

The fourth day of General Cronje's fine defence of the Boer laager opened in a startling manner. Soon after dawn a terrific rattle of rifle fire broke out, waking everybody. Information came that the Gloucestershire and Essex Regiments had lost their way and bivouacked in error close to the Boer laager on the north side of the river. When they were perceived, the enemy opened a heavy fire upon them. Wonderful to relate, our casualties were practically *nil*. The incident proves again what our soldiers have always contended—that the Boer shooting is bad.

Desultory firing continued on the north and south banks of the river, General Knox's Brigade holding the containing lines on the south side, while General Smith-Dorrien on the north worked towards the laager.

General French had meanwhile advanced far in an easterly direction, and approached a kopje which was held by a strong force of Cronje's men reinforced by a contingent from Ladysmith, while General Broadwood's Brigade, with a Battery of Horse Artillery, was on the left and rear of the same kopje. The front of the hill was thoroughly searched from every side. Suddenly, the Boers bolted in the direction of General French, who headed them towards the drift, shelling them vigorously. A great number escaped, but many were killed by shrapnel, while about 50 prisoners were taken.

As soon as the kopje was evacuated I visited the position, which is one of wonderful natural strength, and really forms the key of the fighting area in case we have to defend ourselves against the enemy's reinforcements advancing from the east. The first contact of the Boers from Ladysmith with our force was thus singularly unfortunate for them. A quantity of forage, provisions, and equipment fell into our hands. Frequent marks of blood showed where the wounded and dead who had been removed had fallen. The Boer method of taking away the dead is to tie two reins round the body, which is then carried off at full gallop by two horsemen.

Several *pourparlers* passed between us and the enemy during the short armistice in the middle of the day. It appears that Cronje is willing to surrender, but that the young Transvaal Boers refuse to give in. The rest of the beleaguered force are said to be anxious to surrender.

One of our doctors, who visited the Boer lines to see the wounded, found the trenches near the river full of them. He also saw many dead.

A deserter who came in last night states that yesterday's bombardment was deadly and terrible in its effects, the howitzers especially battering the river bed with an enfilading fire. The position, nevertheless, remains the same. The Boers are strengthening their intrenchments round the laager, but their case is hopeless.

The capture of the kopje which we effected to-day has given us a splendid position, and will prevent any relieving force from marching to join hands with Cronje.

To-day Lord Roberts sent a message to Cronje offering a safe-conduct for the women and children, and a free pass anywhere. He also offered a loan of doctors and medicine. General Cronje's reply was a curt refusal, and desultory shelling followed.

February 22.

The scene of the last five days' fighting is one of the prettiest spots in South Africa. The river where General Cronje is ensconced and fighting for his life resembles parts of the Thames. The ground all round slopes towards the river. All the higher ground is covered with our Artillery, so that General Cronje is faced, front and rear, on both banks by our men, while General French's Cavalry, operating far from our flanks, prevent any sudden inrush of Boer reinforcements.

The Shropshire Regiment occupied the bed of the river from Sunday till to-day. Yesterday the Artillery continued firing till dark. During the night, after the last gun had been fired, the Shropshires rushed forward and seized nearly 200 yards of the new ground, where they spent the remainder of the night in intrenching themselves. As the Shropshires ever since Sunday had been under a galling fire and had done good work, they were to-day relieved by the Gordons.

In the course of our Artillery fire last evening, the mules of the 82nd Battery, which remained hitched to the carriages, were startled by a sudden discharge, and the whole of them stampeded and galloped off, but to-day all except one wagon have been recovered.

General French has sent in 75 men whom he had taken prisoners, while a patrol eight miles to the west has captured 30 Boers found wandering away.

Altogether this force has taken 460 prisoners, while numbers of Boer dead have been seen.

The prisoners all comment bitterly on General Cronje's persistence, which they say is simply murder. They are extremely depressed by the course the war is now taking, and by our refusal to attack their strong positions.

To-day a German ambulance attached to the enemy was allowed to pass through our lines from Jacobsdal.

We have captured large quantities of cattle, sheep, and trek oxen which had wandered from the Boer laager.

February 23.

Yesterday afternoon there was a terrible thunderstorm, accompanied by rain. During the night our guns fired several rounds. The position of General Cronje is now more hopeless than ever. We are gradually closing in on all sides.

In last Sunday's fight the Canadians, who were heavily engaged, behaved with great gallantry.

Colonel Martyr has been appointed to command a Brigade of Mounted Infantry.

From the *Times* special correspondent :—

Paardeberg, Feb. 23.

The cordon around General Cronje is being daily drawn a little closer.

To-day the Gordon Highlanders pushed up a distance of 200 yards of the river bed, beyond the point gained by the Shropshire Light Infantry on Wednesday night.

In the afternoon a balloon ascended from the river west of the Boer laager.

Meanwhile, General Cronje's investment is rapidly drawing the Boers together from every quarter, and several thousands are now hovering in the neighbourhood of Paardeberg. At half-past five o'clock this morning, 50 of the 9th Lancers on Poplar Farm were attacked by 500 Boers with a Vickers-Maxim gun. The Lancers, supported by a Battery of Artillery and a Squadron of the 12th Lancers, succeeded in keeping the enemy at a distance.

At the same time a large force made a very determined attack on the south-easterly kopje captured on Wednesday, which is now known as

Kitchener's Hill, and is held by the 1st Yorkshire Regiment, and drove in the picquets. The Yorkshires, who were under good cover, held the position till they were supported by the King's Own Scottish Borderers and a Battery of Artillery from the east. By 10.30 most of the Boers were routed. The Buffs, working round to the west, surrounded and captured the remaining 87 Boers, including two Field Cornets and one Commandant belonging to the Johannesburg and Heidelberg commandos, who had just come from Ladysmith, which place they left four days ago.

Through Reuter's agency :—

February 26.

This is the eighth day of General Cronje's resistance. General Smith-Dorrien's Brigade has now worked up the river bed to within 300 yards of the Boer laager.

Our stay here is in no way due to Cronje. Supplies and rest for the troops had become absolutely necessary. The daily arrival of large convoys now allows full rations to be given to the men. During the past three days heavy rain has fallen intermittently, causing great discomfort to our troops, but still greater discomfort to the Boers. The cold winds which sweep across the veldt have killed many sick animals. Last night the river rose, bringing down a great number of Boer dead and horses.

When the history of Lord Roberts's movement comes to be written, it will be found that the marching power and endurance of the British soldier are as great as ever. The distance covered, according to the map, seems nothing very marvellous; but it must be remembered that the whole original plan of the march was changed when General Cronje made his dash from Magersfontein. The whole army immediately swung to the left in hot pursuit. Some Regiments marched 27 miles in 24 hours, outstripping the transport and supplies, and living for days on almost quarter rations. The hardships and fatigue were borne with wonderful cheerfulness.

The troops have been lying fully exposed to the drenching rain of the last three days, and the terribly cold winds at night have severely tried them. They have borne all with admirable patience.

Last Monday afternoon the Gloucesters approached within a short distance of a Boer kopje and contained the enemy until nightfall, when 120 men charged the kopje with the bayonet and drove off the Boers with loss. The positions taken were evacuated during the night.

Diary continued :—

February 18th.—Moved off at 3 a.m., without food or water; after a little there was some brisk firing on our right front, when the 6th and 7th Divisions and the Highland Brigade extended. The Boer laager was now sighted across the river, and our Artillery set to work to shell it, soon setting some wagons on fire. We now advanced towards the river, which was held in a sort of semi-circle by the Boers. We got into action at about 8 a.m., and pushed on as far as we could under cover of the ant-hills. Bullets came dropping in most unpleasantly, and soon fell in storms. The left flank moved down to the river, where there was absolutely no cover, and of course suffered terribly, though they reached a point within about 400 yards of the laager.

The enemy was intrenched on the opposite bank of the river amongst trees, and could not be seen, so that it was quite impossible to turn him out, even if the river could have been crossed, and the fire was kept up all day. Fortunately their Artillery fire was ineffective, as their shells did not burst, but their "pom-pom" was rather a nuisance, and their rifle fire throughout the day was like the independent firing preliminary to the final assault on a good old Aldershot field-day. We were under it for nearly twelve hours, without food or water. The casualties in the Regiment were heavy; Bright and Ball-Acton were

SERGEANT E. LUDLOW
(One of the Wounded).

shot dead, Day mortally wounded, Hammick shot in the leg, Watt shot in the shoulder by a Martini bullet, which passed along under the skin of his back and out at the other shoulder, while F. J. Henley had the skin of his leg carried away by a bullet, and Porter escaped by a veritable hair's breadth, a bullet grazing the left side of his head just above the ear. Of the men, 6 were killed and 26 wounded. At dusk all firing ceased, and we all moved back and bivouacked for the night. The Battalion fired during the day 17,260 rounds of ammunition.

February 19th.—Up at daybreak, having had hardly any sleep, owing to the cold. Moved to two different bivouacs, and then to a third, where we remained. Lords Roberts and Kitchener rode by and inspected our Brigade, being loudly cheered by the men. At 3 p.m. it was announced in camp that the Boers had surrendered; the men cheered, threw their helmets into the air, and there was wild excitement. However, after about three-quarters of an hour, we heard our guns hard at work again, as some of the Boer wagons had been seen to be on the move : and it turned out that ,there had been some mistake about their surrender, as Cronje had sent in to say that he had no intention of doing anything of the kind.

The Regiment paraded in the evening, and moved off with the object of driving the Boers from a kopje two or three miles away. We joined the Gloucesters on the way, and then advanced, ourselves working round to the right, the Gloucesters on our left. We were hotly peppered from the kopje, and had five or six casualties in the Regiment. The Gloucesters captured the lower kopje (at the foot of the big one) and occupied it until 3 a.m., when they were ordered to evacuate it, as Lord Roberts did not consider it safe with the Boers in possession of the higher kopje. We were ordered to return to camp when darkness came on ; but by 1.30 a.m. we were hopelessly fogged as to our whereabouts, and the men were so done up, that we halted and went to sleep on the veldt.

Colonel Dalzell writes :—

On the 19th February—the day after the battle of Paardeberg—I was sent out in command of a small Brigade of ourselves, the Gloucesters, the Yorks, and a Battery, to try and capture a kopje (five miles off) known as " Kitchener's Kopje," on which the Boers were intrenched. We did not start until 6 p.m., and my great fear was that I might lose my force, or some of it, in the dark. I sent the Regiment round to the right to try and get at the Boers' left, whilst I attacked with the Gloucesters in front and Yorks in support. The Gloucesters worked uncommonly well, and got up in spite of a pretty heavy fire, and the Boers retired to a higher hill behind. After being under fire from 7 a.m. until dark the day before, the amusement had begun to pall, and I was glad to get off with only nine men killed. Six men of the Regiment were wounded—two mortally.

Diary continued :—

February 20th.—Got up at 4.30 a.m., and marched a mile to the Brigade bivouac, very hungry and thirsty, as we had had no food or water since 5 p.m. yesterday.

At 3 p.m. the whole of the troops paraded, and the Infantry took up a position along the ridge facing the laager ; guns in front ; the Cavalry advanced across the plain on the other side of the river ; while the Howitzer Battery and two naval guns got into position. The idea was to make a demonstration of the whole force. The guns shelled the laager till nearly dusk, and the Infantry nearest the Boers opened fire. The Regiment returned to camp, but went out again later on, and bivouacked for the night in rear of the naval guns. Everyone put on half rations from this date, owing to the loss of a convoy at Waterval Drift.

February 21st.—Returned to camp in the morning, but went out again and took up the same position, and remained there all night.

February 22nd.—Bivouacked on the outpost line day and night. Kitchener's Kopje, which we had captured but again evacuated on the 19th, and which was still held by the Boers, was surrounded by our Cavalry and taken, and then occupied by the Yorkshires. The possession of this kopje completed the cordon round the Boer position. In the morning French drove back a force of the enemy, killing 150 and capturing 90. One man of the Regiment was hit while going to the picquet line. Heavy thunderstorm at about 5 p.m. Six men of the Gloucesters were struck by lightning, not a hundred yards from our bivouac; one was killed, and the others badly injured; they were all lying under a cart containing lyddite! A flag of truce went to the Boer lines, to suggest the removal of their women, but Cronje refused to allow them to leave the laager. A salvo of all the guns was fired at night into the enemy's position.

February 23rd.—Remained in camp for the morning. The enemy from outside tried to capture Kitchener's Kopje, and the Buffs and the Scottish Borderers, who went out to help the Yorkshires, had a very smart little fight, capturing 71 Boers and a lot of horses. F. J. Henley and his Company escorted 85 prisoners to Klip Drift. Terrific thunderstorm at 6.30 p.m., just as we were going on picquet; everyone soaked; then another on the way out at 7 p.m.; and again a third in the night. All the trenches well filled with water. The river rose tremendously in the night, and more than a thousand dead horses from the laager were seen to float down. The Boers kept up a steady fire from their trenches during the night.

February 24th.—Returned to camp at 5 a.m., all very wet and played out. The guns fired occasionally during the day. Lord Kitchener left for Naauwpoort. We are sapping towards the laager by the river, and are already within 400 yards of the Boer trenches. The Regiment went on picquet at 6.30 p.m., and passed a miserable night of almost continuous rain, lying in two or three inches of water in the trenches.

February 25th.—Back to camp at 5 a.m. Boers not doing much shooting this morning (possibly because it is Sunday); occasional rain during the day, but a fine night for a wonder. Took up our usual picquet line at 6.30 p.m. Heard some heavy firing up the river,

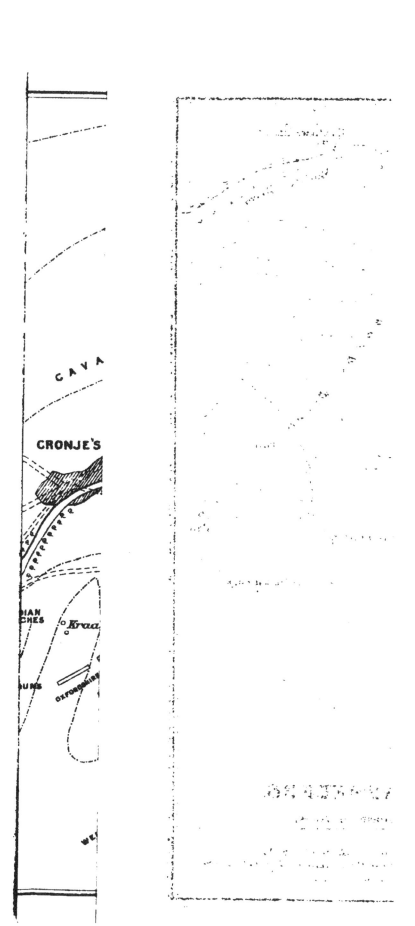

about a mile away, at 9 p.m., but it did not last long. Dead horses been floating down from the laager all day, and they cannot have many left now. Captain Rattray, R.A.M.C., relieved Major Pike as Medical Officer to the Battalion.

February 26th.—Returned to camp at 5 a.m.; a nasty morning. Went on picquet at 6 p.m., earlier than usual, as there was an idea that the Boers meant to attempt to break out during the night. The guns shelled the laager at intervals from 7 to 9 p.m. At about 9 p.m. there was some heavy firing near the laager, and a few shots came over our heads. At 2 a.m. there was a regular fusillade from our sapped position down by the river, also firing further up stream, which continued at intervals till 3 or 4 a.m. Heard later that the Canadians had had 35 casualties.

SHELTERS.

CHAPTER VII.

CRONJE'S SURRENDER.

Lord Roberts' telegraphic despatch ran as follows :—

Paardeberg, Feb. 27, 7.45 a.m.

General Cronje and all his force capitulated unconditionally at daylight this morning, and is now a prisoner in my camp.

The strength of his force will be communicated later.

I hope Her Majesty's Government will consider this event satisfactory, occurring as it does on the anniversary of Majuba.

11 a.m.

From information furnished daily to me by my Intelligence Department, it became apparent that Cronje's force was becoming more depressed, and that discontent among the troops and discord among the leaders were rapidly increasing.

This feeling doubtless accentuated by the disappointment caused when the Boer reinforcements, which tried to relieve Cronje, were defeated by our troops on the 23rd inst.

I resolved therefore to bring pressure to bear on the enemy. Each night trenches were pushed forward towards the enemy's laager so as to gradually contract his position, and at the same time I bombarded it heavily with Artillery, which was yesterday materially aided by the arrival of four 6 in. howitzers, which I had ordered up from De Aar.

In carrying out these measures, the captive balloon gave great assistance, by keeping us informed of the dispositions and movements of the enemy.

At 3 a.m. to-day a most dashing advance, made by the Canadian Regiment and some Engineers, supported by the 1st Gordon Highlanders and the 2nd Shropshires, resulted in our gaining a point some 600 yards nearer the enemy, and within about 80 yards of his trenches, where our men intrenched themselves and maintained their positions till morning —a gallant deed worthy of our Colonial comrades, and which I am glad to say was attended with comparatively slight loss.

This apparently clinched matters, for at daylight to-day a letter signed by Cronje, in which he stated that he surrendered unconditionally, was brought to our outposts under a flag of truce.

In my reply, I told Cronje that he must present himself at my camp, and that his force must come out of their laager after laying down their arms.

By 7 a.m. I received General Cronje, and despatched a telegram to you announcing the fact. In the course of conversation he asked for kind treatment at our hands, and also that his wife, grandson, private secretary, adjutant, and servants might accompany him wherever he might be sent. I reassured him, and told him his request would be complied with.

I informed him that a General Officer would be sent with him to Cape Town to ensure his being treated with proper respect *en route*. He will start this afternoon under the charge of Major-General Pretyman, who will hand him over to the General Commanding at Cape Town.

The prisoners, who number about 3,000, will be formed into commandos under their own officers. They also will leave here to-day, reaching Modder River to-morrow, when they will be railed to Cape Town in detachments.

1.5 p.m.

Boer prisoners amount to about 4,000, of whom 1,150 are Free Staters, the remainder Transvaalers. The officers are as follows :—

TRANSVAALERS.

General Piet Cronje.

Chief Commandant M. J. Wolverans.

Commandants F. J. Roos, J. T. Maartens.

Assistant Commandants R. Woest and J. P. G. Verster.

Camp Commandant W. L. Jooste.

Field Cornets Alberts and Vande, J. H. L. Bosman, W. A. Lemmer, H. J. Badenhorst, Früs (who is a Scandinavian), D. H. Hattings, and Venter D. J. Terblanche.

Acting Field Cornets P. V. de Villiers, G. J. Du Plessis.

Assistant Field Cornet R. J. Sneyman.

War Commissioner Arnoldi.

Assistant War Commissioner B. J. Jooste.

Magazine Master A. K. Enslin.

Adjutants J. M. A. Wolverans, A. D. W. R. Jolverans, A. Uing, M. S. Maree, J. A. Botha, and G. H. Grobler, in charge of Artillery.

Farrier Thomas Moodie.

FREE STATERS.

Commandants J. P. Wordaan, J. K. Kok, J. C. Villiers, R. J. Sneeyman, S. Meintjes, J. Greyling, Smith.

Field Cornets J. Cronje, C. Oosthuisen, C. Van Lÿl, J. Nicuvenhal, M. Kvick, J. Kvick, J. Van der Walt.

Commandant of Artillery, Major Albrecht.

Lieutenants Vaen-Heister, Van Dewitz, Van Angersteins.

Guns captured are as follows:—From Transvaal.—Three 7·5 centimètre Krupp 9-pounders (?) and one Maxim. From Orange Free State. —One 7·5 centimètre Krupp, one Maxim.

Paardeberg, Feb. 28, 11.55 a.m.

Cronje with his family left [here] yesterday in charge of Major-General Pretyman, and under an escort of the City Imperial Volunteers Mounted Infantry. Later in the day the remaining prisoners [left], under the charge of the Earl of Errol, and escorted by the Gloucestershire Regiment and 100 City Imperial Volunteers.

The women and children are all being sent to their homes.

I understand that grave dissatisfaction was felt by the Boers at Cronje's refusal to accept my offer of a safe-conduct to the women and children and medical care of his wounded, 170 of whom are now in our hospital. Very many of them are in a terrible plight from want of care at an earlier stage.

I inspected the Boer laager yesterday, and was much struck by the ingenuity and energy with which the position was made almost impregnable to assault.

Reuter's Agent telegraphed from Paardeberg on the 27th February :—

At three o'clock this morning our camp was awakened by the continued rattle of musketry fire. When day broke the news came that the Canadians were building a trench quite close to the enemy, who were firing at fifty yards' range. The Canadians worked forward, and occupied the edge of the Boer trenches along the river, entirely enfilading the rest. Then, with the exception of an occasional solitary shot, there followed a complete cessation of firing on all sides.

Suddenly the Regiment stationed on the crest of the hill, which first caught sight of the white flag, burst into cheers, and the news rapidly spread that General Cronje had surrendered. Shortly afterwards a note arrived for Lord Roberts stating that General Cronje had unconditionally surrendered. General Pretyman was thereupon sent to take his surrender.

At about 7 a.m. a small group was perceived crossing the plain towards the British headquarters. Lord Roberts, who was walking to and fro in front of the modest cart in which he sleeps, ordered a guard of the Seaforth Highlanders to make a line. As the group of horsemen approached nearer, it was seen that on the right of General Pretyman rode an elderly man clad in a rough, short overcoat, a wide-brimmed hat, ordinary tweed trousers, and brown shoes.

This was General Cronje, his face almost burnt black, and his curly hair tinged with grey. Lord Roberts and his staff stood awaiting him.

General Pretyman, addressing the Commander-in-Chief, said, "Commandant Cronje, Sir." General Cronje touched his hat, and the salute was returned by Lord Roberts. The whole group then dismounted, and Lord Roberts, stepping forward, shook hands with the Boer Commandant.

"You have made a gallant defence, Sir," was the first salutation of Lord Roberts to the Boer leader, who was then ushered into the headquarters, where he was entertained with food and refreshment.

Later the *Times* Special Correspondent wrote :—

The events of the early morning of the 27th can best be told from outside.

Brigadier-General MacDonald sent from his bed a note to Lord Roberts reminding him that Tuesday was the anniversary of that disaster which, we all remembered, he had by example, order, and threat himself done his best to avert, even while the panic had been at its height ; Sir Henry Colvile submitted a suggested attack backed by the same unanswerable plea. For a moment Lord Roberts demurred to the plan ; it seemed likely to cost too heavily, but the insistence of Canada broke down his reluctance, and the men of the oldest colony were sent out in the small hours of Tuesday morning to redeem the blot on the name of the mother country.

From the existing trench, some 700 yards long, on the northern bank, held jointly by the Gordons and the Canadians, the latter were ordered to advance in two lines—each, of course, in extended order—thirty yards apart, the first with bayonets fixed, the second reinforced by fifty Royal Engineers under Colonel Kincaid and Captain Boileau.

In dead silence, and covered by a darkness only faintly illuminated by the merest rim of the dying moon, " with the old moon in her lap," the three Companies of Canadians moved on over the bush-strewn ground. For over 400 yards the noiseless advance continued, and when within eighty yards of the Boer trench, the trampling of the scrub betrayed the movement. Instantly the outer trench of the Boers burst into fire, which was kept up almost without intermission from five minutes to three o'clock to ten minutes past the hour. Under this fire the courage and discipline of the Canadians proved themselves. Flinging themselves on the ground, they kept up an incessant fire on the trenches, guided only by the flashes of their enemy's rifles, and the Boers admit that they quickly reduced them to the necessity of lifting their rifles over their heads to the edge of the earthwork, and pulling their triggers at random. Behind this line the Engineers did magnificent work. Careless of danger, the trench was dug from the inner edge of bank to the crest, and then for fifty or sixty yards out through the scrub. The Canadians retired three yards to this protection, and waited for dawn, confident in their new position, which had entered the protected angle of the Boer position, and commanded alike the rifle pits of the banks and the trefoil-shaped embrasures on the north.

Cronje saw that matters were indeed desperate. Many Boers threw up their hands and dashed unharmed across the intervening space; others waved white flags and exposed themselves carelessly on their intrenchments, but not a shot was fired. Colonel Otter and Colonel Kincaid held a hasty consultation, which was disturbed by the sight of Sir Henry Colvile, General of the Ninth Division, quietly riding down within 500 yards of the northern Boer trenches, to bring the news that even while the last few shots were being fired a horseman was hurrying in with a white flag and Cronje's unconditional surrender, to take effect at sunrise.

Of the three Canadian Companies the foremost, and that which suffered most, was the French company, under Major Pelletier.

Meanwhile a few formal preliminaries were being arranged at Headquarters, and General Pretyman went out with a small escort to meet the Boer Commander and his secretary.

Lord Roberts, in the plainest of khaki, without a badge of rank except his Kandahar sword, awaited the arrival of his distinguished prisoner. "Commandant Cronje," was the brief introduction as the Boer swung himself off his white pony, and curtly answering the Field Marshal's salute, shook hands. "I am glad to see you; I am glad to meet so brave a man," was Lord Roberts's brief welcome, and a formal surrender followed, the conversation being interpreted by Cronje's secretary.

The General, a man of few words, sat deeply sunken in his chair with his hands in the pockets of his overcoat, and sullenly regarded the scene. Every consideration was paid him, but until the last was seen of his bulky form driving away to Modder River in the closed carriage which had been provided for him, his set, hardened face only suggested that the bitterest hour of his life was being barely endured by the man whose pluck, whose capacity, and whose straightforwardness we his enemies are the first to admit.

Major Caunter's account[1] :—

The Free Staters next morning told us that their last ration was consumed on the 26th, and that they had on that day addressed a communication to Cronje, in which they set forth that, escape being impossible, hope of relief abandoned, and food exhausted, they had determined

---

[1] From the *Journal of the Royal United Service Institution*, October 1900.

that, with or without his leave, they would surrender; but that, to give an opportunity to those who were prepared to risk their lives in an attempt to break out during the night, they would defer their purpose until the morning of the 27th.

However this may be, and whatever may have been the determining factor, loud cheering from our men all along the south front soon after daybreak, announced the fact that at last, without a doubt, Cronje had thrown up the sponge.

And it was the dawn of the nineteenth anniversary of Majuba!

The Boers could be seen sitting outside their trenches, white handkerchiefs and pieces of cloth fluttering here and there in the breeze.

To the Sixth Division fell the honour of taking over the prisoners, who were ordered to collect on the south side, after laying down their arms. Each commando was then formed up under its own commandant, and led past General Kelly-Kenny two and two. As illustrating the complete want of order and organisation among them, it may be mentioned that the Boer officers experienced great difficulty in getting their men to carry out this not very complicated manœuvre. Altogether the standard of intelligence, as judged by their physiognomy, manner, and movements, was of a very low order, the Free Staters, however, comparing favourably with the Transvaalers. Far from being dejected or appearing to feel the ignominy of their position, the majority were in high spirits, and nearly all saluted the General with a smile as they filed past. The official numbers with commandos and commandants were as follows:—

O.F.S. Artillery—Major Albrecht, 45 men.

One Vickers-Maxim, three 7·5-centimetre Krupps, one Q.F. 12-pounder.

Commando.	Commandant.	Men.
Kroonstad	J. V. Meantages	134
Ladybrand	R. J. Sneyman	134
Ficksberg	De Villiers	44
Winberg	J. W. Kok	193
Hoopstad	J. Greyling	373
Bloemfontein	Fouri	202
Jacobsdal	A. Smit	16
Boshof	J. W. Grunewald (field cornet)	112
Petrusberg Fauresmith Vryburg		67
Total Orange Free Staters		1,320

Transvaalers :—

Commando.		Commandant.						Men.
Potchefstroom	-	Roos	-	-	-	-	-	- 615
,,	-	Wolmarans	-	-	-	-	- 646
Gatsrand -	-	Maartens	-	-	-	-	- 446
Scandinavians	-	Früs (field cornet)	-		-	-	49
Bowyk	-	-	Terblanche (field cornet)	-	-	-	318
Bloemhof -	-	Woeste	-	-	-	-	-	- 518
		Total Transvaalers	-	-	-	-	-	- 2,592

Making a grand total, with 160 wounded, of 4,072.

Conversations with the various Commandants elicited some interesting facts. Albrecht appeared somewhat depressed. He said he had repeatedly warned Cronje that he was getting himself into a trap from which there could be no escape, by remaining in the bed of the river, but that his advice was of no avail. As an Artilleryman he had a high opinion of the so-called pom-pom on account of its range, accuracy, mobility, and moral effect. He stated that lyddite both at Magersfontein and here had done little damage. Roos, who had been most kind to two of our officers taken prisoners on the 18th, sharing his tobacco and coffee, and making them as comfortable as the circumstances would permit, was anxious to know what we thought of his management of the rear-guard action at Klip Kraal on the 16th, and was delighted at our warm encomiums. Others told us that Cronje never anticipated the arrival of our Infantry on the 18th; that had he done so he would have occupied the kopjes; that he was about to inspan when he realised their presence, and that in their absence he did not consider it would have been a difficult matter to have pushed on in spite of the Cavalry.

Diary continued :—

February 27th.—At 6 a.m. the Regiment retired under cover of the hill, where we remained until 7 o'clock, a few shots coming over our heads. Half-an-hour later we returned to camp, and shortly afterwards the Boers sent in a flag of truce, offering unconditional surrender, and then Cronje rode into Lord Roberts' camp. The Buffs went down to the laager during the morning, and brought in the prisoners—upwards of 4,000 of them—with a "pom-pom," four guns and two Maxims, and Mrs. Cronje and some women and children. The Boers had run out of food, and, after a Council of War, had agreed to surrender if they could not escape last night. The Gloucesters marched the prisoners to Klip Drift in the evening. It was pleasant to see the last of them. There was a nice collection of captured weapons—rifles and carbines—including Mausers, Martinis, Lee-Metfords, and various others, with about half-a-million rounds of ammunition. At 5.30 p.m. the officers of the Regiment and portions of two Companies went down to the river to the funeral of poor Bright and Ball-Acton.

February 28th.—Quite a relief to have no enemy about, and to have a day off.

Night picquet at the usual place. Very short of food now; half rations hardly enough to keep one going, and we all feel quite sick sometimes for want of a decent meal. I have made a vow never to grumble at the quality of the food again, as long as there is enough of it.

PIQUET AT DINNER.

CHAPTER VIII.

THE ADVANCE ON THE FREE STATE CAPITAL.

Diary :—

March 1st.—The Brigade marched at 8 a.m. to Osfontein, about four miles off, where we bivouacked near a farm, with excellent well-water. Heavy storm for an hour or two at mid-day. Heard of the relief of Ladysmith. Lords Roberts and Kitchener now at Kimberley.

March 2nd.—Halted.

March 3rd.—Lord Roberts arrived, and took up his headquarters at the farmhouse. We got a few supplies from Modder River—most acceptable.

March 4th.—Two Companies of the Regiment on picquet. Heavy rain and thunderstorms most of the day and night; our shelters and kits soaked. An English mail arrived, as well as some stores from Kimberley.

March 5th.—Halted. The Boer position is said to be about five or six miles away, along a line of kopjes.

March 6th.—Still halted at Osfontein. Received orders in the after-noon to move to-morrow, in order to work round the left of the Boer position, and if possible roll them up. French, with the Cavalry Divi-sion, is working right round to the enemy's rear; and the 7th Division and other troops are to take the right and centre of the position. General Knox returned from hospital and took over command of the Brigade.

March 7th.—Paraded at 2.30 a m.; marched at 3.30. The 7th Divi-sion moved on the left by the river, the 9th Division and Guards Brigade in the centre, and our (6th) Division on the right. We had previously heard and then seen a field gun firing on French's Cavalry. Our 24 field guns (viz., three field batteries and one howitzer) opened fire on the " Seven Sisters " kopjes, held by the enemy on our flank. The position was almost at once abandoned, the Boers evidently not liking the appearance of French's Cavalry in their rear; their guns ceased fire and disappeared. Our Infantry now advanced and occupied the position, the 6th Division moving right round to the rear, and then through the line of kopjes. The Boers had apparently imagined that we were going to make the usual frontal attack, and had dug shelter trenches all along the crest of the high ground connecting the kopjes. They left in rather a hurry, as we found several wagons, ponies, and tents abandoned. We then halted for a bit, and in about an hour's time advanced again, passing the centre of the enemy's late position —a high kopje, on which they had had a gun. We had now gone 16 miles, and it was another four to the river, which we eventually reached at 3.30 p.m. The men had suffered considerably from the

ARRIVAL OF STORES.

exertion, as they were carrying 150 rounds of ammunition and a whole day's rations, and the heat was intense ; they stuck to it however manfully, though 70 men of the Regiment had fallen out from sheer exhaustion. Other Regiments suffered equally, 700 having fallen out when the force reached the river. We immediately settled down in bivouac, as we thought for the night, but we had been in barely an hour when we got orders to be ready to move on at 5.30 p.m. At the appointed time we were off again, eventually reaching Poplar Grove at 7.20 p.m., having done 25 miles in the last 16 hours. Had no blankets or great coats, and consequently put in little sleep ; the men walked about most of the night, and lit fires to keep themselves warm.

French reports 50 casualties in his force to-day. He hunted the Boers the whole day, and pounded them with his guns, but he was never really able to get well into them, as they broke up at once. Two foreign attachés were taken prisoners, and stated that the Boers had 9,000 men, but were rather disorganised, the Transvaalers having quarrelled with the Free Staters.

March 8th.—Marched at 12 noon eight miles, to Roodepoort. Halted half way for half-an-hour. Very hot to start with, but clouded over later, and had a shower of rain. On the way we passed the Mounted Infantry and some of French's Cavalry near some kopjes, the remainder having gone ahead. Reached our bivouac at 4.30 p.m. ; the men got their blankets, and had a good night's rest.

March 9th.—Halted at Roodepoort ; the Regiment on picquet at night.

March 10th.—The Division marched at 6.30 a.m. to Dam Vallei (near Driefontein), the Regiment forming the rear-guard, and getting away about an hour later. The force moved in three Columns by the three roads to Bloemfontein, the 6th Division on the left, and Lord Roberts with the centre Division. All quiet until about noon, when we heard heavy firing to our left front, and eventually saw a Field Battery in action some way ahead. We, as rear-guard, did not get into the fight, but about a dozen shells were dropped by the enemy from a Creusot gun into the baggage just in front of us, doing no damage, however, as only one or two of the shells burst. We heard later that the rest of our Division had been fighting all day, and had had over 400 casualties ; though they had the satisfaction of getting home with the bayonet, and doing terrible execution. We reached our bivouac at 7.30 p.m., having covered only 12 miles in the 12 hours. Very cold night, but we got our blankets. On picquet duty.

March 11th.—More than a hundred dead Boers were buried this morning. The Regiment marched at 7 a.m., on rear-guard again. As we have hardly 400 men fit for duty now, we are not considered strong enough to move in front. First four miles over open veldt to a kopje ; then three miles slightly down hill, with another four up. Very open country, with one or two farms about. Transport animals in rather a bad state. Bivouacked near a farm at Salisbury Plain (Kaal's Spruit) at 4.15 p.m. Day's march, 13 miles.

March 12th.—Marched at 5.45 a.m. ; Regiment right flank guard. The 6th Division moved on the left, 9th Division on the right, and 7th Division in rear of the 6th. No opposition, the Boers having cleared off, probably to make a stand near Bloemfontein. We halted for an hour at six miles, and reached a tributary of the Modder at 10 miles. Reached Venter's Vallei at 2.30 p.m., after 15 miles marching from the

Lieut. Hon. G. W. F. S. Foljambe   Capt. Mareseaux, A.D.C.   Lieut. C. F. Henley
Lieut. L. F. Scott   Capt. Rattray, R.A.M.C.   Lieut. S. F. Hammick   Major Pike, R.A.M.C.
2nd Lieut. G. A. Sullivan   Lieut. H. L. Wood.

Capt. H. E. Watt   Capt. F. J. Henley   Lt.-Col. Hon. A. E. Dalzell   Major-Gen. C. Knox   Major R. W. Porter   Capt. F. G. L. Lamotte
Lieut. A. G. Bayley   Capt. E. A. Lethbridge   Lieut. and Quartermaster W. Ross

OFFICERS, 1st BATTALION.
BLOEMFONTEIN MARCH, 1900.

last bivouac.   French well ahead of us, and reported to have struck the
railway at Leeuwberg.

March 13th.—Ordered to march at 5.30 a.m., but the order was can-
celled, and the 9th Division went on ahead, instead of the 6th.   Heard

FARM OF EX-PRESIDENT STEYN'S BROTHER.

that French had met with resistance on arriving at the railway ; but he
planted a few shells into the Boer laager, and the enemy went off north
at once, taking all the rolling stock, and passing through Bloemfontein
to Kroonstad.   Our other half Division (18th Brigade) marched at
3 p.m., and our Brigade (13th) followed at 5 p.m., the Regiment as
advanced guard.   We soon caught up the tail of the 18th Brigade,
which delayed our march the whole way.   Heavy rain for a couple of
hours, and we got wet through.   Marched all night, and reached our
bivouac at 2 a.m.   The name of the place was Brand Dam Kop, near a
large farm (deserted) belonging to President Steyn's brother.   Got our
blankets, and managed to put in three or four hours' sleep in spite
of rain.

March 14th.—Marched at 9 a.m., the 18th Brigade leading, and the
Regiment rear Battalion of the 13th Brigade.   Moved through the

farm, and then from the high ground got our first sight of Bloemfontein —three or four miles off. Each Regiment marched through the town, and had a great reception from the English residents, who had been cooped up here for the last five months, and must have had rather a poor time of it. We found the " Union Jack " flying over the Residency ; Lord Roberts, with French's Division, and the Guards' Brigade, having occupied the town yesterday. The 6th Division marched to bivouacs, about a mile north of the town, under the Fort, at 1.30 p.m. Bloemfontein is rather a pretty little place, close under a kopje, on which the North Fort is situated. The houses are mostly in the Swiss cottage style, of brick, with tin roofs. The public buildings are good, and one or two of the churches fine ; the streets broad, but badly looked after. There is electric light throughout, but not in working order at present. No doubt the place will improve a good deal after we have had it for a year or two.

We expect to stay here for about a fortnight, until the line is thoroughly repaired, and the bridge at Norval's Pont rebuilt ; then we shall be off after the Boers again. They are reported to be preparing to oppose our advance somewhere about Kroonstad. A good many of the farmers have come in and given up their arms. I don't fancy that the Free Staters will bother us much more.

CAMP AT BLOEMFONTEIN.

MARCH OF THE 6TH DIVISION FROM ENSLIN TO BLOEMFONTEIN.
12TH FEBRUARY TO 14TH MARCH, 1900.

Date.	From	To	Hour of Start.	Hour of Arrival.	Miles.	Remarks.
12 Feb.	Enslin / Graspan }	Ramdam	6.0 a.m.	1.0 p.m.	10¼	
13 „ ..	Ramdam	Waterval Dft.	5.0 a.m.	11.0 a.m.	10	
14 „ ..	Waterval Dft.	Wegdrai......	1.0 a.m.	11.0 a.m.	10	} Including detours, 27 miles in 24 hours.
14 „ ..	Wegdrai......	Klip Drift	5.0 p.m.	12.30 p.m. 15th	12	
16 „ ..	Klip Drift	Brandvallei ..	5.0 a.m.	12 noon 17th	11 {	13th Bgde. engaged with enemy's rear-guard.
17 „ ..	Klip Drift	Brandvallei...	3.0 a.m.	12.30 p.m.		18th Brigade followed.
17 „ ..	Brandvallei ..	Paardeberg...	5.0 p.m.	9.30 a.m.	5	
18 „ ..	Paardeberg ..	Boer Laager ..	3.0 a.m.	7.0 a.m.	2	Battle of Paardeberg.
1 Mar. .	Boer Laager..	Osfontein.....	—	—	4	
7 „ ..	Osfontein.....	Poplar Grove .	5.30 a.m.	7.0 p.m.	22	Including detour; drove enemy from his position.
8 „ ..	Poplar Grove .	Roodepoort Farm	12 noon	4.30 p.m.	7	
10 „ ..	Roodepoort...	Driefontein (near)	6.0 a.m.	6.0 p.m.	10	Battle of Driefontein.
11 „ ..	Driefontein...	Kaals Spruit..	5.30 a.m.	3.0 p.m.	14	
12 „ ..	Kaals Spruit .	Venter's Vallei	5.30 a.m.	2.30 p.m.	12½	
13 „ ..	Venter's Vallei	Brand Kop ...	3.0 p.m.	1.0 a.m. 14th	13¼	
14 „ ..	Brand Kop...	Bloemfontein.	9.0 a.m.	2.0 p.m.	6	

6TH DIVISION.
DIFFERENCE IN STRENGTH BETWEEN 12TH FEBRUARY AND 14TH MARCH, 1900.

Units.	Strength on 12/2/00.			Strength on 14/3/00.			Decrease.			Explanation of decrease.											
										Killed.		Died of Wounds.		Wounded.		Sick.		Missing.		Other Causes.	
	Officers.	W. Officers.	N.C.O's and Men.	Officers.	W. Officers.	N.C.O's and Men.	Officers.	W. Officers.	N.C.O's and Men.	Officers.	N.C.O's and Men.	Officers.	N.C.O's and Men.	Officers.	N.C.O's and Men.	Officers.	N.C.O's and Men.	Officers.	N.C.O's and Men.	Officers.	N.C.O's and Men.
Divisional Troops ...	38	2	1006	36	2	877	2	-	129	-	4	-		1	17	-	65	1	1	-	42
2 Bn. Buffs.	18	1	786	10	1	575	8	-	211	2	25	-	-	6	105	-	81	-	-	-	-
2 Bn. Glouc. Regt.	23	1	716	19	1	572	4	-	144	-	9	-	3	3	46	1	80	-	3	-	3
1 Bn. W. Rid. Regt.	23	1	789	17	1	596	6	-	193	-	23	1	1	4	124	1	45	-	-	-	-
1 Bn. Ox. Lt. Inf.	20	1	595	14	1	430	6	-	165	2	16	1	1	2	74	1	74	-	-	-	-
1 Bn. York. Regt.	21	1	953	12	1	723	9	-	230	1	46	-	-	7	131	1	42	-	11	-	-
1 Bn. Welsh Regt.	23	1	875	10	1	660	13	-	215	2	32	-	-	10	165	-	5	1	13	-	-
1 Bn. Essex Regt.	23	1	936	11	1	757	12	-	179	1	21	1	-	5	128	3	8	-	15	2	7
Totals ..	189	9	6656	129	9	5190	60	-	1466	8	176	3	5	38	790	7	400	2	43	2	52

THE 1st OXFORDSHIRE LIGHT INFANTRY,
After the Occupation of Bloemfontein, March 1900.

The following order was published to the troops after the entry into Bloemfontein :—

ARMY ORDERS—SOUTH AFRICA.

Bloemfontein, 14th March, 1900.

It affords the Field Marshal Commanding-in-Chief the greatest pleasure in congratulating the Army in South Africa on the various events that have occurred during the past few weeks, and he would specially offer his sincere thanks to that portion of the Army which, under his immediate command, has taken part in the operations resulting yesterday in the capture of Bloemfontein.

On the 12th February this force crossed the boundary which divided the Orange Free State from British territory. Three days later Kimberley was relieved. On the 15th day the bulk of the Boer army in this State, under one of their most trusted Generals, were made prisoners. On the 17th day the news of the relief of Ladysmith was received, and on the 13th March, 29 days after the commencement of the operations, the capital of the Orange Free State was occupied.

This is a record of which any army may well be proud—a record which could not have been achieved except by earnest, well-disciplined men, determined to do their duty, and to surmount whatever difficulties or dangers might be encountered.

Exposed to extreme heat by day, bivouacking under heavy rain, marching long distances (not infrequently with reduced rations), the endurance, cheerfulness, and gallantry displayed by all ranks are beyond praise, and Lord Roberts feels sure that neither Her Majesty the Queen nor the British nation will be unmindful of the efforts made by this force to uphold the honour of their country.

The Field Marshal desires especially to refer to the fortitude and heroic spirit with which the wounded have borne their sufferings. Owing to the great extent of country over which modern battles have to be fought, it is not always possible to afford immediate aid to those who are struck down; many hours have indeed, at times, elapsed before some of the wounded could be attended to, but not a word of murmur or complaint has been uttered ; the anxiety of all, when succour came, was that their comrades should be cared for first.

In assuring every officer and man how much he appreciates their efforts in the past, Lord Roberts is confident that, in the future, they will continue to show the same resolution and soldierly qualities, and to lay down their lives if need be (as so many brave men have already done) in order to ensure that the war in South Africa may be brought to a satisfactory conclusion. By order,

(Sd.) W. F. KELLY, Major-General,

Deputy Adjutant General, for Chief of the Staff.

25°

brahams
Kraal

Driefontein
Pan

25°

CHAPTER IX.

ON THE LINES OF COMMUNICATION.

Diary :—

March 15th.—General C. Knox inspected the Brigade in bivouacs. Two Regiments of the Guards' Brigade went south by rail.

March 16th.—Troops put on full rations. Hear that we shall be here two or three weeks. A rest is much needed ; men want feeding up. We only have about 400 men now.

March 19th.—Inspection of the Division by Lord Roberts, who addressed every two Regiments in turn. Heavy rain all the afternoon.

March 20th to 30th.—Routine work ; picquet duty in the Fort ; route marches ; a good deal of rain. The effects of Paardeberg water showing up now in enteric.

March 31st.—Our Brigade got sudden orders to march. Buffs, Gloucesters, and West Riding left at 2 p.m. We were rear-guard, and brought the carts, wagons, etc. Started at 5 p.m., and arrived at Steyn's Farm, Roodeval (due east) at 2 a.m. 12 miles.

April 1st.—Other three Regiments left at daybreak ; we (rear-guard again) marched at 10 a.m., arriving at Krantz Kraal Bridge at 2 p.m. Left again at 3.30 p.m., and at 5.30 p.m. bivouacked on a kopje (Mokesberg), two Regiments on the kopje, and two below. Day's march 9 miles. Information received soon after midnight that General Colvile (9th Division) had retired at midnight to Bushman's Kop—about seven miles from us, as the Boers were supposed to be trying to cut his communications with Bloemfontein.

April 2nd.—Heavy rain in early morning. The Regiment moved at 7.30 a.m. to a kopje, two miles off, where we took up a position. Two Regiments occupied another kopje, and the other Regiment remained with the convoy. We left our position at 1.30 p.m. and returned to Krantz Kraal Bridge (3 miles), the remainder of the Brigade following. Halted, and marched again at 5.30 p.m. for Springfield Farm, said to be 10 or 12 miles off, but which turned out to be a good 17 miles for us, as we were rear-guard and had to keep to the road. Got in at 1 a.m., and found the 9th Division and some Cavalry also here. Springfield is eight miles south-east of Bloemfontein.

April 3rd.—Left at 10 a.m., and reached Bloemfontein at 3 p.m., having marched 50 miles, without any apparent object, as we had no Cavalry, Mounted Infantry, or guns. However, we hear now that, on the 30th, Broadwood's R.H.A. fell into an ambush, losing seven guns near the Bloemfontein Waterworks on the Modder, about 20 miles from the town, and 10 miles or so from the kopje that we occupied yesterday; that Colvile had gone to his assistance, and that we had been sent to protect Colvile's left flank. The Boers damaged the Waterworks a bit, so water is scarce at present.

The 18th Brigade left at 5 p.m. for Springfield. We thought we were

THE BRITISH FLAG AT BLOEMFONTEIN.

going to get a night in bed, but at 10 p.m. we were warned for parade at 4 a.m. to-morrow.

April 4th.—The Brigade marched, at 4.30 a.m., to Tempey Farm (three miles). Two Regiments went a little further, to Fischer's Farm, the Boers having threatened to seize the owner, who had given up his arms. No Boers appeared, so we left at about 10 a.m. The Brigade then took up a line of picquets on the kopjes commanding Bloemfontein, and remained out the day and night. The 12th Brigade (Clements) rejoined the 6th Division in the evening, and the 18th Brigade ceased to belong to the Division.

April 5th.—Off picquet at 8 a.m. Part of the 9th Division sent down to help Gatacre, who has had five Companies captured. Want of boots is our great trouble now. We are beginning to get tents.

April 7th.—200 men of the Regiment (under Mockler) strengthening the Supply Stores with intrenchments—digging all day.

April 8th to 10th.—Took up alarm-post positions for defence of Bloemfontein.

April 11th.—Draft from England joined headquarters. Childers, Paske, Christie-Miller, Logan, and White, and about 300 men.

April 12th.—Five Companies on outpost duty.

April 13th.—Enteric is increasing, and there is a lot of dysentery. Numbers of men are dying.

April 16th.—Ward and Simpson arrived with a draft of 100 men from England.

April 19th.—Our tents all up now; had been without them since leaving Modder River on February 10th.

Extract from a letter, dated Bloemfontein, 25th April, 1900:—

We are still here, and nothing startling has happened in these parts since I last wrote. You know that both our drafts have turned up, and we are once again a Regiment, having a good 800 men ready for the job; and when we get the Volunteer Company (which is on its way up) we could march 900 strong. The men are as hard as nails, but there is no doubt that the Reserve men have stuck it better than the younger men. Pears, the Sergeant-Major, is very ill with enteric. I sincerely hope he may weather it; but it will be about as much as he can do. Lamotte and Lethbridge are better, and should be out of hospital soon. Porter is still in hospital with dysentery, and Cobb has gone down to Cape Town to pick up after his go of fever.

Extract from letter, dated Bloemfontein, 12th May, 1900:—

The Regiment moved on the 7th to Sussex Hill Camp, four miles out of the town, to relieve some Mounted Infantry. The Gloucesters went to the Waterworks, and two Regiments of Clements' Brigade are out in the country round the town; so our Division is pretty well split up, and I am afraid there is small chance of our moving on towards Pretoria. [Our Volunteer Company turned up from England on the 8th;

there are a lot of Oxford Undergraduates in the ranks.[1] Life here is a bit slow now, though we have a nice roomy camp, a bit higher than the town. We keep the men fit by playing football when we are not on duty ; but there is a heap of enteric about, and a certain number of officers are down with it.

We discovered in the cemetery here the other day, the grave of a 43rd soldier who died of wounds during the Kaffir war.   The stone, like many others, has evidently been used as a target by the Boers at musketry practice in the old fort (some 700 yards away), but it was still in fair preservation, and the surrounding ground and the mound were soon put in order by willing hands.   The following is the inscription on the stone :—

Sacred to the Memory of
JOHN DELAP,
Late of H.M.'s 43rd Regiment
Light Infantry,
Who died from wound received in
Action, on the 28th December 1852,
Aged 27 years.

This Tablet was erected by the Detachment
45th Regiment, as a token of respect to a
Brother Soldier.

Extract from letter, dated Bloemfontein, 27th May, 1900 :—

Still here and kept pretty busy, loading and unloading stores, and one thing and another. We hear that Roberts has crossed the Vaal with little opposition. It is rather sickening being left behind like this, but of course someone had to stay to look after this place and the communications. Seven of our officers are in hospital with enteric now, and of course an equal proportion of the men. We got another draft of 100 men and an officer (Kirkpatrick) to-day, which will help us along for a bit. We are to have a big parade next Monday for the reading of the Proclamation annexing the old Orange Free State.

---

[1] The Volunteer Service Company was enlisted for one year, or until the end of the war.   Date of attestation, 19th January 1900 ; embarked 10th March 1900 ; arrived at Cape Town, 31st March 1900. Officers: Captain M. F. Lathy (1st V.B.) in command, Lieut. L. C. Hawkins, and Lieut. C. A. Barron (1st Bucks).   Strength : 1st (Oxford University) Vol. Battn., 1 Sergeant, 15 R. and F. ; 2nd Vol. Battn., 25 R. and F. ; 1st Bucks, 1 Colour-Sergeant, 3 Sergeants, and 66 R. and F. Total of all ranks, 114.

Diary :—

June 6th.—Received orders to move at once to Kroonstad, as De Wet is threatening the railway at Rhenoster River. Porter, with 500 men, left at 4 p.m., remainder followed at 7.30 p.m. in coal trucks. Cold night and rain.

June 7th.—Reached Kroonstad at 3.30 p.m. ; heavy rain and hail. Detrained and moved into bivouac, north-west of the town. Heard on arrival that Christian De Wet had already cut the railway line, captured Roodeval and its garrison, as well as the Derbyshire Militia at Rhenoster. Reinforcements of the Buffs, and 4th Argyll and Sutherland Highlanders arrived a little later, but no guns or Cavalry. Got to the bivouac ground in the dark ; no baggage and only one blanket apiece. Cutting wind

ARRIVAL IN CAMP.

and hard frost ; sleep out of the question. Took up a strong outpost line, as there was a probability of being attacked ; but, owing to the lateness of our arrival and ignorance of the country, it was quite a chance whether the outposts were in the right place. However, nothing happened, though we could see the reflection of the Boer signal lights in the sky all night.

June 8th.—Hard at work intrenching ourselves all day. General Charles Knox arrived and took over command. The kits came in the evening, and blanket shelters put up, but of little use, as they would not keep out the driving cold wind and frost. No. 17 Battery, R.F.A., and a few Yeomanry and Prince Albert's Guard joined us.

June 9th.—Very cold and freezing hard.   At 4.15 a.m. paraded for a
reconnaissance in force (viz. : the Battery, Yeomanry, half our Battalion,
half the Buffs, and half Argyll and Sutherland Highlanders).   Moved
north, up the railway to America Siding.   Enemy had left that morning,
but our Basuto scouts tracked them on a kopje about three miles north.
Returned to camp at 7 p.m.   Day very hot.

June 10th.—At 5 a.m. 6 officers and 100 men (under command of
Mockler) left by train, and went down the line to Ventersberg Road ;
reconnoitered the country round, and returned about 8 p.m.

KROONSTAD.

June 11th and 12th.—Busy intrenching the camp ; made ourselves
fairly secure, and have now got three 5-inch guns.   No tents ; days very
hot, and hard frost at night.

June 13th.—At 11 p.m. orders came for headquarters and 500 men of
the Regiment, with two guns of the Battery, to entrain at once for
Ventersberg Road.   The remainder of the Battery and some Yeomanry
started by road.   News had come in that the Boers were gathering
round Zand River—a post on the railway to the south of us—where
there is a quantity of stores and ammunition.

June 14th.—Reached Ventersberg Road Station at 6.30 a.m.   The
stationmaster reported that a loud explosion had taken place at 6.15 a.m.,
and after that telegraphic communication with Zand River had ceased.
We wired up for the remainder of the Battalion and some Mounted
Infantry.   About 7 a.m. we heard heavy firing in the direction of Zand

River (about 13 miles). Set to work at intrenchments, and when the Yeo-manry and the remainder of the Battery reached us, we moved on, leaving Mockler and a Company to hold the Station. The guns and Yeomanry went by road, we by rail, pushing on as fast as possible, as we could still hear heavy firing, and knowing that our Zand force had no guns, we fancied that the Boers would be giving them a bad time. Firing ceased suddenly at 3.30 p.m., and we imagined that it was all up with the Zand garrison. We pushed on to Riet Spruit, where there is a big bridge which the Boers had previously blown up, and which had been repaired. Here we detached the Battery and one Company (under Porter), and they set to work to intrench themselves, while the rest of us went on down the rail. We had to stop to examine every culvert, so progress was necessarily slow. At last we reached the break ($1\frac{1}{2}$ miles from Zand)—a culvert blown up and the telegraph wire cut. We sent some Yeomen into Zand with information that we were at hand if any help was wanted, but the answer came back that the garrison had repulsed the enemy with small loss to themselves. On hearing this we returned to Riet Spruit (about two miles), where we bivouacked for the night, six of our men and a sapper going back when it was dark and mending the break and laying new rails. About midnight Ballard and 50 men, escorting some sappers to mend the telegraph, marched into the bivouac from Ventersberg Road.

June 15th.—The C.O., Adjutant, and the Volunteer Company railed down to Zand River. The garrison had had a tremendous fight, but the officer in command had got wind of the coming attack, and had made his plans accordingly. His camp was on the top of a hill, but after dark he evacuated it, and took up a position lower down. The garrison dug hard all night, and in the morning had excellent cover. The con-sequence was that the Boers came along and blazed all they knew into the deserted camp, then walked unexpectedly up to the trenches, where they got more than they bargained for. The Zand people lost five killed and the same number wounded, took eight Boer prisoners, and picked up about a dozen corpses within ten yards of the trenches. Porter, with two Companies (Lamotte's and Watt's) and two guns, remained at Riet Spruit Siding, the remainder returned to Venters-berg Road. [N.B.—Most maps reverse the positions of these two places : Ventersberg Road is six miles *north* of Riet Spruit].

June 16th.—Mockler and his Company and the Maxim gun were left at Ventersberg Road, and the rest of the Battalion went back by rail to Kroonstad, which was reached at 10 p.m. Bivouacked on new ground in pouring rain.

June 17th.—Got our tents and pitched camp, and we were fairly comfortable for some days, though the weather was wet and cold.

June 25th.—The Regiment went out to America Siding to escort back two guns of the 17th Battery. Out till 6 p.m.; nothing happened. The Regiment has had 30 deaths from disease up to date. After this we had comparative peace for about a month, though, as Christian De Wet was hovering about, we always had 400 men ready to turn out, and guards and picquets stood to their arms at 5 a.m. daily.

July 12th.—Our detachments came in from Riet and Ventersberg Road, where they had not a very happy time. Always in a state of intrenching and expecting attacks, which never came off.

July 26th.—Piet De Wet and his staff came in through our outpost line, and surrendered to Lathy (Volunteer Company), who was on picquet. Piet said that his brother, Christian, would not give in as long as his old friend Steyn held out, and that Kruger wanted to make peace directly our troops crossed the Vaal; but Steyn persuaded him that, as he had ruined the Orange Free State, it would be a mean thing to cave in directly the Transvaal was invaded.

Our original Brigade has been split up long ago. General Knox is here in command of the Station; General Kelly-Kenny is at Bloemfontein; the Buffs are at Pretoria, the Gloucesters at Bloemfontein Waterworks, and the West Ridings somewhere about Lindley or Winburg.

Rough estimate of regimental casualties up to date :—*Killed in action and died of wounds,* three officers and 31 men ; *wounded,* three officers and 74 men ; *died of disease,* 52 men ; *invalided home,* six officers and 150 men. This does not include casualties in the Mounted Infantry Company.

AFTER THE SURRENDER.

CHAPTER X.

OPERATIONS AGAINST DE WET.[1]

Diary :—

August 1st.—Got sudden orders to leave Kroonstad at 2.30 p.m. Rendezvous, on the other side of the line, near our old camp. General C. Knox in command. Troops : Oxfordshire Light Infantry, 600 ; Royal Scots Militia, 400 ; five guns and a "pom-pom," and 250 of Sitwell's Mounted Infantry. Marched due west, nine miles, and bivouacked near a spruit. No tents with us. Carried four days' rations. The officers who marched out with the Battalion were :—Lt.-Col. Dalzell ; Major Mockler ; Captains Lamotte, Childers, and Lathy ; Lieutenants Scott, Ballard, Foljambe, Sullivan, Simpson, Ward, Hawkins, and Barron ; Captain and Adjutant Cobb ; Lieut. and Quartermaster Ross ; Captain Rattray, R.A.M.C. Captain Watt and Lieut. Hammick remained in Kroonstad in charge of the Depôt of the Battalion ; and Major Porter and Captain Lethbridge in hospital.

August 2nd.—Stood to arms at 5 a.m., and marched at 6.30 north-east towards Rhenoster Kop (a large wooded kopje, six or seven miles round the base, and 340 feet high—a favourite Boer stronghold). Sitwell found about a hundred Boers on the kopje, and drove them off towards Bothaville. Halted for a couple of hours near a farm, and then marched north, passing to the right of the kopje. Halted at Belmont. Day's march, 19 miles.

August 3rd.—Stood to arms at 5 a.m. (a standing order now) ; waited for news all the morning, and marched west at 2.30 p.m. Left the kopje on our left, and halted on top of a rise called Boschkopjes (seven miles). Laagered for the night in form of a square. As we got into camp in the dusk, heard Sitwell firing his guns on our right front. Hard frost all night ; blankets stiff and white in the morning.

August 4th.—Marched north at 6 a.m. After about six miles, heard the Mounted Infantry engaged. About a mile further on, and when within a mile and a quarter of Rhenoster River, the Boers opened fire on us. Halted on the ridge overlooking the river, the Battery shelling the river bed, and driving out what Boers there were (fifty or sixty), who cleared out across the open plain. A sergeant of the Royal Scots was mortally wounded.

---

[1] *Vide* Map, page 106.

The troops formed up, had some food, and fell out until 3 p.m. Then crossed the drift, and advanced across the open towards a line of kopjes two or three miles on. Reached the top of the highest kopje (Rhebokfontein—wooded, rocky, and covered with sheep-pens) at 5.30 p.m., Mockler's Company remaining there on outpost duty for the night, while the remainder of the force bivouacked on the ground below. Day's march, 10 miles.

August 5th, Sunday.—Halt. Kitchener and Broadwood visited the

THE VAAL, NEAR VENTERSKROON.

camp. Any number of troops about here—after De Wet, who is said to be north of us, in the Wit kopjes.

August 6th.—Halt.

August 7th.—Received orders to move in early morning. Marched at 10.30 a.m., mostly over rough undulating ground. The Mounted Infantry were fired on, just before reaching camp, from a kopje above a farm-house. Encamped at Doornhoek, on a rise near Kaffir Kraal, and intrenched ourselves, which took till nearly midnight. Opened up communications with Broadwood by lamp. Just as we got to camp, we heard a lot of firing in the direction of the hills, where we could see our Cavalry. They came across about 40 of the enemy, and were fired on at close quarters; one man wounded and two missing. Hard frost at night. Day's march, 12 miles. Heard afterwards that Scott-Murray and a draft of 100 men joined our depôt at Kroonstad to-day.

August 8th.—At 7 a.m. Cobb took 100 men to a farm about two miles away (from which we had been fired on yesterday) and burned it, bringing back a good stock of poultry. Marched at noon to the north, up-hill for four miles; then halted at a pass overlooking the Vaal for about two hours. The General got a despatch from Methuen. Moved on down hill, and then up to some low kopjes, where one or two shots were fired at the Mounted Infantry. Halted on the top of a rise looking down on Rietzburg (one or two farm houses in a big valley), four miles or so from the Vaal. Put on half rations, being short of supplies. Came out originally for four days, and have had only one convoy since leaving. Heard that Methuen had a fight in the morning, with 13 casualties (including six officers). A line of rocky kopjes runs from here to the Vaal. Night outposts. Day's march, eight miles.

August 9th.—Marched at 2 p.m., leaving Rietzburg on our right; then over open country, with range of kopjes on each side. Hit the Vaal River for the first time, after about five miles. Followed the bank for another six miles; camped opposite to Venterskroon (about a dozen houses). Hard frost at night. Day's march, 13½ miles.

August 10th.—Started east at 8.15 a.m., first along the river and then inland, between high hills. Met the Vaal River again at Rensburg Drift. Bivouacked half a mile from the river. Boers supposed to have crossed by this drift. Fine scenery along the river; high, rocky hills, and a good many trees. Day's march, seven miles.

August 11th.—Terrific wind and dust all the morning. Two or three veldt fires in camp, one nearly reaching our bivouac lines, after passing through the gunner lines and doing some damage to saddlery. At 2.30 suddenly ordered to march; crossed the drift (knee deep) and marched for about a mile into the Transvaal, then returned, fairly soaked, to our old bivouac at 5 p.m. Hard frost at night.

August 12th.—Halt at Rensburg Drift. Scouts out all day trying to discover whereabouts of Kitchener and Methuen, but without success.

August 13th.—Marched at 1.30 p.m., south-east, to Vredefort (a small town with a few shops); got in 5 p.m.; seven miles. Bought up everything in the town, though not much to be had. Orders from Lord Roberts to proceed to the drift at Scandinavia.

August 14th.—Moved at 7.30 a.m.; halted at Rietzburg for two hours in the middle of the day. Went on to Vlackfontein, which was reached at 6.30 p.m.; 14 miles.

August 15th.—Left at 7.30 a.m.; through open country; reached the

Vaal River at Scandinavia (Forssman's Drift), at noon. About a hundred Boers came to the Kaffir kraal on the opposite side of the river, and inquired who we were. River here about 100 to 150 yards wide. Day's march, 10 miles.

August 16th.—Halted. Sharp night.

August 17th.—Halt. Heard that De Wet had trekked to Rustenberg.

August 18th.—Halt. Hammick, Ballard, and 100 men of the Regiment brought in a convoy from Kroonstad. On full rations again, though nothing but water to drink still.

August 19th.—Halt.

August 20th.—Marched at 7.15 a.m.; open country all the way; passed Doornhoek, and then approached the Rhenoster River. Crossed at Kerr's Drift. Got in at 3.30 p.m., after a 16 mile march. Ox convoy did

BROKEN BRIDGE NEAR RHENOSTER.

not arrive until 7 p.m. Heard that mess cart of Royal Scots, returning from Kroonstad, was captured yesterday at Rhenoster Kop.

August 21st.—Marched at 7.15 a.m., as usual. Kept along the left bank of the river till we came to Honing's Spruit. Crossed, and encamped half a mile off, at Wet Kop. Day's march, 13½ miles.

August 22nd.—Marched at 7.15 a.m., for nine miles; crossed a dry drift, and then a mile on to camp (Gansvlei), arriving at 1.30 p.m. A Mounted Infantry patrol went to Rhenoster Kop and burned the farm near which the Royal Scots' cart had been captured.

August 23rd.—Marched at 6.30 a.m. After seven miles came to a lot of low kopjes and the Rhenoster River. Passed De Wet's burnt farm; marks of old encampments about; some shells picked up—probably the remains of Roberts' advance. Crossed the river, and $1\frac{1}{2}$ miles further on struck the railway at Kopjes Station. Encamped on kopjes about a mile from the station. Day's march, 12 miles.

August 24th.—Halted. Made walls all round camp. Strong cold wind blowing all day. The General, Colonel, and Quartermaster went off to Kroonstad to get supplies, etc. Heard that Lethbridge and 100 men have gone to Holfontein. Severe frost at night.

August 25th.—A warm day, no wind. Halted.

August 26th.—Halted. The General and party returned from Kroonstad. "Coats, warm, British," served out, and very welcome.

August 27th.—Left at 12.30 p.m.; proceeded along the railway to some hills overlooking Vredefort Station. Got in about 4.30 p.m., after nine miles march. Dug shelter-trenches round the bivouac until 11.30 p.m. A lot of thunder and lightning in the evening, and a little rain. Heard that Bruce Hamilton had captured Olivier near Lindley. All farms along the line have been destroyed.

August 28th.—Marched at 6.30 a.m. Some Boers were reported to be at a farm on the road; the pom-pom went after them, but they cleared off. Crossed a spruit and encamped at 10.30 a.m. near a store-house known as Shepstone's Farm. Day's march, 10 miles.

August 29th.—Heavy rain at 6 a.m., in spite of which we marched at 7.30, wearing greatcoats over everything. The coats, of course, did not meet in front, so were of little use. Rained in torrents the whole march. We had been intended to march to Vredefort Town, but as the convoy could not be brought out from Vredefort railway station on account of Boers being about, we had to march back to Vredefort Station. The going was very bad, both for men and animals, and we lost several mules —already weakened with continuous trekking. Halted at a kopje with English farm $1\frac{1}{2}$ miles from the station at noon, after marching 13 miles. Rain cleared off a bit in the afternoon, but came on again at 6 p.m., and poured hard all night. We got no dinner. Watt and Higgins, with a convoy from Kroonstad, met us as we reached camp. They went out half-way to Shepstone's Farm, but then got orders to return.

August 30th.—Cleared up in the morning, and the sun came out, at which all the men cheered. Heavy shower at noon, after which we managed to dry our kits to a certain extent.

August 31st.—Cloudless morning, following a dewy night, which had made all our things wet again. Marched at 7 a.m. north-west; thought we were going towards Parys, but route altered at the last. March through open country, in places a perfect swamp. Ox transport could not get along, so halted on some high ground after going six or seven

VILGEBOSCH DRIFT.

A HORSE DOWN.

miles. Took a lot of cattle, carts, ponies, etc., from the farms. Barron went into Kroonstad to do duty with the depôt.

September 1st.—Halted.

September 2nd.—Marched at 7 a.m. After six miles passed a lot of farms and kraals, and drove in a good quantity of cattle. About four miles further on, struck the road by which we had formerly marched to Kopjes Station. Another two miles brought us to our destination (Gansvlei) at 2 p.m. De Wet reported to have been here last week, and now to have gone off to Winkle's Drift. Natives say he has no wagons, and only 200 men, but we believe nothing that we hear now.

September 3rd.—Marched at 7 a.m. Crossed Rhenoster River at a mile from our bivouac ; it was dry when we crossed here before, but now knee-deep. Took two or three hours to get all the transport across. Bivouacked at Kristal Kopje (Kitchener's camp when we were at Rhebokfontein). Heard seven explosions in the evening, which we learned later were caused by the blowing up of the line at Honing's Spruit. Day's march, five miles.

September 4th.—An empty convoy went off to Honing's Spruit to get supplies. Mockler went off on this job with 300 of our men, two guns, and 50 Cavalry. They had a fairly good march of 10 miles to the railway, looting some burnt farms of geese, fowls, and pigs on the way, and turning half-a-dozen Boers out of the river bed, though without bagging any of them. The remainder of us moved at 10 a.m. to Roodeval Vlei. Just after crossing the drift over the Honing's Spruit we came to a farm, where the men who had blown up the line the night before had slept. The farm was burned, and the woman and her family arrested. March, 5½ miles.

September 5th.—The men of the Regiment left in camp, with two guns, a pom-pom and Mounted Infantry, went out in the morning to clear Boers off Rhenoster Kop, but after marching all day saw none of the enemy.

September 6th. – Marched early and reached Driekopjes at 4.30 p.m., where we bivouacked. Found Mockler's convoy had arrived at 1.30 p.m., having marched from Honing's Spruit to our old camp yesterday, and on here, with General Knox and the rest of the column, by Lace Diamond Mine and Valsch River to-day.

September 7th.—Marched at 7 a.m. ; reached Blesboklaagte at 11.30 a.m., after an eight mile march. The Mounted Infantry and the pom-pom went out at 9 p.m.

September 8th.—Marched at 7 a.m. Thought we were going south-west to Smalldeel, but on starting the direction was altered to north-east. The Boers hearing that we had gone west yesterday trekked north. Day's march, 15 miles. Bivouacked at Tweekuil.

September 9th.—Parade postponed until 7.30 a.m., then moved to ground near dam, and bivouacked for the day. Started for a night march at 6.45 p.m., by road all the way ; halted, after doing 12 miles, at 11.30 p.m., and bivouacked near a farm. Three Boer prisoners were caught yesterday with valuable information regarding De Wet ; one was carrying despatches to the Boer Commandant at Bothaville, telling him to be at Paardekraal on the 12th.

September 10th.—Off at 3.30 a.m. in the dark, and marched to surprise Rhenoster Kop. Reached the kopje at daybreak, and marched all over it without seeing a sign of a Boer (though plenty of game was put up). Moved on to a bivouac near Belmont, and halted at 10 a.m. Started again at 1 p.m. for Honing's Spruit, and arrived at 5.45 p.m., blowing up two farms on the way, and having completed 31 miles in the 23 hours.

September 11th.—As we were within the picquet lines of the Honing's Spruit Garrison, we did not stand to arms at 5.0 a.m., the first time for six weeks. Marched at 8 a.m., crossed the line, and then on to Boschpoort (nine miles) ; bivouacked near a dam. Watt went into Kroonstad sick.

September 12th.—Started on a night march last night at 11 p.m., the idea being to surprise Paardekraal, about ten miles away. The convoy was left behind with a guard to come on afterwards. Halted every hour for ten minutes. We were to have marched till daylight, and consequently carried no coats or blankets. At 2.30 a.m., however, the force was found to be only a mile or two from Paardekraal, so was formed up and bivouacked in strict silence, and a good deal of shivering until 5.30 a.m. The Regiment then led the way to the farm, which was empty, except for one of our Mounted Infantry, who told us that the rest of the Mounted Infantry had passed at 4 a.m. There was nothing further to be done, so we halted, and our transport came up in the afternoon. The Boers had left the place yesterday.

September 13th.—Marched at 5 a.m. towards Kroonstad. Halted at Hout Kop at 10.30 a.m. after 15 miles.

September 14th.—Halt.

September 15th.—Marched at 4 p.m. four or five miles nearer to Kroonstad, and halted for the night at Welgevenden.

September 16th.—Marched at 5 a.m. to Kroonstad. Crossed the drift, and halted half a mile from the river. Went into our Depôt camp in the afternoon to get kit, etc. Been out 47 days, instead of the original four days. Distance marched, roughly, 350 miles.

September 17th.—Off again on another job at 5 a.m. Marched along the Senekal road (14 miles), and bivouacked at 10.30 a.m., at Ranjeslaagte, on the Bloem Spruit. The Cavalry of the 3rd Brigade, and four R.H.A. guns, now forming part of our force, preceded us over-night, and moved on ahead again as we arrived at our bivouac. News was brought in later that the Cavalry had located the Boers on Klompje Doorns, and that an officer of the 16th Lancers had been shot in the arm from a farm-house.

September 18th.—Marched at 5 a.m. Heard on the march that a laager had been sighted by the Cavalry, and after we had gone about eight miles the R.H.A. and our battery opened fire. The Royal Scots moved round the right flank, and fired a few rounds at some retreating Boers, while we moved round the left flank, but saw only a few Boers in the far distance. The laager had cleared off in the early morning. Our advanced Cavalry, we heard, nearly came to grief ; a party of Boers *dressed in khaki* beckoned to them, and then opened fire, but made away

EMPTY.

as soon as they saw the Infantry advancing. The casualties were two men of the 16th Lancers killed, five Cavalry men and one gunner wounded. Two dead Boers were found. We halted from 11 a.m. till 2 p.m., then bivouacked for dinner, and moved in the evening on to higher ground (Blaauwboschbank) for the night. There are now seven Columns advancing from the south, and the object of our force is to prevent the enemy breaking north.

September 19th and 20th.—Halt.

September 21st.—Marched at 5 a.m., and reached Kroonstad at 5 p.m., having marched the whole 25 miles straight off, in order to get a day's rest in tents at our Standing Camp.

September 22nd.—Had an easy morning ; did not stand to arms.

September 23rd.—Away again at 5 a.m. on the Heilbron road (by which we had returned from Paardekraal). Were to have gone this trek to Bothaville, but the route was changed last night. Halted on our old ground at Hout Kop (15 miles).

September 24th.—Moved at 5 a.m. to Paardekraal, 15 miles.

September 25th.—Mockler sent into Kroonstad hospital with fever and ague. Marched at 5 a.m. to Paardekraal North. Came across De Lisle's force at the drift over Rhenoster at Vaalkrans ; 14 miles.

September 26th.—Heard guns to the north. General Knox rode on to join the 3rd Cavalry Brigade, who were engaging the enemy near Heilbron. Our C.O. assumed command of the Column, and we moved on to Leeuwfontein, on the Heilbron road, 5 miles.

September 27th.—Moved at 5 a.m. due west to Uitkijk, where we met Dalgety's Colonials. 15 miles.

September 28th—October 1st.—Halted at Uitkijk.

October 2nd.—Marched at 6 a.m. to Hartebeestefontein, 15 miles.

October 3rd.—Marched into Heilbron and bivouacked on the south side of the town, re-opening the railway, which had been closed for seven months. Childers (with H Company), Lathy (with I Company), and Barron and Sullivan went off at 3.30 p.m. by armoured train on detachment to Gottenberg, a bridge on the Heilbron—Wolvehoek line (about 17 miles from Heilbron). A few miles from Gottenberg, the train was attacked by a party of Boers who, however, soon dispersed when our men opened fire.

A correspondent writes to the *Times* as follows :—

Heilbron, O.R.C., Oct. 15.

As the result of there being no press-men in the Orange River Colony, where all the real fighting has been and is going on (the Free Staters being the men who have made the stand throughout), the doings of the troops south of the Vaal have been but little chronicled. The public have thus been left in the dark regarding the movements of the different Columns operating against the now notorious De Wet and the many marauding bodies and commandos of Boers still at large. As I think it will interest very many of our friends at home, I send you an account of the last "trek" of Major-General Knox's Column which left Kroonstad on the first of August and "fetched up" at Heilbron on the 3rd of October, after having marched over 500 miles, part of the time on half rations, and covered nearly every yard of country lying between Bothaville and Heilbron, west and east, and between the Vaal River and Ventersburg, north and south. The Column was engaged in rounding-up cattle, burning farms, searching for arms, and generally clearing the country, besides pursuing De Wet's and other commandos. Owing to the extraordinary "slimness" and mobility of the enemy the course of the Column was necessarily very tortuous. We were constantly on the heels of the enemy or endeavouring to effect a surprise. The passage of the Rhenoster River on August 4, which was strongly opposed by De Wet's rearguard, being the point where the greatest resistance was encountered. With the exception of 100 Yeomanry (77th Company), the Column was destitute of mounted men, the force being composed of 17th Battery R.F.A. (Major Johnson), 1st Oxfordshire Light Infantry (Lieutenant-Colonel Hon. A. E. Dalzell), 3rd Royal Scots (Colonel Grant), and a section of Royal Engineers (Captain Barrington). It is wonderful the mobility this force exhibited, and how frequently it came in touch with the enemy, though it was never able to crush the Boer commandos, owing to its composition being entirely of Infantry and Artillery.

Major-General Charles Knox, who must not be confounded with W. G. Knox, now at Kroonstad, undoubtedly deserves great credit for the manner in which he carried out his arduous task. It must be admitted, however, that the officers and men under him would have preferred to see him use more drastic measures with the enemy, and ruthlessly destroy all farms harbouring rebels, rather than allow his kind heart to be imposed upon by weeping women left behind for the purpose. The fact is, that in this country mounted men are an absolute necessity. Our Cavalry and Mounted Infantry have disappointed us. The first are still armed with lance, sword, and carbine, the two former weapons being relics of the Middle Ages, and the latter useless against the Mauser Rifle. In our action of Blauwbosch Bank, on September 18th, the 16th Lancers, who had joined us for a short time, left their cumbrous spears on the veldt until the affair was over, and then went back to fetch them. During all this period it must be remembered that the troops have had nothing to eat but "trek-ox"—no one knows the oak-like character of the ox that daily treks who has not sampled him—and ration biscuit, with an occasional pig, goose, or hen commandeered *en route;* that they lay every night in the open, and were exposed all day to the ever-varying whims of the South African climate. Here, at Heilbron, there is comparative rest. We have had our tents sent up, and as a big supply depôt is being formed here, we are not likely to starve. When we marched into the place the Boers had just marched out, and we found everything in a state of siege. The shops were closed and empty, the post-office and other public institutions wrecked, the railway a bare line with no rolling stock, and everything chaotic. Now we have a train in every day heavily laden with supplies, the shops are open, the Dutch conventicle taken over for Church of England services, the offices reorganised, and things generally put straight. Heilbron is quite a small town, but is cleaner and better built than most South African places, and the water supply is excellent. In ransacking the railway station soon after we marched in, I found a large number of invoices for the despatch of arms and ammunition, showing how fully prepared the Boers were. Their dates were in September and October of last year. We have now got this place into a good state of defence, and strongly intrenched. On October 13th we got news that a large commando had collected between this and Frankfort, and the General despatched 400 Oxfordshires with two guns at 3 a.m. to attack them and co-operate with Colonel Le Gallais, who was moving from the Frankfort side. At 7 a.m. we saw the Boers retreating towards us before Le Gallais, but unfortunately, they all turned off, riding on the spur, four miles from our position, and we only bagged five odd ones. Yesterday a few of them rounded up 70 oxen belonging to the Royal Scots while the canny ones were in kirk. The Boers are very hard up for food, and would "round up" anything now, even Oom Paul himself! As for ourselves, we are a collection of "prehistoric peeps," and I shall hardly know a decent meal or bed when I see one.

FOR THE OFFICERS' DINNER.

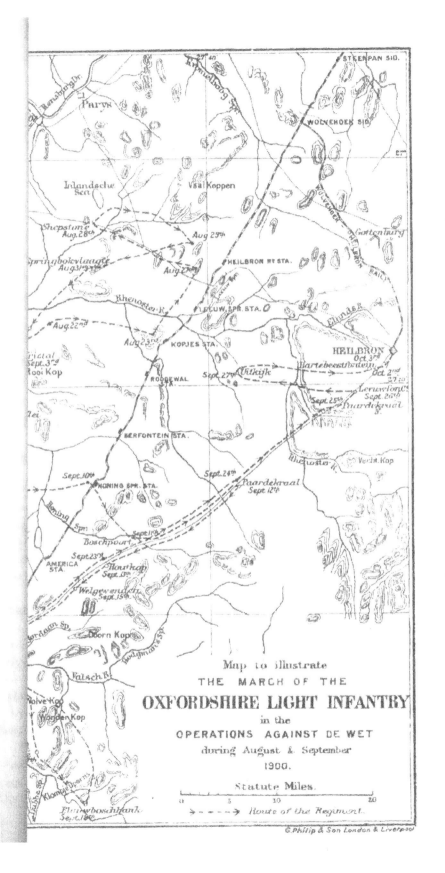

Map to illustrate

THE MARCH OF THE

OXFORDSHIRE LIGHT INFANTRY

in the

OPERATIONS AGAINST DE WET

during August & September

1900.

Statute Miles.

0   5   10   20

→ – – – – → Route of the Regiment.

G.Philip & Son London & Liverpool

CHAPTER XI.

HEILBRON AND DETACHMENTS.

FROM October until the end of the year the head-quarters of the Regiment were at Heilbron, with four Companies out on detachment in the neighbourhood, guarding the railway line. Nothing of great importance took place during this period, though the Headquarter Companies were constantly called upon to make sudden marches to endeavour to cut off small parties of Boers, and destroy farms that harboured the enemy, and the isolated detachments were occasionally attacked, and were frequently threatened.

Extract from a letter from Major R. W. Porter, dated Heilbron, 5th November, 1900 :—

We are anchored down here for a bit, I fancy, and not sorry that the trekking after De Wet is over, as far as we are concerned. We are left here with a 5-inch gun, two field guns, 40 or 50 Yeomen, and ourselves, as a garrison for this town, Roberts having promised the inhabitants that it shall not be again evacuated. Colonel Dalzell is in command of the Station; Cobb, Station Staff Officer; and myself, Provost Marshal. The Regiment is well up to strength again, since the draft of 140 men joined us on the 22nd October, and we can turn out 820 men, including all the detachments. Lamotte and 60 men are at a bridge four miles from here; Childers, with his Company and part of the Volunteer Company, at Gottenberg (half-way to Wolvehoek), and the other half of the Volunteer Company is at two small posts close by. I was out a fortnight ago with 200 men and a " pom-pom " for four days, trying to locate a laager about 15 or 16 miles from here. I found it all right, and there was to have been an attack on it in combination with another force from this place; but at the last moment the plans were altered, as we were wanted to go off to Vrede-fort Road, so I had to march straight back to Heilbron. It was a pity, as we might have got a few. The Boers tried to see me home to camp the day I spotted their laager ; and when I was about four miles on my way back, about a hundred of them came after me and opened fire on my Yeomen, who were doing rear-guard. But the moment I said " pom-pom " to them, they bolted for their horses and were off to a man, and I saw no more of them. There are lots of them in small parties all round us—tens, twenties, and so on—but I don't believe they mean business at all ; they are just waiting about till the job is over, so as to avoid being sent away. They have a shot or two at long ranges at our picquets now and then, but nothing else. We are very nearly cut off from the world here, as we only get two trains a-week with supplies, consequently we hear little or no news. Fanshawe and his lot got a couple of guns and a few prisoners off De Wet last week. He (Fanshawe) is making a great name for himself, and I hope he will get something out of it. Hamilton is quite fit again now, but had a near shave, I believe, as he was hit on the side of the head by a splinter of a shell.

MAJOR R. W. PORTER.

Diary :—

November 5th.—Moved at 10 a.m. with 200 men of the Regiment, 2 guns, and 20 Yeomen. Visited Hartebeestefontein, burned the house (good substitute for fifth of November bonfire !), and took the family back to the town. Then proceeded to Brakfontein farm, which had been already burned by a former Column, but which had been re-roofed and occupied by several families. We took all the women and children back to Heilbron.

November 6th.—Sent out a wagon at 7 a.m. this morning, with an escort of 12 men, under Sergeant Bibby and 6 Yeomen, for the purpose of destroying the roof of Brakfontein farm, and bringing away the iron work. About noon heard firing in that direction, and 20 Yeomen, 100 Infantry, and 2 guns went out, and took up a position on a ridge above the farm. Found the wagon in the low ground, and the escort taking cover in a spruit. Located enemy in a kraal, about 3,000 yards away. Shelled them, and the rocky ridge above the farm. Enemy cleared off, and we brought the wagon in. The escort had been attacked soon after leaving the farm on the return journey, and, being surrounded, took cover in the spruit. The Boers kept up a continuous fire, but only

OFFICERS' MESS.

killed one mule and wounded four (of which three had to be destroyed). When first attacked, one of the Yeomanry galloped back to give the alarm to camp, but his horse was killed before he had gone 70 yards.

November 7th.—Hammick's outpost on Kraal Hill heavily fired on at 5 p.m.

November 9th.—Foljambe went out with a party of our men and some Yeomen to destroy farms at Skeit Kraal and Damplaats, both of which were the resort of Boer sniping parties. The enemy kept up a brisk fire from a distance during the operations.

November 12th.—Burned two farms—Luyts and Badenhorst. Drove in a quantity of stock. A good deal of resistance from Boers, who had to be shelled out of their positions.

November 13th.—Wagon sent to Luyts Farm to fetch in wood, etc., attacked by a party of Boers. Simpson took a party out and drove the enemy off. No casualties.

November 26th.—The Holfontein detachment (Watt and Hawkins) came in. Fuller rejoined from sick leave in England.

Writing on the 7th December, an officer of the Regiment says :—

One day last week, one of our small posts, five miles from Gottenburg, got into a mess. Four men went out from camp to collect fuel, and apparently strayed too far, being suddenly surrounded and fired on, with the result that one man was killed and the other three were taken prisoners. The subaltern at the next post, hearing of it, went off, with 15 men, to the rescue, but met with a warm reception, having four men wounded and four missing. The Boers sent back one of our men to have the wounded taken away, which was done—one poor chap was hit in three places. Two days later the three prisoners turned up, having been released ; but we have not heard anything of the four missing men.[1] Mockler has relieved Childers at Gottenburg.

Diary :—

December 8th.—The sentry at Leeuwpoort bridge was fired on at about 11 p.m., and had a narrow shave, one of the three shots they had at him passing through the skirt of his jacket.

December 12th.—A small mixed force went out at Leeuwpoort and Steyn's Halt to try and round up some Boers. Saw about 20 of them in the far distance and shelled them. Killed one and wounded another. Drove in about 800 head of cattle, horses, and sheep.

December 18th.—Two armed Boers came in and surrendered. Both had Lee-Metfords, bandoliers, and ammunition. One rifle belonged to the Lancashire Fusiliers, the other to the Royal Scots Fusiliers. Some refugee women also came in.

December 19th.—Tried to come the "slim" over the Boers, by hiding some men in farms which the enemy were known to frequent. They were too cunning to be caught, however, and they gave our Yeomen a bad time. Eventually Lathy and 50 men went out to cover the retirement, and the guns did a bit of shelling. Hot day and rain all night.

---

[1] They eventually came in to Frankfort, 30 miles from Heilbron.

Our last letter of the year is dated Heilbron, 31st December, 1900, and the following is an extract :—

Not a very merry Christmas, perhaps, but merry enough under the circumstances. Since my last there has not been much excitement ; a few farms have been destroyed round about ; a few Boers have surrendered, and a certain number of Boer families have come in or been brought in. Attempts have also been made to induce troublesome parties in the neighbourhood to give themselves up. The latest proclamations have been freely distributed among the burghers, but they all seem to be a bit shy. However, I suppose they will get sick of it in time. We had our sports on the 27th—quite a good show, and we have started a real live weekly newspaper, called the *Pom-pom*, which will probably have the largest circulation in—Heilbron.

The following competition took place at Heilbron, Orange River Colony, on the 27th December :—

Inter - Company Sharp - shooters' Match.—Teams :

ON FULL RATIONS AGAIN.

Eight men (including Corporals and Lance-Corporals) under a Sergeant. *Dress :* Drill order, with braces and two pouches. Eight targets, 8 inches in diameter, two paces apart. Distances unknown.

Conditions.—Two teams will be drawn up in extended order, about 350 yards from the targets, and will number off from right to left. On the signal to commence from the superintending officer, the teams will advance at the double to the firing point and open fire. One minute allowed from time of starting until the "Cease-fire" is ordered by the superintending officer. On a target being knocked down or broken, the corresponding man of the opposite team will be ordered to fall out as a casualty, and will take no further part in the competition. The team with most men in at the end to win. Position, any military. Ties to shoot again.

Prizes (presented by Major R. W. Porter).—1st, 5*l.*; 2nd, 2*l.* 10*s.* Won by E, or Major G. F. Mockler's Company; 2nd, B, or Captain F. J. Henley's Company.

The Annual Athletic Meeting was held on the same day.

Committee:—Captains Lamotte and Childers, Colour-Sergeant G. Bryan, and Private Simlin.

Events and results:—

High Jump.—Lance-Corporal Muddle, 1st; Bugler Williams, 2nd; Bandsman Balls, 3rd.

Wheelbarrow Race.—One man to carry another on his back, run about 60 yards, and return wheelbarrow-fashion, blindfolded. Sergeants Gear and Aldridge, 1st; Corporal Broome and Private C. Faulkner, 2nd.

Long Jump.—Private Sheehy, 1st; Private Greenaway, 2nd; Lance-Corporal Brannagan, 3rd.

Quarter-Mile.—Regimental Challenge Belt, to be inscribed "Won on Active Service."—Lance-Corporal Brannagan, 1st; Private Sheehy, 2nd; Private Witcher, 3rd.

Veterans' Race.—200 yards handicap.—Colour-Sergeant Baldwin, 1st; Private Speakman, 2nd.

Alarm Post.—Inter-company.—Teams, 10 men commanded by a N.C.O. below the rank of Sergeant. Dress: Field Service Marching Order. Conditions: A tent complete will be placed on the ground, and the team will be marched up to it. The team-commander will then post one man on sentry, and the remainder will pile arms, take off their equipment, and proceed to pitch the tent. The men will then go inside and take off their boots and putties. The alarm will then be given. Three men will get dressed, double out, and lie down alongside the sentry. The remainder will strike the tent, pack it correctly, and join the others, after getting dressed. The whole will then advance about 100 yards. Points will be given for time, style, turn-out, and manner of pitching and packing the tent. Won by B, or Captain F. J. Henley's Company; F and I Companies divided 2nd prize.

One Mile.—Regimental Challenge Belt, to be inscribed "Won on Active Service."—Bandsman Welch, 1st; Private Timms, 2nd; Private F. Smith, 3rd.

Band and Buglers' Race.—Walking. Competitors to play their own instruments.—Bandsman Balls, 1st; Grant, 2nd.

Artillery Driving Competition, open to teams from 17th Battery, R.F.A.—Won by Gun Team and Wagon Team of E Sub-Division.

Tug-of-War. — Inter-Company. — H Company, 1st; E Company, 2nd.

Half-Mile.—Private Witcher, 1st; Private Sheehy, 2nd; Bandsman Welch, 3rd.

In addition to the above there was a *Lucky Bag Competition;* and *Tilting at the Ring* went on during the afternoon. " The sports," writes a correspondent, " were a brilliant success: The band played, the officers gave tea and cake to the *élite* of Heilbron, and Boer refugees came up in their hundreds and were much interested."

THE MESS WAITER'S SIESTA.

CHAPTER XII.

THE MOUNTED INFANTRY COMPANY.

FROM ALDERSHOT TO PRETORIA.

By C. E. Forrest.

THE Regiment mobilised on December 4th, 1899, at Aldershot.

The mobilisation was half completed when an order was issued to the effect that each Regiment of the 6th Division would find a Mounted Infantry Company. This Company was to consist of one Captain, three Subalterns, and 140 rank and file.

G Company was chosen to form the nucleus of our Mounted Infantry Company, those men who did not wish to become Mounted Infantrymen being transferred to other Companies. The men of the Regiment who already possessed Mounted Infantry certificates, were then transferred to G Company. The total was reached by means of Volunteers from other Companies. The officers were Captain G. N. Colvile, Lieut. C. E. Forrest, and 2nd Lieut. R. R. M. Brooke.

The Regiment sailed for South Africa on board the *Gaika* on December 23rd, the Mounted Infantry Companies of the 6th Division being left behind to follow when they had received their horses. A lot of hard work had to be got through before orders to sail were received; saddles, nosebags, hay-nets, horse-shoes, wire-cutters, sandbags, a field forge, and innumerable straps, were a few among the many different articles to be drawn in addition to the usual tents, blankets, etc.; then "stables" at 7 a.m. till 8 a.m., again from 9. 30 a.m. to 12, and 5 p.m. to 5.30. p.m. ; and lastly, parades and inspections for the General.

FUNERAL OF A HORSE.

Major Evelegh was in command of the Mounted Infantry of the 13th Brigade and remained so till our arrival at Maitland Camp, South Africa.

Three weeks after the Regiment had sailed, orders were received for the Mounted Infantry to embark on the *Pindari* at the Albert Docks on January 13th, taking 84 cobs with them. The deficit in cobs was to be made up at Cape Town. A certain amount of difficulty was experienced in finding the required number; as, although there were over 400 to choose from, most of them had strangles.

The *Pindari* belonged to the Brocklebank Line, Liverpool, and had already made one voyage with troops to the Cape. The troops on board consisted of the Mounted Infantry Companies of the Oxfordshire Light Infantry and the West Riding Regiment, and a draft for the Inniskilling Dragoons. The number of horses on board was 480, and Major Evelegh was in command of the troops.

There was sufficient work to be done at stables to allow of physical drill being practically dispensed with. Except when it was rough every horse was taken out of its box and groomed daily. On the voyage 23 horses died; but when the *Pindari* arrived at Cape Town she had the second best average for horse-ships from England.

On arrival at Cape Town we found the bay full of transports, hospital ships, and yachts. On February 8th, the *Pindari* was laid alongside the docks; the disembarkation commenced; and after half-a-dozen hours' work a start was made for Maitland Camp. The horses at once showed their appreciation of being again on *terrafirma*, and more than one unfortunate tram passed on the road bore the marks of their hoofs. On reaching Mait-

THE M.I. COMPANY DISEMBARKING.

land Camp, the cobs were turned loose into wire kraals, and it was with the greatest difficulty that they were prevented from breaking out, though after a time they settled down.

The cobs of the West Riding Mounted Infantry Company, however, ran clean over the wire of the kraal in which they were placed, some being badly cut about, and having to be shot. Next day additional horses were received, thus making the Company complete.

Parades were held every morning. Men who could not ride were taught to ride, fresh bandoliers were drawn, and unnecessary baggage was stored at the base.

On February 13th, the Company left by train for De Aar at 9.5 p.m. The scene on mounting when leaving Maitland Camp for Cape Town Station was most amusing. Men mounting from the near side; mounting from the off side; men lying on their backs on the ground; men with their arms round their horses' necks, and the horses kicking and squealing all over the field.

The sleeping accommodation was good. Early next morning the train slowly climbed up the Hex River Pass—the line is a most wonderful feat of engineering. More than twenty horses were placed in most of the trucks. One or two were continually falling down, and the train had to stop at stations until they were put on their legs again. The country through which the train passed is called the Great Karoo. It has a very sandy soil, and is covered with small bushes, which are its only kind of pasture. Water is very scarce, sheep being the only animals which can be reared. On nearing Magjesfontein the guard pointed out General Wauchope's grave. At the station Mr. Logan made his appearance, and with great kindness asked the officers to lunch. He had been wounded at Belmont, and gave a graphic description of the battle. He was there as a sight-seer.

De Aar at last! after two nights and a day in the train. The usual stoppage for watering and feeding horses. Up to now the Company had expected to join

Lord Roberts's Army at Orange River, but at De Aar fresh orders awaited it. After two hours stop the train left for Naauwpoort. At Hanover Road Station the Victoria Mounted Rifles were passed. On arriving at Naauwpoort orders were received to go as quickly as possible to Arundel, which place General Clements had just reached in his retirement from Colesberg. Expectations ran high as to whether the Mounted Infantry Company, although starting three weeks after the Regiment, would see service first. By this time, however, we learned afterwards, the Paardeberg campaign had begun. The train reached Arundel at 9 p.m., when the horses and baggage were unloaded, and the Commandant pointed out the camping ground. The Wiltshire Regiment provided tea, food, and so forth. They were very despondent, having had two Companies captured the day before during the retreat. Having reached Arundel they thought they had got a good position, and would not have to retire on Naauwpoort, as was at one time . feared.

The position at Arundel consisted of a range of kopjes running east and west. The Boers occupied the range running parallel through the north of it, distant about $4\frac{1}{2}$ miles. Innumerable smaller kopjes dotted the whole country. (The country in Cape Colony was far more mountainous than any afterwards encountered in the Free State.)

The troops at Arundel consisted of the 12th Brigade, 6th Division, the Inniskilling Dragoons, J Battery R.H.A., two Batteries R.F.A., four 5-inch howitzers, and about 700 Volunteer Mounted Infantry, consisting of South Africans and Australians. General Clements was in command. Two nights after arrival the Company found two picquets, each consisting of one officer and 25 men. A plain extended between the British and

Boer positions. About 2¾ miles from Arundel Camp side, and therefore about 1½ miles from the Boer side, were three small hills, called respectively Inniskilling, Australian, and Epsom, on which the picquets were posted.

From all three the Boers were distinctly visible. It was a standing order that no horses were to be unbitted or ungirthed. It was a most jumpy kind of game. The picquets arrived back in camp at 8 a.m., having been relieved by some Colonials. One hour for breakfast, and then off on a two days' reconnaissance. The force making the reconnaissance consisted of one Battery R.F.A., Inniskilling Dragoons, and the Oxfordshire Light Infantry and West Riding Mounted Infantry Companies. This was the first time the Company had seen any fighting. After getting about two miles beyond the picquet line on the west flank, the Boers put in an appearance. They opened fire from a big gun on Taaibosh Hill, and from a couple of pom-poms. These last when heard for the first time, and even at any time, give one a most uncomfortable feeling. The Battery had soon to retire, the remainder of the force following more leisurely. The Boers then came out into the open, and compelled the whole force to retreat behind the picquet line. One object of the reconnaissance was to open up communication with Hanover Road.

Although several other reconnaissances were made, they generally had the same result, namely, that after getting a few miles beyond the picquet line, the Boers compelled the force to retreat. During one of these reconnaissances, Captain Wallis, commanding the West Riding Mounted Infantry Company, was killed.

Another picquet found by the Mounted Infantry was on the extreme left. One day Brooke with 25 men was on picquet there. There was a long low kopje from 1,500 to 2,000 yards away facing his position, which was on a high kopje overlooking a farm. Suddenly, and without any warning, 300 Boers appeared over the kopje facing him. Luckily a squadron of the Inniskillings was in sight, and he sent back to them for assistance, at the same time sending back word to camp. The Boers endeavoured for a long time to find out whether there was a picquet on the kopje, and if so, of what strength. As our people kept quite still, the enemy found out nothing. Their intention was to seize the kopje on which the picquet was posted, and then turn our left flank. They approached the farm

SECOND-LIEUT. BROOKE AND HIS CHARGER.

very carefully, and two old gentlemen (one in a black frock coat) rode up and dismounted at the farm, which was vacant. The picquet fired a volley at them, knocking over one man and a horse. The remainder of the Boers then retired to the kopje in the distance at their best pace. All the troops in camp had now been turned out, and the remainder of the Mounted Infantry arrived on the scene. Orders were given to find out whether the Boers were still on the kopje in front, and whether in any strength.   Four men started to go round the right of the kopje and four round the left.   Directly the patrols made their appearance, the Boers opened fire.   The patrols went on until within 200 yards, when some of the Boers could be seen. Owing to a locust storm, the patrols made a bad mark to shoot at, which was a mercy.   Having found out what was required, they came back as quickly as possible, and, on dismounting, one of the horses was found to have been shot in the shoulder.

The Infantry which had arrived was now sent back to camp, and the Mounted Infantry was placed on detached kopjes to prolong the left flank.   Next morning a battery came up, and, after carefully concealing the guns, shelled the Boers out of the kopje in front. In the evening the battery and the extra picquets on the left flank were withdrawn.

At Arundel four cold-shoers were attached to the Company; two coming from the gunners, the others being Indians.   Colvile thought the latter would make an excellent body-guard to him, as one was a Central India horseman, and the other a Madras Lancer, and both were very keen to fight.   The General, however, did not see it in the same light.

Towards the end of February news arrived that Kimberley had been relieved, and a few days later that 68 wagons belonging to Cronje had been captured. After that confused reports flew about, some saying that Cronje was captured, and that Ladysmith was relieved.

Shortly after these rumours, Lord Kitchener came and inspected the troops.

On the 27th February a general advance of the troops at Arundel was ordered, its objective being Norval's Pont.   For the last week the Boers had been much quieter, and at a reconnaissance on the 25th showed signs of being in largely reduced numbers; in fact they were already retreating; the majority, with their General (Delarey), having gone to try and succour Cronje.

The Company was attached to a force under Major King-King, ordered to guard the right flank of the advance. The force consisted (besides ourselves) of one section of J Battery R.H.A., one Company West Australians, and two Companies Prince Alfred's Guard. Each Company of Mounted Infantry had two buck-wagons as transport, each wagon being drawn by ten mules. The West Australians, under Major Moore, were a splendid body of men; they compared more than favourably with any other Colonials met with afterwards.

The advance began early in the morning, and the force slowly approached the original Boer position. A sharp fire opened on nearing it. Some of the Boers were still there. The guns were unlimbered, and after shelling Taaibosch Hill for half an hour the advance continued, and no other opposition was met with. A halt was made at mid-day at Jasfontein, a farm where the Boers had watered their horses for over three weeks in sight of the picquets. Later on their laagers were passed, and by their appearance the Boers must have lived as well, if not better, than the British troops; sardine tins being especially noticeable. Khaki coats, minus their field-dressing and identification cards, were found lying about. A halt was made at Jasfontein for the night. The farm had evidently been deserted in a hurry. Clothes, etc., were strewn all over the rooms— from the old frau's black Sunday dress to the farmer's brown slouch hat. There were two harmoniums in good working order.

Next day Rensburg was occupied. A mile beyond the station was an overturned train, which in the previous retreat from Colesberg had carried three days' rations for the whole force. The station-master had treacherously pushed it down the hill towards the Boers, but luckily, the points being crossed, it had upset after going a mile. A force had to be sent down to burn the train to prevent the provisions falling into the enemy's

THE MESS CART.

hands. Upon one of the doors at Rensburg Station a Boer had written up the following riddle :—

Q. How many kinds of fools are there ?

A. Three. The fool ; the —— fool ; and the British General.

General Clements saw this, and was much amused at it.

The next place of interest was Slingersfontein, round which a lot of fighting had taken place during the retreat. Colesberg was then occupied. The Boers had been in possession here for over 100 days. Most of the population were Dutch, and the few remaining British residents had had a very bad time. Coleskop could be seen overlooking the town. Two guns had been placed on the top of it when General French was in command.

A halt was made here for a few days to rest the horses and repair the line, every single bridge of which was blown up. Very little fighting had been done since leaving Arundel, the General's intention being not to attack as long as the Boers kept retreating. This may appear to have been wrong, but the positions were tremendously strong, and as long as the Boers continued to retreat there was no need to hurry them. If an attack had been made it would probably have failed, and if it had failed, it would have put fresh life into the Boers, who could then have remained at Norval's Pont, and cut Lord Roberts' lines of communication. However, all went well, and the Boers retreated.

When Colesberg was left, the Company still remained on the right flank, generally about 14 or 15 miles from the main body. A great many of the people in the farms were unable to speak English, although this was still Cape Colony. Anyhow, they were most polite to the troops; but in spite of this, a great number were sent into Colesberg to answer the charge of disloyalty. At one farm, called Hebron, the people were particularly kind, and one felt very sorry when they had to go to Colesberg with the rest. The farms about here were very fine, this being a great horse-breeding and ostrich-rearing district. On arriving at Hebron, which was distant 12 miles from Norval's Pont, a loud explosion was heard, and a column of dust rose in the air. The Pont was blown up!

After this there was no hurry; the next thing to do was to get across the river. The force gradually approached, and at last caught sight of the Orange Free State. The Boers were still in force on the north side of the river. The bridge had cost £99,000 to build, and the three centre arches and piers had been blown down. It took two months before these were replaced and the bridge was again ready for use.

The Intelligence Department expected a big fight to take place. The river was commanded on both sides by steep kopjes. The banks, which were covered with trees (thus affording good cover for snipers) were low, and good

NORVAL'S PONT.

for bridging purposes. The current was very strong, and Dent, an officer of the Inniskillings, who came out on board the *Pindari*, was drowned whilst bathing.

Major King-King's force, to which the Company still belonged, was sent along to the east to make a demonstration. This took place at Kruger's Drift. Several farm houses were visible across the river, about a mile inside the Orange Free State. A few Boers were seen walking about. The guns were unlimbered and a shot fired, which fell short. The next shot burst in the middle of the Boers, who were galloping away; two men and horses being left on the ground. The guns then shelled the farms, when a white flag was immediately hoisted. A big reconnaissance was made at the same time opposite the main Boer position. This last was shelled for some time, but there was no response. Volunteers who could row were then asked for, and the West Australians were able to send in, among others, the name of the champion sculler of Australia.

The crossing was to be attempted on the 15th March. On the evening before a concert was held, at which several of the Company took part. Up to now everyone had thought that the passage was going to be contested. The Company was ordered to prevent any Boer reinforcement coming to assist those opposing the main column. A pontoon bridge was to be thrown over in a re-entrant bend towards the British side. The Company was posted on the eastern flank of this bend and marched down to its position very early in the morning. Sangars were built, and all expected to have a warm time. The covering party had been sent over before daylight. The sun rose and still there was no firing, and after half-an-hour it was known that the passage was not going to be disputed. The bridge was the longest one that has ever been built on active service by the British Army. By the afternoon all the Infantry had crossed, and in two days the whole force was over the river. On the second day after crossing General Pole-Carew came down from Bloemfontein by train, thus showing that communications between the Colony and Bloemfontein had been opened up.

The Company was moved on March 18th to Donkerpoort, this being the first station within the Orange Free State. During its stay of several days, patrols were sent out to visit the farms and collect arms. The farmers, although they had been fighting, were most friendly, and wanted to keep their Mausers for " sporting purposes," as they said! One man told a patrol how he had been at Colesberg, and when asked if he had ever shot at the British and killed any of them, he answered, that one afternoon he had assisted in a small fight, but when a number of men were firing together it was very hard to say if one hit anyone. He was a Scotchman, and seemed quite delighted to tell the tale!

After waiting three days at Donkerpoort, orders came to proceed to Bloemfontein by way of Philippolis and Fauresmith. There were to be two mobile columns, to act as an advance guard. The Company was attached

CAMP AT NORVAL'S PONT.

to the one under the command of Major Dauncey, Inniskilling Dragoons. The force consisted of one squadron of Inniskilling Dragoons, one Battery R.A.,

the Oxfordshire Light Infantry and the West Riding
Mounted Infantry Companies, and the West Australians.

Philippolis was reached in three or four days. The

RIET RIVER.

Company discovered a large quantity of ammunition
buried under a kopje, two or three miles from the town,
and destroyed it all next day. Whilst here the weather
was awful, raining for 40 hours without stopping ; and
as there was only one blanket apiece it was most uncomfortable. At Philippolis, as at the other towns
afterwards visited, it was impossible to get luxuries in
any shape or form. When the ground became dry
enough for the wagons to move, a start was made for
Fauresmith. On leaving Philippolis the whole force
marched past the General, the bands playing. This was

done to impress the burghers with the true state of affairs. President Steyn's daughter was among the crowd looking on. Major Dauncey's Column had orders to call at Jagersfontein on the way to Fauresmith. During the march, an old Armstrong gun and a Maxim were found down a disused mine-shaft. On the Column entering Jagersfontein the people were intensely pleased, a great many of them being English, or having English sympathies. The force was accommodated in the mine compound. All night long the strains of " Rule Britannia " and " God Save the Queen " could be heard all over the town. Next day Fauresmith was reached. Got news that the remains of a commando had been heard of at Koffyfontein. General Clements with a small force went to attempt its capture, but it had dispersed. Petrusburg was then visited, and the next point was Bloemfontein, which every one was very anxious to see. Signs of a large force having marched this way were evident; old camping grounds, distinguished by " bully " beef and biscuit tins were passed; dead horses marked the line of advance, and the smell from them was sickening. Their presence could be detected at a considerable distance, and one endeavoured by filling one's lungs as full as possible with air, and by holding one's nose, to escape more than the first sniff. One's breath, however, generally gave out when one was exactly opposite the object, and it was then possible to know how a *dead* horse *could* smell. No opposition having been met with during the march, the affair of Sanna's Post (the news of which came during the last march but one before reaching Bloemfontein) was a great surprise to most.

The force reached Bloemfontein April 3rd, and was broken up on arrival there. The Government Buildings in the town we found to be decidedly handsome, and there was a good Club. Provisions were already beginning to run short, and it was extremely hard to get a bath, owing to the Boers being in possession of the waterworks. The Company met the Regiment here and learned all about Paardeberg; and although one would have liked to have been there on account of the fighting, one was glad *not* to have been there on

PARLIAMENT HOUSE AT BLOEMFONTEIN.

account of the food — or rather its absence. At Bloemfontein the Mounted Infantry was formed into a Division, consisting of two Brigades; each Brigade having four corps. Our Company belonged to the 8th Corps, commanded by Colonel Ross, Durham Light Infantry. After waiting three days at Bloemfontein, it went to join the remainder of its corps at Karree Siding, twenty-four miles north.

The Corps was composed of four Companies of other regiments, with Lumsden's and Loch's Horse. The Oxfordshire and West Riding Mounted Infantry Companies were stronger than the other four regular Companies, who never seemed to have recovered from Paardeberg. The work consisted for a long time in doing outpost duty day and night, and nothing else. Brandfort could be seen towards the west, and the Boer picquets could be discerned at a distance of two or three miles, on the top of a long grassy slope. One morning the Boers got close to the picquets, and a lot of firing took place. After using two and a half boxes of ammunition, with apparently little result, the firing ceased. Shortly after, however, the Boers sent down an ambulance, which showed that the firing had not been altogether unsuccessful.

One morning a raid was made on the enemy's cattle, which used to feed in front of their picquets. It resulted in the capture of over 2,000 sheep, about 50 oxen, and three Cape carts. During this raid, and while it was still dark, Colvile came across a wire fence. He dismounted and cut the wire, when he suddenly heard some one talking at a distance of about thirty yards. It was a Boer picquet. He thought it was time to get on his horse, which he did quickly, and galloped away, followed by the bullets of the picquet, who were now awake.

Our Company and the West Riding Company were now sent to General Maxwell's Brigade at Krantz Kraal. On the third night after arrival there, and whilst it was dark, General Broadwood's Cavalry Brigade, with three Batteries of Artillery, joined the force. Early next morning an advance was made on the Boer position in front, the Cavalry being on the right, the Infantry on the left rear, and the two Companies of Mounted Infantry keeping up communication between them. The Boers, after firing a few shots, retreated, and the Infantry occupied their position. The Cavalry still continued its advance, the Mounted Infantry following; and late in the afternoon a shower of pom-pom shells fell in the former. The Cavalry retired a short way, and bivouacked for the night. Owing to the turning movement being a large one, the Mounted Infantry had lost touch with the Infantry, and no one knew where one was! The only thing to be done was to bivouac at the nearest farm, commandeering what food and forage there was. Picquets were posted, no fires being allowed, and a sharp look-out was kept, as the enemy was believed to be quite close, and the whole force of Mounted Infantry was barely 150. Nothing happened in the night, and next morning the Infantry was rejoined. Next day another short advance was made, and the Boers could be seen trekking in the distance. The object of the operations of these two or three days was to straighten out the line before making a general advance on Brandfort.

Early next morning the Company was joined by the 4th and 8th Mounted Infantry Corps, the intention being to work round to the north of Brandfort, and to cut off the Boers' retreat. The advance had barely begun before the Company received a volley from a Boer picquet. As one section after another galloped across a piece of open ground the volleys continued. The picquet commander could be heard giving the command to fire, in English. The range was taken, and the Boers soon retreated. The men mounted, one section advancing towards some Kaffir kraals, another along a spruit. It was necessary to dismount after going a short way, as rifle fire again opened, this time supplemented by two guns. The section advancing along the spruit saw some Boers, who appeared from the formation to be Zarps, marching calmly along to take up a fresh position. Riding their horses into the spruit, and thus getting cover and concealment from its banks, the men again dismounted and fired two volleys at the unconscious enemy. The range was 1,800 yards, but the Zarps extended quickly, and disappeared into the spruit higher up. The section then advanced into the open to get closer, but directly it appeared bullets whizzed around, so it returned to the spruit and walked along it for three or four hundred yards, having excellent cover all the way. A few volleys soon turned the Boers out of their shelter; and, as they retired up the hill, another volley caused them to go at their best pace.

The 8th Mounted Infantry had now to wait till the 4th Mounted Infantry, which had been hanging back, came up on the right. The advance continued, and the top of the ridges was reached without further opposition. Directly the Mounted Infantry appeared over the crest, the Boer guns (which had been moved to another range of kopjes) opened fire, and nearly hit one of the Mounted Infantry pom-poms. Brooke had gone on with one section to a kopje in front, and as he reached it the firing again commenced sharper than ever. No one could make out what had happened; but on reaching the kopje a Boer gun was seen disappearing in the distance, and the firing had come from its escort. Whilst waiting here for a short time to reform, Maxwell's Brigade could be seen some distance away on the left flank. After re-forming, a move was made towards a farm in front; but on reaching it the Boer guns, which had its range, opened again. Men were dismounted and advanced towards the Boer position, but after going a short way, and partly owing to night coming on, this was abandoned. The Mounted Infantry marched back, and bivouacked for the night about three miles on the right flank of the Infantry. The attempt to cut off the Boer retreat from Brandfort had failed, but the latter place had been occupied by the Guards' Brigade with very little loss. The casualties in the Mounted Infantry were only six, although they had been firing at the Boers, and the Boers at them, from six o'clock in the morning till dark. A Boer ambulance was captured during the day, with three badly wounded Boers inside, and the doctor in charge (an Englishman) said that the enemy's gunners were Frenchmen.

Next day a halt was made to allow the wagons to come up; and when the advance continued, the 4th and 8th Corps, which from now to Pretoria worked together, were ordered to join Ian Hamilton, who was marching on Winburg. An early start was made, but at about two o'clock an order came from Lord Roberts for the Mounted Infantry to wheel to the left, as General Maxwell was being strongly opposed by the Boers at Vet River. The two corps started at the trot, and came in on the Boer left as they were retreating, General Maxwell having crossed the river. From here a patrol (April 5th) of one officer and twenty men was sent off with a message from Lord Roberts to General Hamilton, who was supposed to be where the Bloemfontein-Winburg road crossed the Vet River. The only guide was the telegraph wire between Winburg and Brandfort, on the north side of which were the Boers. It was necessary, therefore, to keep well to the south. The patrol had no map or compass, the former of which would have made matters a great deal easier. A deserted farm by the telegraph wire was reached just before dark; the horses were fed for the first time during the day, and several chickens afterwards adorned the saddles, as the men were without food.

It was now dark, and nothing remained but to move
on in a south-east direction till someone or something
was seen. After a time, camp fires were made out;
whether they were Boer or British it was impossible to
tell; but the patrol made towards them. After marching for a couple of hours, and twice crossing a river
(which proved to be the Vet) the patrol crawled up on
their stomachs, and found that they were British, and
the Highland Brigade.   General Hamilton was not

THE WORK OF THE BOERS.

where he was supposed to be, but twelve miles further
on, at Winburg. After this the way was easy enough,
there being a good road.

Winburg was reached at 3.30 a.m.; every one very
tired, having been in the saddle from 6 a.m. the previous
day. The horses were dead beat. It took four days to
get back to the Company, which was at Smaldeel, one
night being spent at a deserted farm belonging to Steyn's
brother. Next day a short march was made close to

Zand River; and during the afternoon, while making a reconnaissance towards the station, the Boers opened a heavy fire. At an early hour next morning the Mounted Infantry marched down to the drift. They waited here till Gordon's Cavalry Brigade, Tucker's Division, the guns, and Headquarters' Staff arrived. About a mile further back the captive balloon rose in the air. The Mounted Infantry were the first to cross the drift, and were able to advance for half a mile beyond it, the enemy's shell fire then stopping them. The gunners could not see the enemy's guns for a few moments, and the shelling still continued. Luckily it was common shell, and no one was hurt, although they kept bursting all among the horses. The Horse Artillery then opened fire, and in a couple of minutes the Boer guns, which were previously invisible, could be seen retreating. The Mounted Infantry then galloped on to the kopje the Boers had just left. After our people had occupied several more kopjes the whole of the Boer army could be seen retreating. It was the first and last time the Boers were visible in any great numbers. The Mounted Infantry pom-poms came into action against some Boers behind the railway embankment. In a minute they were scuttling out like rats. The Company then advanced with the rest of the 8th Corps against a long, low kopje, in front of which was a mealie patch. The ground was open, and the horses were left behind. On getting close to the mealie patch, the Boers (who were concealed in it) opened fire. There were no ant hills to give cover, and the fire was too hot to allow any one to raise his head in order to return it. The only two men who moved about were shot. Captain Head, commanding the 8th Mounted Infantry Regiment, was mortally wounded; and Sergeant G. Watson of our Company was shot through both legs. He was the Company's first casualty. After a time the firing slackened, and one was able to return it. The Mounted Infantry then advanced, but the Boers had gone. They had been protecting the removal of one of their guns. When it was all over, a squadron of Lancers and a battery of guns came up. After that there was no more firing, and the Mounted forces moved on to Ventersburg Road Station, where they camped for the night.

Next morning an early start was made, and at twelve

KROONSTAD BRIDGE.

o'clock the Company was lying along a grassy ridge firing at the Boers, seven miles from Kroonstad. Two Horse Batteries came up, but no further advance could be made. The firing continued till night, when the Infantry came up and camped four miles in the rear. Picquets were left out all night, and next morning the Mounted Infantry again crept up the ridge. Each man picked out the biggest ant-heap he could find, and all waited for the enemy's fire to break out, and the expected battle of Kroonstad to begin. The scouts went slowly forward to the position held by the Boers the day before, but still there was no firing. The position proved to be unoccupied, and in a quarter of an hour's reconnaissance not a Boer was seen. · The enemy had retreated, leaving Kroonstad to its fate. The Mounted Infantry was formed up, and rode with Lord Roberts to the drift outside the town. As they approached the town, General French's force could be seen coming in from the north, while other forces came in from the east and west. Lord Roberts halted outside the town, and the Mounted Infantry camped, and waited anxiously for their wagons. The Company had been two and a half days without them, and all were hungry and tired. After three hours the Guards' Brigade marched up, and Lord Roberts entered the town at their head.

The bridge over the Valsch River having been blown up, a deviation was made alongside the drift. It was at this drift that President Steyn had taken up his stand the evening before the British troops entered the town, and with his shambok endeavoured to instil courage (*i.e.* Dutch!) into the minds of the burghers.

The next day Colvile, armed with a pass from the Commissariat Department, endeavoured to buy a few things in the food line; but this he found to be impossible, as there was nothing to be had. The troops stayed for a week at Kroonstad, and during this time the Company received remounts, which were badly needed. These remounts (which were Argentines) followed the army up from Bloemfontein and had apparently been fed on the veldt most of the way. They were received the day before a fresh start was made, and having had little or no corn, were absolutely unable to do the work required of them. Their main idea seemed to be to kick anyone who happened to be behind their heels, or to lie down and refuse to rise.

The advance continued about the 20th May, and for the next three or four days no opposition was met with. Farmers came in from the surrounding country, and gave in their arms and ammunition—a great deal of the latter containing expanding and explosive bullets. By dint of great exertions, the Army Service Corps had managed to bring up some rum, and on 24th May a double ration was issued, the Queen's health drunk, and " God Save the Queen " sung. From this all the way to Pretoria, the Boers burnt the grass after them, and every night the whole veldt was ablaze. The Intelligence Department prognosticated a battle at Rhenoster River, but on arriving there, it was found that the Boers had decamped. This was owing to the left flank of their position having been turned by General Hamilton, and their right by General French. The enemy, it was evident, had made great preparations to fight at Rhenoster. Trenches, after the Paardeberg type, had been dug, and a siding for a big gun had been laid down. The position was of considerable strength, and it appeared doubtful if shell fire would have had any effect on the trenches.

On nearing the Vaal the good news came that General French had crossed into the Transvaal at Parys. General Hamilton's Column now crossed and took up the centre position, Lord Roberts taking the right of the line of advance. Every bridge from Kroonstad to the Vaal was blown up, and at Rhenoster the line was torn up for over a mile. On reaching Wolverhoek, orders were received that next day the Mounted Infantry, supported by a section of guns, would cross the

Vaal at Viljoen's Drift. The orders stated that there were twenty-five Englishmen shut up in the coal mines at Vereeniging, and that no help was to be expected from the Infantry.

On starting next morning the 8th Corps marched on the left of the line, the 4th on the right. The coal mines at Viljoen's Drift were sighted after two hours' marching, mostly through mealie fields. As the 8th

BRIDGE OVER VAAL RIVER.

Corps neared the buildings the Boers opened fire. A few minutes afterwards there was an explosion, and an arch of the railway bridge over the Vaal fell into the river. The Boers had blown it up. The Company was on the left of the line, and after a quarter of an hour's skirmishing reached the river. On the Transvaal side, and close to the water's edge, was a high

bank of slack. From the top of this the Boers, who
had now retreated to that side of the river, continued
their fire. The men dismounted and skirmished along
the river bank, and a Boer could be seen coming out
of the doorway at intervals, and firing off his rifle. It
was soon made too hot for him to stay there. A drift
had meantime been discovered on the left flank, and
Colvile went over with half the Company. The remainder lined the bank of the river in order to cover
his retreat if necessary, and still kept up a warm
fire at the slack bank. The two guns now opened
on the same object, and Colvile's party rode towards
the slack bank in widely extended order. The remainder of the Corps hurried across, but the Boers
had retreated to Vereeniging Station, which they
at once set on fire. The ground was too open to
attack them with the small force at Colonel Henry's
disposal; and as the passage of the river had been
gained, it was only necessary to prevent them gaining
command of it. When the Boers had done as much
damage as possible to the Station, they retreated,
and the Company camped there that night. The
English people at the mine were delighted to see their
fellow countrymen, and were most kind to the officers
and men.

At noon next day the main body crossed the river.
The Mounted Infantry had been hoping to have a day's
rest; but directly the Infantry had crossed they were
ordered to go down to Engelbacht Drift and engage
the enemy if they saw them, Gordon's Cavalry Brigade
being supposed to be held up by some Boers. This
entailed a march of some twenty miles, all of which
had to be done at a walk, as the horses were worn out,
and could only canter in presence of the enemy. The
Boers were seen, but did not wait to fight; and on

arrival at Engelbacht Drift Gordon's Cavalry Brigade
was found to have extricated itself and to have gone on.
The force turned round and commenced to retrace its
steps; but night came on after going ten miles, so it
camped in a mealie field.   There were no wagons, nor
any forage, and one was told if one wanted water to
march on a certain star for three or four hundred
yards—to find in the end stuff unfit to drink.   The
horses were fed at two o'clock next morning, and the
Mounted Infantry cut in in front of the main body
at about 6 a.m.

Soon after this a big plain was reached, on the
further side of which was a long and high kopje.   It
looked as if there was going to be a real good fight,
and the heavy guns, with their teams of sixteen oxen,
where hauled out into the open.   At this display of
force the Boers retreated, and the march continued to
Klip River, where a halt was made for the night.
Throughout the last hour before reaching the camping
ground, the sound of General French's guns could be
heard away on the left flank, and as the sun went down
the last sound to fill the air was produced by a pom-pom
firing off a dozen of its shells.

The orders received that night were that the Mounted
Infantry were to go on next day at their best pace and
seize Elandsfontein at all costs, and to capture as much
rolling stock as possible.   Accordingly, next morning
the 8th Corps started, the 4th Corps following in reserve.
The Company led the way on the right of the line, the
West Riding Company on the left.   The pace was much
quicker than usual.   On reaching Natal Spruit, one of
the scouts brought in word that a train could be seen
coming up the Natal line, on its way to Elandsfontein.
Here was a chance of capturing some rolling stock.   Up
to now only smoke had been seen; but, as the first

section came over a rise, the train itself, steaming along at a slow pace six hundred yards away, became visible. The remainder of the Company galloped up, the men dismounted and opened fire, and the train put on full steam. The railway lines ran in a curve; one section started across, so as to reach a small station higher up the line before the train, but a wire fence intervened. *There were no wire cutters*, and as the men rode up and down the fence looking for an opening, a sharp fire broke out from the train. Half the Heidelberg commando (300 men) was in it. It was impossible to go further, and the train disappeared round a corner. The remainder of the Corps had now come up, and the advance continued. There was a long range of hills on the left flank, and from this three guns at once opened fire, one being quite close, as could be told by the sharp crack it made. There were no guns with the Mounted Infantry, as one of the naval 4·7 guns had fallen through the bridge at Klip River, thus blocking the way to the rest of the army. Lumsden's Horse deployed to the right, and could now be seen advancing in skirmishing order. The Company moved on, and in a few minutes reached the top of the ridge of hills on the left. As it arrived there, two men opened fire upon it. The men took cover in a Boer trench which was close at hand, and did not return the fire. The two men who were firing belonged to the West Riding Company, and it took some time to make them understand that they were firing *at their own side!* This was at last accomplished by sounding their regimental call, white handkerchiefs and helmets on the ends of rifles having failed to stop them firing.

Elandsfontein Station, and several gold mines, could be seen from the top of the hill. The remainder of the Corps now received orders to cut the line further to the east, and not to go into the station, as was at first intended. The Company never received these orders, so it proceeded straight down the line towards the station. As Colvile went in with one section on the left side of the station yard, the Boers again began firing. The horses were got under cover as quickly as possible, but three were hit, one receiving six wounds. The men got behind a tin shed, but the Mauser bullets easily found their way through it, causing them to retire with three men wounded. No more headway could be made, and reinforcements were anxiously looked for, but there were none in sight. Doctors from the Russian ambulance now came and dressed the wounded, and, after waiting for some time, a fresh attempt to reach the station was made. This second attempt was successful; but sniping broke out, and was only put a stop to by the appearance on the scene of the Grenadier Guards. The Company bivouacked in the yard for the night, and next day rejoined the 8th Corps.

On the 30th of May there was a twenty-four hours' armistice, to allow the people in Johannesburg to decide whether they would surrender the town or stand a bombardment. The result, as everyone knows, was that they chose the former alternative, and on the 31st the troops marched through the town. The march began through Jeppe and the mines, and after five miles the Government buildings were reached. The English flag was hoisted, and there was a certain amount of cheering.

The troops camped at Orange Grove for the night, and two days after they fought near Pretoria.

The writer is unable to give a further account of these two or three days, as he was not there.[1] Amongst the

---

[1] He was wounded at Elandsfontein, and invalided home ; see next chapter.—ED.

different things learned during the period that this account covers are the following :—

   1. Never to trust a white flag.
   2. To get cover as quickly as possible.
   3. That one volley was worth ten rounds independent per man.
   4. Long range volley firing was useful.

These are only opinions, and must be taken as such.

CHAPTER XIII.

THE MOUNTED INFANTRY COMPANY—*(Continued)*.

EXTRACTS from letters written home by Captain G. N. Colvile, commanding the **M. I. Company**, Oxfordshire Light Infantry :—

Near Johannesburg, 2nd June, 1900.

Here we are, about four miles out of Johannesburg on the Pretoria road. We have had a very hard time since leaving Kroonstad, pursuing the Boers' best pace ; consequently the wretched horses are done, and I have lost a lot, the poor brutes dropping down on the way from exhaustion and want of food. We expected a fight at the Rhenoster Spruit, where the Boers had made entrenchments, but they all cleared out in a hurry, and we did not fight till we got to the Vaal River.

We have been marching since leaving Kroonstad with the 4th and 8th Mounted Infantry in front of the main body, and on reaching the Vaal we were fired on from a big coal mine on the Transvaal side.

We had rather an exciting time, as I got over the river, with some of Lock's Horse and a few of our men, and worked round the back of the mine. We fought all through the mine buildings, and the Boers cleared off pretty quick.

I never saw anyone so pleased to see us as the English people left in the mine. They rushed at us with open arms ; in fact, I was much embarrassed by two old women, whom, however, I managed to dodge round the dining-room table.

They had certainly had a bad time, as their houses were between us and the Boers, so the bullets were coming both ways. The mine was to have been blown up, but luckily they had not enough dynamite, and we just got there in time.

We had a very good lunch (with champagne), and I bought some food for our people.

Next day we made a march of 24 miles up the banks of the river to help General Gordon to cross a drift ; we didn't get unsaddled till 8 p.m., and were off next morning at 4 p.m., and that really finished our horses. We kicked them along to a place called Klip Drift, about 14 miles from here, and next day had a most exciting time. We started before daylight, and, with the W. Riding Company, had orders

K 2

to go first along the line to seize the telegraph office at Elandsfontein, a suburb of Johannesburg. After going about five miles, we saw a train passing slowly from a branch line on to the main line, and a most exciting chase began. I got half the men on a hill blazing away at the

CAPTAIN G. N. COLVILE.

train, and the others galloped down to try and cut it off, but it couldn't quite be done. It was great fun, the Boers blazing away out of the train at us, and we galloping along to try and get in front of them. The Boers were astonished at our getting on so quick, and never expected the English near them till the next day. After chasing the train, we pursued our way along the line, and got detached from the other troops, who had got orders (which I never received) to go round clear of the line, as the Boers had their big guns and a strong force in front.

So on I went gaily up the line, with Forrest and some men on my right, and Percy-Smith on the left. We got right up to the town of Germiston, and within half a mile of Elandsfontein Junction, where we saw the Boers loading up their train in a desperate hurry. I had about twenty men with me, as neither Forrest nor Smith had got up, and we had just dismounted and collared the signal-man at the shunting station when our exciting time began. We saw the Boers riding quietly about the place, having no idea we were so close. We got in the first shots, but the Boers soon tumbled to the fact that there were only a few of us, and we had to retreat from one building to another, and eventually back to the trench where Forrest and his men were.

We all had very close shaves; three men were wounded, but only one badly. One man was hit in the back behind the heart, and the bullet travelled round his ribs to the front, and he is little the worse; it was a lucky escape, as it was only about 100 yards' range, and I think the cartridge must have been a bad one.

One man had his rifle hit as he was firing it, and his water-bottle shot through; and I had a bullet through the sleeve of my coat. Anyhow, in the pick up afterwards, the English doctor got three dead Boers and three others wounded. We had three horses shot, too.

I was jolly glad to get back to the trench where Forrest was, as it was very warm work for those few minutes. Poor Forrest got shot after this as he went down the line with Beddington and two men, to see about a

IN JOHANNESBURG.

man of ours, who we thought was shot, as he was lying out behind a heap of stones. As a matter of fact, like a sensible chap, he was lying low, but Forrest got shot through the calf of his leg, and Beddington, who is an Intelligence Officer, got his arm badly smashed. After this the Boers cleared off, and we got hold of a Russian doctor working with the Boers to attend to the wounded, and, later on, we got into Elandsfontein Station and caught several trains before they got away; but it was a great pity that reinforcements could not come up sooner, to stop all the trains clearing off to Pretoria.

Next day we rested in the Gold Fields. We expect to move on to-morrow.

I was in Johannesburg yesterday and saw Forrest, who is very comfortable. It is a fine town, but of course many of the shops are shut up. I got my beard shaved off, and feel quite clean; also I bought a few things, but the prices are ruinous. I expect we shall enter Pretoria, a queer rabble of men and horses.

Near Pretoria, 6th June, 1900.

Well, we entered Pretoria yesterday and had a good fight the day before, as the Boers held a long ridge about five miles out of the town, and the Mounted Infantry had to hold the opposite ridge till the guns and Infantry came up. I had one man killed in my Company. We got into Pretoria yesterday morning, but only passed through the edge of it, and are now on the Johannesburg side, about fourteen miles out, guarding the railway, and we think we are going back to Johannesburg, which I rather hope we do, as I have fought enough for the present, and I think everyone wants a little quiet.

I think the war is far from over, but by the time you get this, you will know more; but I believe there are lots of Boers, all about, to the south of us, and it will be an awful job clearing them out of the mountains north of Pretoria, if they have supplies, and mean fighting. I got a young Boer prisoner to-day, who said the war had only just begun, and that the taking of Pretoria was nothing. They all say that, but still there is a lot in it, for we caught none of their men on entering Pretoria. It was a fine sight seeing the big naval guns shelling the Pretoria forts and our old guns shelling the Boer trenches.

Elandsfontein, 11th June.

Here I am, living in the lap of luxury. As I think I told you in my last letter, the 8th Mounted Infantry are distributed on the railway between the Vaal River and Pretoria, and we are at this Elandsfontein Junction with the West Riding, as a sort of reserve, to go up or down the line as required. Smith-Dorrien's Brigade is here too. I hope we may be here some time; it is most peaceful, but we may be sent off at any moment.

The men are all in a bit of waste land with the horses, and we officers are all in houses side by side. The house where we mess and I live in, is fitted with electric light. It was unfurnished, but I found a good bed, and got a table and some chairs out of other houses. You have no idea how nice it is being in a house again ; I now have a warm bath in the morning, and keep quite warm at nights, and don't care if it freezes, or anything else, outside. Yesterday Smith and I went into Johannesburg to see Forrest and the other wounded, who are all doing well. One poor chap has a wound through the knee and shin bone, but will not lose his leg, I hope.

I am sick of looking at the horses ; five died in the quiet march back from Pretoria ; the fact is, they are done, and want six months' rest and feeding, but I don't think even then they would be much good.

Johannesburg and all this country is very weird. We are about eight miles from the town, and there are deserted mines the whole way ; while, except for a few odd black boys, nearly all the houses are empty.

I got a new rig-out of clothes for the men before we left Bloemfontein, but could not get them up until just now. Now they have new coats, breeches, putties, and shirts ; their old clothes were a sight, so I had them chucked in a heap and burnt.

I had a long talk with an Englishman living here, who is a burgher, and has been fighting against us. He was fighting round Arundel, so we compared notes. We are camped close to the place where we had our little fight when Forrest was wounded. I look at the place, and think we were lucky not all to have been caught, but the Boers were on the run, and did not know, I suppose, how few of us there were.

13th June.

No peace ; we are just off by special train in cattle trucks, with the Gordons and four guns, to Irene, this side of Pretoria, to join on to Roberts' force ; whether we come back or not, we don't know. I have only 45 horses fit to take. The idea is to cut off Botha.

Elandsfontein, 15th June.

I wrote a short note two days ago, to say we were off to Pretoria again. We went by train to Irene, near Pretoria, to join Roberts' army again, and on reaching there after dark, we were told to march at 12 midnight—however, a wire came to say we were not wanted, so we were sent back here next morning.

I hear De Wet has captured 2,000 mail bags somewhere near Rhenoster Spruit. I'm afraid it's true ; if so, I suppose he has got several of my letters, besides my boots and breeches.

To-day I have been out commandeering horses, which is rather fun. I sling on to every horse I see, and look in every stable and barn, but the people are very cute at hiding them. They get paid by Government, but have to give them up whether they like it or not. I like taking a horse from a sleek old Jew; they do lie so, and tell me their horses are only two years old, and exalt them in every way—quite a change to the usual order of things out here.

19th June.

We are still comfortably in a house, but I don't know how long it will last, as I expect to be sent off somewhere at any moment. We are collecting a few remounts —of sorts—and getting rid of the poor brutes that are utterly done.

WHAT THE HORSES LOOK LIKE.

We have occasional scares and rumours of Boers in the neighbourhood, and do a good lot of patrolling looking for them. I was in Johannesburg yesterday, and saw Forrest, who was very cheerful, but I don't know if his wound is going on altogether well; it festers such a lot, and there is a big hole where the bullet came out.

One poor chap, who, I told you, was wounded through the knee and shin bone, had his leg amputated last week, and died two days later of enteric. Nearly all the mines round here are closed, and the Boers disarmed all the natives at the beginning of the war; there are a few mines open, but they are only just having the water pumped out of them. The Kaffir compounds belonging to the mines are interesting places. Last Sunday we went down the New Primrose Mine.

We have a man with us now, half a Dutchman, who is most interesting, and as he knows both the Dutch and Kaffir languages, is very useful. It is a rum thing how these Dutchmen are mixed up; half this man's relations are fighting against us, and his brother-in-law, who was lunching with us the other day, was sort of secretary to Botha, and fought at Spion Kop and round Ladysmith, but chucked it, like many others, when Botha got back here.

We hear very little news now, but they seem to have had a lot of fighting with Botha near Pretoria and with De Wet down south.

Klip River, 26th June.

We are now at a railway station called Klip River (about 15 miles south of Elandsfontein), where we have been these last four days. We were sent off in a hurry with the idea of joining in with the troops that have gone to Heidelberg; anyway, we are stuck here, but shall very likely go back to Elandsfontein again—possibly to-morrow. I hope we do go back, as this is a most uninteresting place, and we were very happy in our house at Elandsfontein. The cold at nights is awful, but I am still sleeping in a tent, and wear all the warm clothes I possess. The water in one's basin is frozen right through in the morning. In the day time it is just right—nice hot sun and beautiful air.

We have heard a bit of fighting the last two days about ten miles off; we hear too, that Ian Hamilton has got round the Boers who were in these hills, but one can never believe these reports.

I am told the mails that were destroyed were set on fire by the train being shelled, and that letters were picked up all over the veldt; I only hope De Wet is not wearing my new breeches. His farm was full of the best Egyptian cigarettes, sent out from England. There are a lot of Irish Rifles (released prisoners) here, dressed in the most weird clothes. All these stations along the line have troops in them, and are very strongly intrenched.

Boksberg, 29th June.

We are now at a place called Boksberg, about four miles to the east of Elandsfontein. We came on here from Klip River, rather more than 15 miles off, last Monday, as they did not want us there any longer. This is rather a better place than Klip River, there being a little town, and we have shanties of a sort to live in.

Yesterday we were wired for to reinforce at the Springs, ten miles further east, where we heard a bit of firing going on, so off we went in a desperate hurry, and had gone about six miles, when we were stopped, as the fight was over. All these scares bore me; the Boers now are simply hanging about in the hills, looting cattle and picking off any odd patrols that they can, but they will not come out and fight on any account. If things go on like this, it will take a long time to finish the Boers off, unless they get starved out. I believe they have plenty of meat, but are short of flour, coffee, etc. There is a Commando of about

5,00 men round the Springs, who give a lot of trouble. All these Boers in the towns who have given up their arms are crafty devils. I fancy they go out for a few days to the Commandos and fight, and then come to me as if nothing had happened ; and it is of course impossible to stop them going out and fighting, or from telling their pals what we are doing ; the women also take out food. There are all sorts of orders out ; no one is allowed to ride a bicycle or horse without a pass, in fact, they must have a pass wherever they go, but they are very cute.

One finds all kinds of soldier's equipment and things in the houses ; the Boers seem very fond of the little trophies of the war, and I find bits, buttons, badges. shoulder-straps, etc., that they have got off the prisoners and the dead. The Dutchmen pretend they can't talk English, but they nearly all can, and I always make them, and tell them the sooner they learn the better.

Boksberg, 4th July.

We are still here, though we have been up to the Springs meanwhile, as we were again wired for, and spent the night there. Our patrols only saw a few Boers, and exchanged some shots ; we had one horse shot, and we got two prisoners.

Yesterday I found myself in command here, and got a report from a spy that the Boers were advancing on us, besides other alarming rumours, so I wired to the General, and went round and put everything ready in case of an attack. We had a few Canadians here, and had just got our pom-pom. In the evening the Gordon Highlanders arrived with their guns, and we had another report that the Boers were going to attack us last night, but they have not done so.

I think they want food badly, and are trying to raid some of the mine stores. I expect at any moment they may be packed off to some other place to cut the line. We are kept here to go where we are most wanted. There are not more than 1,000 Boers close round here, but I suppose the General means to leave them alone until he has cleared off the others.

It is very cold now by day when we get no sun, and I always wear a sweater.

The Springs, 6th July.

We have just got back to the Springs, 12 miles from Boksberg, with the idea of going for the Boers round here, and I hope we do something with them, as we have scares and alarms nearly every day ; and though nothing comes of them, one never has any peace, and can't move out of the place. I think it's quite likely there are too many Boers here for us to round up, and I only hope they won't round us up instead. In spite of everything being kept very dark, the Boers know everything ; it is impossible to stop them. I expect by now they know to a man how many of us are going for them to-morrow.

Boksberg, 9th July.

Just back again from the Springs. We went 12, 28, and 20 miles these last three days, and now have to go off to-morrow somewhere south, and as our poor brutes of horses are all in a bad way, it's not good enough. We got one side of the Boers on Friday, and saw a fight going on in the distance, but were too far off to join in. We saw about thirty Boers, but they fled before we got within a mile of them. As everything is kept such a secret, I don't know where we are off to to-morrow, but I think south, and shall possibly help round up De Wet. By the time we

AT VEREENIGING, OR VILJOEN'S DRIFT.

reach Vereeniging, I expect we shall have very few horses; it is very disheartening going along with our wretched crocks, and I am sorry for the poor brutes. I suppose we have only about thirty Irish cobs left out of the 130, and they are all more or less done; still, they must be real good ones to have stood the work; they want a year's rest to pull round. Some of the Basuto and Cape horses we have picked up are good ones, but the Argentines are, as a rule, rotters, with no pluck at all; they just lie down and die when they feel done up.

I am just beginning to hear of the men who have gone sick at different times; five have died from disease for certain, but I expect to hear of several more.

The Springs, 14th July.

Here we are still at the Springs, which is a stupid place, and most monotonous. We have to be up by 5.30 in the morning, just before daybreak, for fear of being attacked then, and we can't move out of the place at all.

Yesterday, as a man of Lumsden's Horse was fired on from a farm and hit, we went out in the afternoon and burnt the farm.

I have no news; we only hear rumours of what is going on around. There are a certain number of Boers round about, but there are not enough troops here to go for them. We have to stop here a bit, as there are a lot of stores to watch, it being the terminus of a small railway. Our patrols go out a lot, and occasionally get shot at.

16th July.

We march to Irene to-morrow, probably for the Middleburg column, but don't know for certain.

Irene, 22nd July.

We marched up here from the Springs about four days ago, stopping at Kaalfontein on the way. This is a very nice camp, as camps go, being in a wood, and so a good deal sheltered from the cold, and I have enjoyed the few days' quiet very much. We went out reconnoitring one day, but met no Boers, though two of Lumsden's Horse were caught the day before when they were a good long way off.

I went into Pretoria on Wednesday to try and see E———, but I could not find him. Pretoria is not particularly interesting, but a bigger town than Bloemfontein. Kruger's house is a rotten little place.

There is a nice house near here, called the Irene Estate, belonging to a rich Dutchman. The grounds are very well laid out, but of course left rather upside down since the war broke out. There were enormous beds of violets, of which I picked a huge bunch.

We moved this morning from our nice camp in the wood to a horrid place nearer the station, which is considered safer in case we are attacked. It is a beastly dusty place, and, as this is the windy month out here, everything gets full of dust. I believe it does not get warm till September, and the rains may begin then, which I am not looking forward to at all.

There is a small Commando, perhaps 200 or 300 Boers, in a strong place, about twenty miles off. They caught five or six of Lumsden's Horse yesterday, but let them go after taking away their rifles and horses. One man got three shots through his clothes before he was taken.

I believe the Middleburg column has started, so we are not for that as we thought; it would have been useless to go with these horses.

I expect we shall get some fighting round here, as the Boers are sure to come round when the others get well on the way to Middleburg, and they may have to go on to Lydenberg.

Wolvehoek, few miles south of the Vaal, 29th July.

Since I last wrote we have had rather an eventful time. We left Irene on Monday, the 23rd, and stopped the night about ten miles to the west, intending to join a force under Hickman, to go for some Boers on the hills west of Pretoria. However, next day we were sent on to Pretoria, and joined Hickman there.

On Wednesday we went out after these Boers with the Duke of Cornwall's Mounted Infantry, some other Mounted Infantry, and a battery. We got into a beastly mountainous country in the afternoon, and formed our camp; but after camping for about an hour I was sent out with my Company to help some other Mounted Infantry, who had had some of their men taken. We went along the hill, getting a good deal fired at, and one of my men got on to the top of a hill, and saw a good lot of Boers watering their horses in the river below, but the idiot began firing at them before we came up, so by the time we came up the Boers had cleared off, and began firing at us. We returned to camp, followed up pretty closely by the Boers, who shot two of our horses.

Next day we started out with the whole force, we being among the advanced guard, and soon started fighting : but after being out an hour we got orders to return to Pretoria, as with the small force we had we could never have tackled the Boers in their strong positions in the mountains. One of my men was killed and another wounded, besides some horses. We had to do rear guard going back to Pretoria, so what fighting there was was pretty well all left to us, and I think we got out of a nasty place very well.

Friday we went into Pretoria, and that night at 10.30 we were wakened up and told to go to the Station six miles off, which we started for at midnight, and we arrived here the next afternoon at 3 p.m.

It seems these Free Staters are continually cutting the line, and they started attacking this place the day before yesterday, so that's why we were sent down in such a hurry. Anyway, the country all round here is flat, and I would much rather fight here than in the Transvaal. We are having a quiet day to-day, and I have had a bath, the first for over a week, and it was most acceptable.

It is a rum thing being back in the Free State again, but I daresay we shall be back in the Transvaal ere long.

It seems to be getting a bit warmer, but the early mornings are awfully cold, and Friday night on an open railway truck, and last night on this platform, were very chilly; but to-day we have got a tent pitched.

All the stations down the line are strongly fortified, and we have jolly good trenches to get into in case the Boers attack us.

I lost my best hat when the Boers were following us up the other day, as Castlereagh began to buck when some shots hit the rocks close to him, and I did not feel inclined to stop and pick my hat up just then!

Wolvehoek, 1st August.

We are still here—a most uninteresting place, flat plains for miles round; but that, I suppose, is a good thing, as one can see the Boers coming. They are not likely to attack us here, but if they do they will get it pretty hot.

The day before yesterday I went out with most of my Company to see what we could get from some farms whose owners were still away fighting; some of them had given in their rifles, and sworn to remain on their farms, but had gone out again.

We took two wagons with us, and an Englishman (who had just come out of prison, having been put there by the Boers) showed us round. We collected about 300 sheep, 60 oxen, 2 Cape carts, 1 ox-wagon, besides mealies, geese, hens, and eggs. Some of the women kicked up an awful row, crying and screaming, and I feel rather sorry for them; but they are awful humbugs, and swear a lot of cattle is theirs which does not belong to them at all.

There were a few Boers hanging about; one climbed up a tree to see over the ridge, but when he saw our horses he climbed down again pretty quick. One man had a shot at him as he was climbing down, but did not bag him.

Yesterday the whole Corps went out to try and find out and drive back the Boers who were on the east of the line, as we knew there were a certain number hanging about. The 8th Corps now only consists of the Suffolks, the West Riding, a few of Lock's Horse, our Company, and a "pom-pom"; the rest are stuck all along the line. Lumsden's Horse remained at Pretoria to go on some other expedition.

We divided up into three parties; my lot on the right came across the Boer scouts about three miles from here. We tried very hard to catch them by letting a few of our men draw them on by retiring to where I had hidden most of my men in the grass; but the wily Boer was too cute, and after firing away at our people for some time they made off. A few miles further on we came on a body of 250 Boers about 1½ miles off. I have never seen so many of the enemy together in the open before; as a rule they don't show themselves at all; however, this is the most open country we have yet fought in. We could see these chaps very plainly, and I could easily count them with my field glasses, but they all cleared off before I could get the " pom-pom " up—why, I don't know, as there were only about 40 of us. Their game now is to dodge about the country, and not fight unless they get a jolly good chance of taking you unawares. Some of the others got a few shots with the " pom-pom " into the middle of about forty of them, but don't know whether they killed any. A " pom-pom " is most alarming, but very seldom does any good.

The great objection to this place is the dust; this is the windy month, and the dust blows into one's eyes and ears, and one can't keep it out of one's clothes or blankets. My dismounted men and wagons are coming down by road from Irene, and ought to be here to-morrow, so I hope they will bring us a mail.

8th August.

We have been on an expedition to Parys and back, about 24 miles west of this place, where they are trying to round up De Wet again. There are a tremendous lot of troops out there, but I think De Wet is far too cute, and I expect he will get away again. The day we got to Parys we were sent off to take a kopje near, which we managed very easily, as there were only about six Boers on it at the time, and they scuttled off after firing a few shots, leaving their dinner and a pony behind for us. We held on to the kopje till dark, when we were relieved by some other troops, and we had a lot of shooting at Boers in the distance along the river bank. We only arrived back to-day, as we are wanted to look after some Boers who keep on cutting the railway near here.

It is harder than ever now to tell who are Boers and who are our troops at a distance, as so many Boers are wearing our uniforms that they have got hold of, and so many of our men are dressed more or less in plain clothes.

A regiment has just arrived here, the South Wales Borderers, so that may alter our plans, and we may be sent back Parys way with them. I should like to be at the catching of De Wet, if he is to be caught; he must have several of my letters, and my boots.

Grootvlei, 16th August.

We are now about ten miles south of Wolvehoek, on the railway. Since I last wrote we have had three hard days, taking a convoy out to near Parys; back here the next day, and then an expedition yesterday out to Heilbron; we came across no Boers. To-day, thank goodness, is a quiet day, and I have had a bath and a shave.

Yesterday V. B. and I went out with my greyhound and caught a nice young buck. It was great fun coursing it, but a full-grown buck is too good for any greyhound, though V. B. says they can catch them. To-day, Monday, we went on one of our usual expeditions to find Boers, about seven miles off, and found none ; and in the afternoon I went out to the same place as yesterday after buck. I shot a koran (a bird like a guinea fowl) after about six shots with a rifle.

The Boers cut the line about one and a half miles from Wolvehoek, and not far from us, this morning. The noise of the explosion woke us all up.

Tuesday.

We are now at Vredefort Road, where we came to-day. I don't like this job, messing about on the railway ; we are doing neither one thing nor the other, and to-morrow are to start off towards Heilbron to go for some Boers in that direction, and I expect we shall get back to Rhenoster Spruit.

We are getting a spell of awful cold nights, and have had some bitter cold winds. Getting up at 5.30 in the morning, as we have been doing, with a hard frost, tickles one up properly ; but I am afraid, when the cold weather goes, the rain will begin, which will be even worse.

Bloemfontein, 20th August.

Here I am at Bloemfontein getting a few days' holiday ; I expect to go back on Friday. We came down here in a truck from Roodeval in 22 hours, which is not bad going for these times, and as we had our valises out in the truck, spent a good night, but woke up covered with coal dust. We got some hot water from the engine and made some cocoa. The last place we were at, Roodeval, is on the Rhenoster Spruit, the place where the Derbyshire Militia got cut up by De Wet some time back. I rather fancy we shall join on to Hunter's force, which is now pursuing a gentleman called Olivier, but I don't know for certain yet.

The line, I hear, was cut just behind our truck last Sunday night. I don't at all want to be caught by the Boers that way : they only give you a chunk of raw meat to eat, which you have to cook as best you can, and one has to walk miles and miles while they ride.

24th August.

We go back to-day, as far as I can make out, to Kroonstad ; but as I don't know what we are going to do, I haven't sent you a wire yet.

Ventersburg Road, 1st September.

Since I last wrote to you from Bloemfontein, we have been dodging about, having joined a fairly big mounted force under Le Gallais, who is working under General Hunter.

I returned by train to Kroonstad last Saturday, where we managed to pick up 30 much-needed remounts, and next day we marched towards Winburg, eventually getting to a little town called Ventersburg, which the Boers had just cleared out of.

We spent two miserable days there, as it rained like blazes, and one night it suddenly started blowing a hurricane, and down went most of the tents that I had just got hold of for the men. Mine luckily held up, but it was a queer sight at daybreak—the tents all flat, and everyone lying about in pools of water. B. and S. are wonders to sleep; they never budged when their tent went down, and were peacefully sleeping at daybreak.

I believe the Boers under Olivier have broken up, Olivier being caught, and they are now in rather a funk of Bloemfontein being attacked, so we are being sent down there by special train as fast as possible. We are now waiting for the trains, but don't expect we shall get off till to-morrow, as a lot of Yeomanry and the 7th Mounted Infantry, who are with us, entrain first.

We have now got a lot of Cape carts with us, captured when Prinsloo was caught, and we carry our blankets and food in them, for four days, with the idea of getting away from our heavy wagons, and getting about the country quicker.

Leeuw River, near Ladybrand, 7th September.

I hope this scrawl will get into Bloemfontein in time for the mail, but I rather doubt it. Since last Sunday we have had a hard time—as far as work goes, I think the worst since the war began. We arrived by train in Bloemfontein Saturday night, and on Sunday, at 4 p.m., we started our march to the relief of Ladybrand. We got within about eight miles of Ladybrand at about 2 a.m. on Wednesday morning, having done 70 miles—and we were going the whole time—with three hours sleep in the day, and two or three at nights.

On Thursday we went for the Boers, but they cleared off as usual with very little fighting. We marched back here, and to-day, so far, are resting, and I had a good 12 hours' sleep last night. This is a very pretty country; Ladybrand is close to the Basuto border. There are nice farms about, and everything is just beginning to grow; the mimosa and apricot trees look very pretty, and I have been able to pick some good oranges.

Half-way between Thaba N'chu and Ladybrand,
11th September.

We have moved from Leeuw River a little nearer Thaba N'chu, and suppose we shall be after the Boers again soon, but I expect they will lead us a pretty dance before they are caught, and I think those still out mean fighting to the bitter end. Nearly all the mounted troops are together here under Colonel Le Gallais.

Ladybrand, which was attacked by the Boers last week, is a very pretty place, and it was most interesting seeing it just after the garrison had been relieved. We only had about 140 men, and the Boers at least 2,000, with five guns; but our men got in a very strong position among the rocks, and we only had five men wounded in three days' fighting. The Boers could easily have taken them all, if they had had the pluck to charge them in the night; as it was, we shot a lot of Boers who were looting the town. It was a sight to see all the dead horses, mules, and oxen lying about on the hill, killed by the Boer shells; they were all killed on the hill, there being nowhere to put them under cover.

This is a nice bit of country, with good valleys, where they grow a lot of wheat.

We are now taking all the cattle, especially the trek oxen, partly for our own use, and partly to prevent the Boers from ploughing, and so bringing them to their senses. The Boers, too, take all they want, and smash up all the Englishmen's farms; it will take years to get the country round again.

Winburg, 16th September.

This endless trekking still continues. We are now resting for one day in Winburg after a 24 hours' march, with only four hours' rest in the middle of the day. I hate marching at night, it is so slow, and so beastly cold. I hope to goodness we catch these Boers before long; we have had no fighting since leaving Ladybrand.

I hear Kruger has fled, and our troops up north are getting on well, but goodness knows when the war will be over. We are far too lenient, and the only way is to burn all the farms and get at the men left in the country, as they only rejoin the different Commandos as they come along. Our men are getting a bit done up, and I don't blame them, as they are always on the march, and eight months out on the veldt is almost enough for anybody.

Winburg is a pretty little place. I now know nearly all these Free State towns, and most of the country as well.

Where we go to-morrow I don't know, but Senekal way I expect. The Boers, I believe, have split up into small parties again.

Senekal, 20th September.

Here we are at a new place. We marched north from Winburg, and had a bit of a fight with some Boers near the Zand River, who were just on the move, as usual. Rundle's Division was near us, and, I hear, captured one of their guns.

The old Boers, with a couple of big guns, made very good shooting at us from a long way off, but did not do any harm, except wound one man. My colour-sergeant got a rifle bullet through his field-glasses, and another cut his breeches; he is very proud.

We came in here last night, and I suppose shall move again to-morrow.

The night after the fight we spent a bad night, as our carts didn't turn up, and it was bitterly cold for the time of year. I sneaked into a farmhouse close by, and made the old frau produce a mattress and a loaf of bread, which, with some cocoa, kept us going till next day.

We hear a rumour that the Transvaal people have given in, but I never believe these rumours. These Boers here I don't think mean giving in till they are caught; most of them have plenty of food and nothing to lose, and those who had have had their farms pretty well wrecked. The young grass is coming up nicely now, which gives the horses good food when not on the march, but they have fared very badly the last few days.

This is a pretty place, but, like the other places, cleared out in turn by us and the Boers.

Lindley, 27th September.

We are actually having a quiet day, though expect we shall be on the move again in an hour or two, as half the force is out after some Boers, who are hanging around.

We have been dodging about since leaving Senekal on the 20th, from 6 a.m. till dark, and as that means getting up at 4.30 a.m., I was very glad of a good sleep this morning.

We have caught a certain number of odd Boers the last few days, but when we get anywhere near them, they divide into small parties and disperse in all directions. I should think the war in the Transvaal will be over before it is here, unless they start the same sort of games up there.

Lindley is the most dilapidated and miserable looking of all the Dutch towns I have yet seen. The houses are very small, there is no food to be got, and the smell of the dead horses is dreadful. We are camped about two miles outside the village. It was close by here that Longford, with his Irish Yeomanry, was taken prisoner.

I don't know when this will be posted, unless we get near the railway or a convoy goes in, and I'm afraid it will be a long time before I get any letter from you.

I am getting on quite well with my Dutch, and can talk quite nicely. I always carry my Dutch grammar in my haversack, and pull it out and study it when we are halted on the march.

L 2

We are burning a certain number of the farms from which we have been fired at, and take most of the cattle, carts, etc., and we have begun very late to try and starve the people out. We ought never to have allowed towns like Ladybrand and Senekal to get in plenty of fresh stores for the Boers to take.

It is getting quite warm now, even at nights, and thank goodness, up to date, we have had no rains for some time; I am dreading them. I am afraid my letters are not very interesting now, as we do

THE STATION FOR HEILBRON.

the same old everlasting marching every day after Dutchmen who are always well ahead of us.

Heilbron, 5th October.

We have just arrived here from Frankfort, and I am writing this in case my other letter should not catch the mail.

6th October.

We are still here at Heilbron, and I was very disappointed to find that the mails for us have gone wrong, and so we have got no letters again. I believe they have all been sent to Lindley, where they thought we should stop a few days, but the Boers cut the wires before we had time to stop them being sent there

Just fancy, we found the Regiment here—at least, most of them—when we arrived, and from all accounts they have had a bad time these last two months trekking about the country, but they are going to stop here to garrison this place. Old Henley is in Cape Town, doing A.D.C. to Sir A. Milner, and Stapleton has got some billet there too. We had fighting all day going into Frankfort, the Boers hanging about in small parties; we had a sergeant of the K.O.S.B.'s killed. All the proper fighting is over, I think, but goodness knows how long this messing about will last.

Our stores ran out a week ago, and we have been living on rations consisting of tough meat, biscuits, and a very small allowance of tea and sugar; it is very hard now to get a chicken, eggs, or anything from the farms.

There is a chance of this getting this mail. I am being continually worried all day long for all sorts of jobs, so can't write any more.

Vredefort Road, about 10th October.

At last we have got some letters, the mails of 7th and 14th September, but the two or three in-between are still missing.

We have been most awfully hustled lately, and had a real bad time. We took a convoy from Heilbron to Frankfort and back, which took three days each way; at it all the time, starting at 5 a.m. two days and 3.30 a.m. the other days. We came in here yesterday.

The Boers hung about us all the way to Heilbron and back, sniping whenever they got a chance. We tried to round some of them up on the way back, but only killed three of them. The Boers caught an officer and some men of the West Riding Company going out, but after taking their horses, saddles, and rifles, let them go.

Goodness knows how long this will go on in the Free State. I am beginning to think that burning the farms does not do much good after all.

We are all pretty well done up, and I don't blame the men, poor devils; they want a real good rest, plenty to eat, and new clothes. They can't keep up this continual trekking, of from 12 to 14 hours every day, besides a lot of out-posts, for ever.

We have had no stores lately, and I had *nothing* to eat one day (on a fourteen hours' march) till 9 p.m., and then—a piece of bread and jam. However, I am sick of fried chunks of meat, but we have found a little condensed milk, jam, and Quaker oats here.

Near Vredefort Road, 12th October.

We moved out of Vredefort Road yesterday about 2½ miles, and are having a quiet day to-day, but it's a horrid day, as it's blowing hard, and beastly hot, at the same time.

I don't know where we are going; they all pretend here that the war is over, still nothing can be done till these small Commandos are caught, or give in, and it is hardly like peace, when one is unable to ride about by oneself without being plugged at.

I am most careful not to get shot, and have got safely through so far. I have seen quite enough men killed, and have been shot at often enough not to have every respect for the Dutchman, and I think the Company has done very well to come so far with only a few killed in action, a few wounded, and none of us taken prisoners.

14th.—We have just arrived at Kroonstad, after two hard days' marching; starting at one o'clock at night, we marched till 7 p.m. the following night, with only a short rest in the middle of the day—we were all dog tired.

We are to start again early to-morrow morning, towards Bloemfontein, I expect. I am just going into Kroonstad to get some things for the men, if possible—they are awfully badly off for clothes, their pants are in rags. No mails here; there should be some, the ones that were sent after us to Lindley have not turned up yet. I will try and write again before leaving here, but doubt having time, I am so dreadfully hustled. I am very fit.

Kroonstad, 15th October.

We are having a day's rest here, thank goodness; where we go to-morrow, I don't know. All sorts of preparations are going on here for the end of the war. Volunteers going home, police being formed, etc., but I suppose *we* shall trek about the country, with what is left of my Company, for some time. I have men going sick every day, so am getting rapidly reduced in numbers. They are quite done up, and when once a man goes, it is very hard to get him back when he is well again. I was delighted to get a mail of the 20th September last night, but there were no papers or parcels; we haven't had any of them for a long time.

My temper is not all good now; I suppose it's the endless marching and hard work. I come in so dog tired, and then I have to go and see after the men and horses, and the odd day's rest, like to-day, is endless work—getting remounts, clothing, and all sorts of things.

We have been awfully put to it for firewood, as the little there was has been used by us all over the country. Cow dung is all we generally have to cook our dinners ; it burns all right if there is a little wind. I drink very little but tea, coffee, or cocoa ; I funk the water, though it hasn't done me any harm yet.

I must post this now, I expect ; but don't know yet whether we take a convoy to Lindley to-morrow or go after De Wet. I am certain we shall never catch him, unless he gives in. I don't think he stops with his commandos, but rides about from one to the other, telling them what to do.

Bothaville, 21st October.

We are now near Bothaville, west of Kroonstad. There were a lot of Boers about when we arrived, but they have dispersed as usual, and beyond a little shooting with the patrols, we have had no fighting.

It is getting beastly hot, and we have had a lot of wind. Yesterday there was a regular sand storm, which makes it horrid in camp, as it gets into one's body, clothes, and food ; still, I am quite content to sit still. We live and eat mostly in the American buggy ; it keeps the sun and wind off better than anything.

We have been what they call "laying the country waste," and have burnt and blown up nearly every farm between here and Kroonstad One day we were sent out with the 3rd Cavalry Brigade, and did about twenty miles of country. It is not a nice job, but the Dutch women take it very philosophically. We help them out with their furniture, then, if it's a big stone farm, blow it up with gun-cotton ; if small, we put a match to the roof of thatch, and soon nothing is left but the bare walls ; all their stock is then driven away. What the poor women and children do I don't know : a lot are living with us in ox-wagons, and will go into Kroonstad. I don't think the Dutchman likes it, but he does not seem to be giving in yet, and the whole country will have to be laid waste, from the Orange River to the Vaal, to starve them out : and then it will take some time, though I think there is bound to be a famine in the country in a short time.

A wire has just come to know how many men are wanted to make up our companies to proper strength. I want about 80 to make up to my 140. What this new game is, I don't know, but I don't look forward to training 80 recruits, and it will be a biggish job, as we shall want new saddlery and everything. We had Church to-day, only the second time since I came out here.

I forget whether I told you, we have been working for some time directly under Ross, and have nothing to do with the W. Riding Regiment. Ross has only got with him us, the Suffolks, and some Bushmen.

The Cavalry are made up in queer ways now ; a squadron of the Greys has men from almost every cavalry regiment.

27th October.

We have now crossed into the Transvaal, and are near Potchefstroom; we have had three very hard days, as we heard a large body of Boers were holding up Barton, north of Potchefstroom ; however, I believe now they have cleared off.

This is a beautiful bit of country, on both sides of the Vaal river ; all round Venterskroon and Rietzburg are mountains and snug valleys,

THE VAAL, LOOKING WEST.

with pretty farms. It is the country where De Wet spends most of his spare time, when he isn't blowing up the line.

29th.—We are now near Rhenoster Spruit, on our way back to Kroonstad. Since writing the previous part of this letter, we have doubled back into the Free State, in pursuit of De Wet, and on Saturday afternoon we came up with about 2,000 Boers, near Parys. De Lisle's lot came up first, and we came out of the mountains a bit late to do much good ; however, the Boers left two of their guns, and we caught about forty prisoners, and must have killed a certain number, though I believe very few dead were actually picked up. The Artillery had great shooting at them, but the Boers, as usual, scattered in all directions. One shell pitched on a big wagon filled with dynamite and ammunition; it did make a row exploding, and little bits of the Dutchman who was driving the wagon were found in all directions. My Company, as bad luck would have it, were doing rear guard, bringing up the wagons and cattle, so saw very little of the show. That night was a real bad one : we trekked on a long way after dark, and at about 9 p.m. a fearful thunderstorm came on, and it being hopeless to go on, I just dumped down with about thirty wagons for the night, tied up the horses, and laid down under the carts. I slept well, though drenched to the skin in a pool of water. It was a real hard day ; we had been going since 5 a.m., the men had had no food, except a biscuit, since their coffee in the morning. I was all right, as I had got three eggs cooked in a farm, but I was jolly glad of some hot cocoa to warm me up. When we came up with the others in the morning, nearly all of them had had an equally bad night, getting lost, and away from their carts, and drenched to the skin. I thought, two or three days ago, things were hopeless, and the war would never end, but this fight, the day before yesterday, must have done some good, and I believe Barton before that had knocked them about a bit ; still I am afraid we have not nearly done yet.

To-day one of my patrols, which had to stop behind, had a bit of shooting, and I think they got a Boer or two, and to vary the monotony the garrison on the railway, seeing us in the distance, thought they were being attacked by De Wet, so plumped two shells into some of our men, fortunately without doing any damage. It is very hard to tell who are Boers, as so many of them are dressed in khaki, and one never knows where anyone else is.

I will post this directly I get to Kroonstad, and do hope I shall get at least two mails from you, and perhaps the ones that went to Lindley by mistake.

I am really very fit, only awfully bored by this continual trekking, and should like a bit more sleep.

Honing Spruit, 15 miles north of Kroonstad, 31st October.

I have just got two mails, September 28th and October 4th. We do not know if we go to Kroonstad to-morrow. I think not, as Master De Wet is supposed to be sitting on a kopje 12 miles off, which I can see from here, and I expect we shall go after him—I bet, though, he is not there when we get to the kopje. I think this war is good for another two months at least, though some of the Generals did say it would be over by the 1st of September.

I expect a lot will be made in the papers of the fight we had a few days ago, but we couldn't have killed a great number of Boers, and only took a few prisoners, while the two guns were of very little use to De Wet, as he has not much ammunition.

I hear Prince Christian has died of enteric, poor chap, and there seem to be a good lot of casualties one way and another still.

COLOUR-SERGEANT J. H. ASPEY,
M.I. Company, Oxfordshire Light Infantry.
Killed at Gredgedacht, 18th March, 1901.

CHAPTER XIV.

BOTHAVILLE, NOVEMBER 6TH, 1900.

THE Mounted Infantry Company of the Regiment took part in the brilliant affair at Bothaville on the 6th November, when Captain G. N. Colvile was severely wounded. The following accounts are all that have come to hand :—

Official Despatch from Lord Roberts. Telegram dated Johannesburg, November 8th.

Colonel Le Gallais surprised the Boer forces on night of 5th inst. three miles south of Bothaville. He was heavily engaged for five hours, the enemy's strength about 1,000. Charles Knox followed Le Gallais with De Lisle's Mounted Infantry and completely defeated the enemy.

We captured one 12-pounder of "Q" Battery, one 15-pounder 14th Battery, four Krupp guns, one "pom-pom," and one Maxim, with all their ammunition and wagons, and 100 prisoners. Twenty-five Boers were left dead on the field and 30 wounded.

Steyn and De Wet were with this force, and left in great haste.

The enemy were pursued for some miles in a south-easterly direction, when they broke up in small parties

Our casualties were :—

Killed.—Le Gallais, 8th Hussars ; Captain F. Engelbach, of the Buffs ; Lieut. W. A. Williams, South Wales Borderers ; and eight men. Wounded.—Seven officers and 26 men.

I deeply regret the death of these three officers, all most promising. Le Gallais is, indeed, a very serious loss, a most gallant and capable cavalry leader.

The officers wounded are—Lieut.-Colonel W. C. Ross, Durham Light Infantry, neck and face, dangerously, but doing well ; Captain Colvile, Oxfordshire Light Infantry, side, severe ; Lieut. D. Percy-Smith, Middlesex Regiment, slight ; Lieut. A. S. Peebles, Suffolk Regiment, seriously ; Captain O. Harris, West Riding Regiment, slight ; Captain G. T. Mair, R.H.A., severe ; and Major N. Welch, Hampshire Regiment, severe.

The fighting must at one time have been at close quarters. "U" Battery, R.H.A., under Major P. B. Taylor, was in action at a range of 400 yards.

Amongst the wounded prisoners is De Villiers, Steyn's secretary, and amongst the dead the Boer doctor with Red Cross on his arm, rifle in hand, and bandolier half emptied.

Letters from Captain G. N. Colvile, commanding the M. I. Company, Oxfordshire Light Infantry :—

Bothaville, 6th November.

I have just been hit in the hip, but don't feel very bad. The parson is taking this to Kroonstad, as they won't be able to move me for a few days. You must not worry about my wound ; it is a clean wound, and not dangerous.

We have had a big fight, with a lot of casualties, I am afraid, but have given De Wet a nasty knock.

You can see from this I am not very bad, as I was only shot this morning ; the bullet went in at my back and out at the front.

7th November.

Brooke has just come in with a patrol, so I am writing this line on the chance of its catching the mail.

I am doing wonderfully well, and don't have much pain, only bad aches. I have not been able to ask the doctor yet how long I shall be lame, but he says I am getting on capitally. He lets me eat anything now, though I was starved at first, as he was not sure that my stomach wasn't hit, but now he knows I am all right.

There are 17 wounded in this little farmhouse, most of them very bad. Poor Le Gallais and a gunner sergeant died last night. I expect to be taken into Kroonstad in a day or two ; they have wired for ambulances. De Wet and Steyn were both here, but cleared off pretty quick.

I have got the rifle belonging to the man who shot me ; he is dead.

9th November.

I hope you will have got the two scrawls I wrote you by the mail, which leaves Kroonstad to-morrow. One I wrote a few hours after I was hit, and the other one the next day as Brooke came back here with a patrol. I also gave Hamilton a wire to send off as soon as possible to say I was all right.

I last wrote to you from Honing Spruit. We thought we were going on to Kroonstad, but were sent off after De Wet, hunting him along the Rhenoster, and eventually round to Bothaville. We had a bad time, as it had been raining like anything the first four days, consequently our mules died, and we had an awful job to get the transport through the mud, besides always being soaked through.

We had next to no fighting till the 5th, but that afternoon I was sent on towards Bothaville with my Company, the Bushmen, and some niggers, to see by the tracks which way De Wet's guns had gone. We tracked them to the river, and there saw a good number of Boers, who made off. We were too few to go for them, and they laid very low, not even firing into our scouts that went into the river bed.

Le Gallais turned up about an hour before dark, and I was just telling him that a few Boers were left behind a kopje across the river (which he did not believe), when the Boers, who had been hiding, began blazing away with their guns and a pom-pom. We were all pretty close to the Boers, who gave us a proper shelling, but they only hit five men, I believe, and some horses.

That night after dark we crossed the river, and stopped in the Boer laager. I could not lie down till twelve o'clock, and was properly tired out, but I luckily got some cocoa before going to sleep.

Next morning we started at 4.30 a.m. with about 250 men, three guns, and a pom-pom, and very soon came up with the enemy. We had a pretty good fight; there were about 800 Boers, I believe, with five guns and a pom-pom. We luckily took the beggars very much by surprise, or should have had a bad beating; as it was, we were nearly done, as the Boers galloped round our flanks, and nearly got round on our left, taking one of our guns—the officer, five men, and the horses belonging to it being all shot. Peebles in the Suffolk Mounted Infantry and Brooke took up half my Company. The Boers fought like blazes; it was with about 100 dismounted Boers in the laager that I had most to do. The fight began about 5.30 and ended at 11.30, De Lisle coming to our aid about 8 o'clock.

I got hit pretty early in the day. I had some men in a kraal and some in a farmhouse, and was going across between the two, when I got wounded by some dismounted Boers.

It was a very bad day for the 8th M.I. officers; I think there were twelve of them, out of which six were badly hit, Colonel Ross very badly, I'm afraid, his chin blown off. His staff officer, Williams, was killed, Peebles badly wounded, Harris and Smith (my subaltern) slightly, besides myself. The men got off very well, only one of mine being hit; several horses were killed, but the men all got remounted afterwards from the Boers. We took 85 prisoners, five guns, and a pom-pom; we buried 11 Boers, but there must have been a good many killed, besides a lot wounded.   I heard both Steyn and De Wet watched the fight from a safe distance.   It has been a good knock for them, our getting all their guns ; still, I don't think they will chuck it yet.

The men got some loot out of the laager.   I have got the rifle belonging to the man who shot me—he was killed, and Brooke has got one of Steyn's shirts.

We are still in the little farmhouse where the fight took place.   There are 17 wounded men here ; all the moveable cases have gone to Kroonstad, but of the 17, poor Le Gallais and a gunner sergeant died last night, and two wounded Boers the second night.

Welch, a man in the Hampshire Regiment, is in the same room with me, also Peebles ; they are both bad, but I think will live.   Welch is shot right through the neck.

Colonel Ross has been taken to Kroonstad, as, if they can get a tube to enable him to eat, he may live.

10th November.

Since writing yesterday, we have been twice visited by the Boers.   They have behaved very well to us, taking nothing.   They looked round their old laager to see if they could find any saddles, etc., that might have been left.   I think they were pleased at our taking care of their wounded.   I fully expected them to take our ambulance horses and the mules belonging to our Cape carts.

I hope the ambulances from Kroonstad will turn up to-morrow, and take us in there.   The doctor is named Newmarsh, and belongs to the New South Wales Hospital ; he is a good man.   He tells me I am very lucky, as the bullet just missed my inside, and he said this morning my wound is doing well.   It doesn't give me much pain, except when I move ; it was very fortunate that it was not caused by an explosive bullet, as most of them were.   I shall be thankful to get out of here, as it is so hard to get any sleep, with the other poor beggars calling out for water, or wanting something, and last night poor Welch got delirious.

The corrugated iron roof is full of bullet holes, so I got Gould to fill them up last night, as we had some very heavy rain.   If you saw me now, you wouldn't be a bit anxious.   I feel very well, and eat plenty.   I am just going to have lunch—stewed bully-beef.   I am sure I shan't be any the worse for my wound.

Kroonstad.

We arrived here safely on Wednesday afternoon, not much the worse for our 50 mile shaking in a bullock wagon.   It was a beastly journey ; we started on Monday evening from the farm, and picked up more wounded in Bothaville that night.   We started at six next morning, and travelled all those days with only a halt in the middle of the day. I was wedged in with Peebles, who is pretty bad, and the bumping over the rocks fairly shook our insides out.

It is very nice getting into a bed with sheets, though I couldn't sleep at all the first night, however, I slept grandly last night. It is quite comfortable here, but the food is not good ; it comes up quite cold, and one can't keep off the flies, of which there are a plague here.

We have a good many visitors, as Le Gallais' old force are still here refitting. Pilcher has taken over Le Gallais' force, and a Captain from the 7th Mounted Infantry, Colonel Ross' ; I should have got that if I hadn't been wounded. The 8th Mounted Infantry were brought into Kroonstad by a Subaltern !

Poor Welch died soon after I wrote my last letter to you. Smith is in the hospital, but is off to-day on six weeks' sick leave, after which he rejoins his own Regiment. His wound was very slight, only a splinter in the face and chest.

Extract from a letter from 2nd Lieutenant R. R. M. Brooke, Oxfordshire Light Infantry, dated Kroonstad, November 13th, 1900 :—

It has been absolutely impossible to write since my last letter. Well, to begin with, I am very thankful that I am alive and well, as we have just arrived here after one of the hottest fights (General Knox told us so a few minutes ago on parade) of the war, though not so very many troops engaged as in some of them. Ever since you last heard from me we have been with a flying Column in the west of the Orange River Colony, forming part of Hunter's mounted troops (under Colonel Le Gallais) in pursuit of De Wet. We have had several fights with him, but he has always retired rather hastily. We had one pretty good fight on the Vaal River, about three weeks ago, killing a lot of Boers, and also blowing up an ammunition wagon with a well-directed shell. Our last and most successful fight was at Bothaville, on the Valsch River, about a week ago. The evening before, we heard that De Wet was laagered in Bothaville, on the other side of the river, with eight guns and 2,000 men. We pushed on at once, arrived at the river, and found that he was occupying the town and all the hills on the other side. He at once commenced to shell us with six guns, and did a good deal of damage, killing a considerable number of horses and wounding a lot of men. Our Artillery came into action, and a pretty hot fight went on until dark, when the enemy retired, and we crossed the river and occupied Bothaville that night. It was a fairly warm show that evening, but nothing to what took place next morning.

At 4.30 a.m. we were ordered to march, and expected to come up with De Wet very soon. After going about four miles, and just as it was getting light, we heard shots coming from a farm in front, and then saw shells bursting in all directions, some dropping uncomfortably close. We then knew that our advance-guard had come in touch with the enemy. The first thing I saw was a party of six old Boers being led back prisoners to the rear. Our scouts had caught a picquet asleep about a quarter of a mile from the laager. There were three farms close together, and behind them De Wet and Steyn (with about 2,500 of the enemy) had laagered for the night, not expecting that we would follow them up. Our rapid advance came as a complete surprise to them, and De Wet, Steyn, and as many of them as could seize horses (which had been turned out to graze) bolted at the firing of the first shot, yelling out to the Boers to save their guns at all costs. They managed to get three guns into action before we could reach the ground overlooking the farms and laager. The Boers hung on all round the laager and in all the buildings and cattle kraals round about the farms, while parties of them worked round our right and left flanks, so that at one time we were almost completely surrounded.

Colvile now took one half of our Company on at once towards the farms, and succeeded in seizing the farm nearest to us, on a level with the Boer laager. Here he had to hold out, 200 yards from the laager, under continuous shell and rifle fire, for four hours. On his right and left were two of our guns, and the 5th and 7th Mounted Infantry Regiments. He said to me before he started, "I am going on with half the Company to seize the farms; you wait a minute, until two guns of 'U' Battery come up; they want you and the rest of the Company as escort." Well, the guns came up, and went out at once to the left flank, under a galling fire from the laager, and also from the Boers who were working round to the left in the attempt to get in on our flank. Here, on the left flank, we had a desperate hot fight for nearly three hours, the Boers showing tremendous dash and enterprise. At one time 200 of them got within 70 yards of one of our guns, and would have captured it but for a magnificent man in the Suffolk Mounted Infantry who was escorting the gun with only six men. He held his ground, gave the order to "fix bayonets," then, looking round, saw a Maxim strapped on the back of a mule. He got up, and calmly walked back and brought the Maxim into action, driving off the Boers at once. I am sorry to say that every horse and man belonging to the gun was shot down. I never saw such a sight as it presented when I went over to it afterwards — the men all lying round it shot, and the horses torn to pieces by the shells.

While this had been going on, I and 25 men of the Company (with the two guns) were hotly engaged further away on the left, in which direction the Boers were gradually working round us. The firing was heavy, and we were running short of ammunition; my groom (Pte. Cross), who was a long way behind with the horses, noticing that we had stopped firing, came galloping up with a horse's nose-bag full of ammunition. But there were many incidents like this, for every man worked his level best all through. The enemy's great object was to get round behind us and capture our convoy, in which they very nearly succeeded. All this time there was a tremendous fight going on at the farm, and also on

SECOND-LIEUT. R. R. M. BROOKE.

the right flank. I must say that the Boers fought wonderfully; the way they held out for three hours in and around that laager, with six of our guns playing on them, was marvellous; and the dash and daring that they displayed was more like what one reads of the onslaught of fanatical savages than anything else. It was something quite new, and different to the usual tactics of the ordinary old Boer, who likes to sit on a kopje and shoot until you get near, and then clear out.

What pretty well ended it all was the arrival of Colonel De Lisle with his Colonial Division and Mounted Infantry, having galloped 12 miles directly they heard the firing begin. The Boers now cleared off from the flanks, and retreated as fast as possible after De Wet and Steyn, leaving a lot of dead and wounded on the field. Then we all closed in round the farms and laager, and the 150 Boers who remained (with their seven guns) continued to hold out for another two and a half hours. It was not until the "prepare to charge" was given, that the enemy caved in, and then they all came running out, holding up their hands. I think that you will consider this fairly successful, though I am sorry to say we lost pretty heavily, both in officers and men. Poor Colonel Le Gallais was killed ; Colonel Ross, commanding the 8th M. I. Battalion, to which our Company belongs, was dangerously wounded ; Williams, our Adjutant, was killed, as well as Engelbach (of the Buffs); Peebles (of the Suffolk M. I. Company) badly wounded ; Colvile (commanding our Company) shot through the leg, but I am glad to say doing capitally (I have just seen him in hospital) ; and Percy-Smith (attached to us) slightly wounded. In fact, we suffered pretty severely—10 casualties among the officers, and, I am afraid, a good many men killed and wounded. But the Boers had a much worse time. I counted 30 dead myself, one to my own rifle. He was a dear old man, dressed in blue pyjamas and jack boots, and he kept darting up from behind an ant-heap and trying to plug me ; but I got him at last. We picked up any number of wounded Boers and took them into our hospital. There were 150 prisoners and seven guns captured (one had been taken by the Boers at Colenso). I am pleased to say that our Company behaved splendidly, six of the men's names being taken for recommendation for the Distinguished Conduct Medal. I got Steyn's shirt as loot out of the laager afterwards, also some proclamations, telling the Boers to continue the fighting, and a visiting card of Steyn's private secretary.

OFFICIAL REPORT OF THE ENGAGEMENT.

From Major Taylor, R.H.A.,

    To C.S.O. General Knox.

                        7th November, 1900.

I regret to inform you that Colonel Le Gallais, commanding M. I., Hunter's Force, died last night at 8.30 p.m. from wounds received in action south of Bothaville on the same day.

At 4.30 a.m. yesterday Colonel Le Gallais' Force marched south from Bothaville across the river, the 5th M. I., under Major Lean, forming the advanced guard. Within two miles of the river Major Lean surprised a Boer outpost and took them prisoners, without their being able to give the alarm. Major Lean grasped the fact that a Boer force was close at hand, and galloped on to some rising ground about two miles south of the river ; he had previously sent back for guns. When he reached the summit of the high ground, he found that he was over-looking a Boer laager, about 300 yards distant, which only then became aware of his presence.

He opened a hot fire, and a large number of men mounted their horses and made off, leaving their guns, wagons, etc., outspanned ; this occurred about 6 a.m.

At the same time Lieutenant Percy-Smith, Oxfordshire Light Infantry,[1] made a dash for the farmhouse (see sketch),[2] which stands on the ridge, and seized it.

About 6 a.m. Lieutenant Otter-Barry's section of " U " Battery came into action on the same ridge as the 5th M. I., but about 100 yards to their right rear. There was no choice of position, as, owing to the ground, the guns had to be advanced to within 400 yards of the laager, in order to see into it, and I considered it all important to do so, to prevent the Boer guns being brought into action. From the ridge I saw the Boer laager with several guns still standing in it, and horses running loose ; to our left of the laager, and somewhat nearer, was a stone enclosure about 100 yards long, the walls of which were two feet thick and three feet six inches high. Into this enclosure most of the remaining Boers had withdrawn, but the house marked[2] and a pig-stye were held, and from all these a very accurate fire was maintained at anyone who showed at all.

Our front was then held by about 40 men and two guns.

The right flank was held by the 17th and 18th Companies Imperial Yeomany, about 42 strong.

On the left was the 8th M. I., 105 strong, 12 of whom, under Captain Colvile, were in a kraal.

About 6.20 a.m., having seen the section of my Battery settled in action, I went to the farmhouse where Colonel Le Gallais was, and found that both he and Lieutenant-Colonel Ross had been seriously wounded. As the senior officer present, I assumed command of the force.

I ascertained that both flanks were being pressed by large numbers of mounted Boers, who came round from the laager and threatened to surround us.

The 5th Mounted Infantry, in front, were getting short of ammunition. I despatched Captain Gale to the convoy to direct them to park,

---

[1] Attached from D.C.O., Middlesex Regiment. [2] Sketch not reproduced.—ED.

and send all possible men to the right flank, and the Ammunition Column to a central position in rear of the front. I also directed him to send a message to you, to tell you that I was pressed and feared my flanks were being turned. I sent to Captain Mair to take the third gun of "U" Battery (the fourth being with the convoy) up to the left front. These orders of mine, I subsequently found, had to a large extent been anticipated by Major Hickie, Colonel Le Gallais' Staff Officer, who had been sent back by Colonel Le Gallais to bring up the remainder of the force.

Two Companies of the 7th Mounted Infantry came up about an hour later, one going to the right, the other to the left flank. This resulted in relieving the right flank entirely, and to a certain extent the left.

Shortly afterwards Major Welch, with two more Companies 7th Mounted Infantry and one gun, came up, and I directed him to execute a turning movement round our left of the farm and enclosure, and to bring a gun into action against the house (marked), and to rake the walled enclosure from the east.

About 8 o'clock Lieut.-Colonel Knight, with two Companies Australians from Colonel De Lisle's force arrived, and I asked him to co-operate in Major Welch's turning movement.

About 8.30 a.m. Colonel De Lisle arrived, and told me to hold on to the farm at all costs, and to endeavour, when possible, to take the walled enclosure with the bayonet, for which purpose he sent me, about 10 a.m., 25 Australian Mounted Infantry, as I said I was too weak in men.

By 9 a.m. the Boers in the farm and enclosure were completely surrounded; and the enclosure and house being shelled from the north and east, and under rifle fire from the north and west, the enemy's fire was much subdued. I despatched officers to warn the troops on the east and west that the enclosure would shortly be stormed.

About 10.15 a.m. Lieut. Darling and 25 Australian Mounted Infantry came up, and I arranged that this party, together with about 25 men 7th Mounted Infantry, were to take the enclosure.

The guns and Major Lean's 25 men were to keep up a heavy magazine fire for three minutes; this was to cease on Major Lean's whistle, and the storming party was immediately to charge.

The magazine fire opened, and after about a minute the enemy hoisted the white flag.

Some 82 unwounded Boers emerged from the enclosure.

Only one of the Boer guns got into action behind the further wall of the enclosure, and the pom-pom fired a few shots; neither, however, was of any service to them, as they did not venture from behind the wall, and from this position they were unable to direct their fire on my front and left.

It was, of course, the timely arrival of Colonel De Lisle's Column that enabled me to bring up so many men from my baggage guard, and that made the Boers draw off from my flanks.

Whilst all the troops under my command behaved with gallantry and determination, I would specially mention those men of the 5th Mounted Infantry, under Major Lean's immediate command, Captain Colvile's Company of the 8th Mounted Infantry, and Lieut. Peebles' Suffolk Company 8th Mounted Infantry ; and the men of " U " Battery behaved as I should wish them to do.

I estimate the strength of the enemy at about 800.

I append a list of what was captured in the laager.

Our casualties were :—Officers killed, 2 ; wounded, 8 (1 since dead) ; N.C.O.'s and men killed, 4 ; wounded, 24 (2 since dead).

We buried 17 Boers, took 17 wounded and 97 unwounded prisoners.

I have the honour to be, Sir,

Your obedient servant,

P. B. Taylor, Major, R.H.A.

Another account :—

Kroonstad, Nov. 18th.

On the last day of October it became known that De Wet was somewhere in the neighbourhood. Immediately Major-General Charles Knox despatched three Columns from different points, all converging towards Rhebokfontein, where De Wet was reported to be encamped, some 50 miles almost due east of Rhenoster Station. Le Gallais's force started from Honing's Spruit. De Lisle, with the Colonial division, marched from Kopjes, the first station north of Rhenoster, but the Colonials, after marching some miles with the Column, diverged off towards the north, so as to make a wider turning movement and cut off De Wet should he attempt to retreat to the Vaal. Le Gallais, by marching all the night of the 2nd inst., in pouring rain and over heavy country, was the first to approach the Boer General's hiding-place. By daylight he was in a position ready to attack, but the bird had flown, and all that was left of De Wet was the litter of his camp. Le Gallais decided to follow his tracks. The whole concerted movement thus became abortive, and General Knox, fearing that De Wet was moving to the valley north of Reitzburg, where his wife is said to be living, despatched the Colonial division to the Vaal. He himself, with De Lisle, followed Le Gallais a day's march to the rear.

Meanwhile Le Gallais continued the chase hot-foot. De Wet's tracks led to Klip Drift, south-west, on towards Bothaville. At midday on the 8th the pursuing force reached Doornbult, while Knox remained at Grootkorn, ten miles off. Le Gallais's force proceeded to camp, but he himself, with 200 men and two guns of "U" Battery, moved forward to reconnoitre Bothaville. On nearing the town, now a heap of ruins, he was saluted by two guns placed on a couple of kopjes north of the town and commanding it. The river, crossed by a good drift, ran between. Le Gallais engaged the enemy for two hours, when night put an end to the fighting. Our losses were five men wounded. We remained on the ground, and Le Gallais sent back orders for his baggage wagons to inspan immediately, and follow with the rest of the force. They arrived at 10 p.m., and immediately the baggage was parked in the deserted square of Bothaville, while the 5th and 8th Mounted Infantry were pressed over the drift towards the kopjes lately held by De Wet. These were found to be unoccupied, and were strongly picqueted that night.

At 4.30 a.m. on the morning of the 6th, Le Gallais's little force moved off in his indefatigable chase after De Wet. The 5th Mounted Infantry led the Column, followed by the 8th Corps, under Colonel Ross. The 5th, 17th, and 18th Companies of the Imperial Yeomanry acted as escort to the three guns of "U" Battery, while the 7th Mounted Infantry, under Major Welch, and one gun of "U" Battery remained behind to protect the crossing of the baggage.

The country to our front was open and undulating, and there were no kopjes to afford a hiding-place to the enemy. The 5th Mounted Infantry, under Major Lean, moved rapidly forward, taking every precaution against accidents. Suddenly they came upon a small picquet of the enemy lying fast asleep. Around them their horses, firmly knee-haltered, were peacefully grazing. In a moment they were awakened, and, after rubbing their eyes, found themselves prisoners. Major Lean and his little force rode straight forward towards the next rise. The enemy's laager lay within 300 yards of him, and beneath him guns, wagons, and horses, all contained in a small space of a few hundred yards square. Immediately despatching a messenger with the news, Major Lean dismounted his men and fired volley after volley into the thick of them. Then arose such a panic as perhaps the Boers had never before experienced. Steyn and De Wet fled incontinently in a Cape cart. Those burghers who had horses at hand leaped on their backs and galloped away, leaving everything—guns, ammunition, and wagons. Only those who could not get their horses remained and fought with the courage of despairing men.

In order to understand the fighting that followed, it is necessary to give a rough description of the ground. Lean's men held the top of a rise, which sloped gently towards the Boer laager. Close to the top stood a farmhouse, with a stone wall extending towards the right. Beyond that, again, was another stone enclosure, while on our extreme left was a Kaffir kraal. The Boer position was stronger. About 250 yards from where Lean fired his first volley there was an enclosure of about 100 yards square, with strong thick stone walls of about 6 feet high. On the right corner of this (from the Boer point of view) was a dam with steep banks facing us. The laager was unprotected on the left. On the left rear of the Boers was another dam, while on the right rear of the stone enclosure, and about half-way up another slope, stood a white house. Immediately the fighting commenced the Boers clambered into the enclosure, and held it stubbornly, as well as a stone wall that projected some way to the left. They also manned the banks of both dams, and occupied the white house. There was a small pig-sty situated only 20 yards from our position. Two men remained in it, and caused us considerable annoyance. Once under the different sorts of cover the Boers opened a heavy, well-sustained fire.

Up to the present we only had 60 men, which was all that Lean had with him. The Boers numbered fully 200, but the unequal fight was kept up with vigour by our men. At this stage of the fight our front was formed as follows: On our left front, where the 8th Mounted Infantry had taken up a position in echelon, stood a Kaffir kraal, where lay 14 men of the Oxford Light Infantry (Mounted Infantry), under Captain Maurice, Le Gallais's galloper, who took command when Captain Colvile was hit. In the centre ten men of the Oxford Light Infantry (Mounted Infantry), held the farmhouse; while 20 Buffs and the Royal Irish Mounted Infantry, under Captain Engelbach, who was killed, held a piece of the wall on the right of the farmhouse. Further to the right 20 of the Worcester Mounted Infantry, under Captain Holland, had secured and held a bit of good ground. Later on 20 men of the Royal Irish, under Captain Brush, held a similar position on our extreme right front. Le Gallais and Ross, hearing the firing, galloped forward to see how things were going. They reached the farmhouse, and, leaving their horses outside, entered the building, whence a good view of the position could be obtained. Le Gallais perceived that about 800 Boers, who had fled at the first volley, had formed up and were working round both our flanks. Le Gallais thereupon ordered Major Hickie, his staff officer, to ride back to the heliograph, and order Major Welch, who was in charge of the baggage escort, to park his baggage between the two kopjes, and send every man available to the left flank. This order was promptly obeyed ; the Cape-cart drivers—mostly men who had lost their horses—outspanned and held the kopjes, while Major Welch took the rest of the 7th Mounted Infantry up towards our left wing. At the same time the 17th and 18th Companies of the Imperial Yeomanry were ordered to move to the right flank. This relieved the situation somewhat, but still it was a difficult position, requiring great coolness and courage to face it.

Major Hickie rode back to the farmhouse, and was greeted by a hail of bullets, five of which hit his horse, and killed it. He, however, was luckily unhurt, and immediately entered the house. It was a terrible sight that met his eyes. The gallant Le Gallais lay mortally wounded. Ross, in another room, was stretched on the floor, with his jaw and a portion of his throat shot away. Captain Williams lay dead, and Lieut. Percy-Smith, of the Middlesex Regiment, wounded, together with four men. Outside the house 14 dead horses testified to the terrible nature of the Boer fire. It had become a perfect charnel-house, for it was a splendid mark for the Boers. The front window, which overlooked the Boer position, was an inferno of whistling, shrieking bullets, spattering the walls and breaking the woodwork and glass. Ross, it appeared, had gone straight to this window to see what was the position of affairs. The door of the room was exactly opposite the window, and unfortunately it had been left open, so that the enemy could see right through the house. When Ross was hit four men picked him up and carried him out, showing up clear against the light of the back doorway. The enemy, although they saw that it was only a wounded man being carried away, opened a terrible fire. But the brave four never flinched, and continued to carry their beloved commander down the passage, when suddenly Le Gallais appeared from another room to see what was the matter, and was immediately hit. The bullet entered his left breast, traversed his body, and came out on his left side. He sank to the ground with a groan, and was quickly put under cover. He was conscious all the time, and never seemed to think about his wound, but kept asking questions about the progress of the fight.

For five hours these gallant men, forming our front, held their ground against an overwhelming fire. Man after man was shot, killed, or wounded, but the others continued firing calmly and steadily. The wounded men in several cases filled the magazines for their comrades still fighting, and handed up the full rifles to them. It wanted courage of a very high order to hold the position. Not only were 200 Boers firing with terrible rapidity at short ranges, but 800 were threatening to cut them off. But the men, with bulldog tenacity, would not yield, and never flinched. As one of the men said afterwards:—"We could see their guns, and we wasn't going to lose them." And so the fight went on in front—the courage of despair on one side, and on the other that dogged, bulldog courage which has brought us out of so many a difficulty.

On our right flank the Boers had made an attempt to get in, but the two companies of Yeomanry, under Captain Coates and Lieut. Bolton, faced them steadily, and drove them off in some confusion.

The arrival of Major Welch with the 7th Mounted Infantry and the Durhams was most welcome. Gradually they drove the Boers back until they got opposite the Boer laager, and were in a position to enfilade them. Quickly a pom-pom was unlimbered, and shell after shell was accurately placed along the sides of the dam and the walls held by the enemy. It was a timely arrival, which considerably relieved our front, and showed the Boers the hopelessness of their position. The two companies of Yeomanry also pushed forward on our right, and soon we held three sides of a square, in the middle of which was the Boer laager.

And now De Lisle and his men were up, and were clearing our front flanks rapidly. At a little after 9 the Boers were surrounded. But their cover was excellent, and they kept firing at everything they could see. But our men were in the highest spirits, and shot coolly and steadily, joking with each other as they fired. Gradually it became apparent to the Boers that their position was absolutely untenable, and at last at half-past 10 the white flag was hoisted, and all round the encircling force there rang out a cheer of triumph. But our men would not leave their cover. " Lay down your arms and come out," they shouted, and immediately the walls became black with clambering Boers, who sullenly walked up to our men. The result of the day's work was seven guns— one 15-pounder belonging to the 14th Battery, captured at Colenso, one 12-pounder belonging to "Q" Battery, taken at Sanna's Post, three Krupp 75mm., one pom-pom, one 37mm. quick-firer—13 wagons, containing immense quantities of gun and small arm ammunition, and a large amount of black powder and dynamite, besides all the Boer supplies. But the victory was dearly purchased. Le Gallais lay dead, mourned sincerely by his men. His dash had won the victory, and everybody felt that it was bitter that he should not have lived to enjoy its fruits. If anything can console a mother for the loss of such a gallant son, it is the last words he uttered feebly to his staff officer, Major Hickie, " If I die, tell my mother that I died happy, as we got the guns."

It is not, luckily, an uncommon thing to chronicle the gallantry of the Medical Corps. Captain Surgeon Naismith behaved throughout the whole day with the utmost coolness. He tended the wounded wherever he found them, regardless of bullets, and apparently unconscious of them. Captain Newmarsh, an Australian doctor, volunteered to stay with the wounded at the farmhouse. The Boers behaved very kindly, and put a sentry on the house with orders to allow no one to approach. When he left, Captain Newmarsh presented them with some provisions in return for their kindness. Ross is now in hospital here, and is going on very well.

CAPTAIN G. N. COLVILE,
Commanding the M. I. Company.
Severely wounded at Bothaville.

CHAPTER XV.

A PRISONER OF WAR.

By Lieut.-Colonel F. J. Evelegh.[1]

In December 1899, on arrival from Staff employment in India, I was ordered to organise and take out to South Africa the Mounted Infantry of the 13th (Knox's) Brigade, 6th Division. This consisted of 15 officers, 560 rank and file, and 520 horses; and we arrived at Cape Town, after a 28 days' voyage, on the *S.S. Pindari*, the 8th February 1900.

On the 11th February I received an order, which had been awaiting me, to the effect that being second in command of the Battalion, I was to rejoin it at Enslin, and to proceed by the mail train that night. This meant that I must travel without my cob, as the train would not convey horses. My soldier-servant appeared to desire that I should also go up country without my saddle and carbine, as he carefully packed them in the main barracks with my store baggage. However, at 8 p.m. I made a fair start, and arrived at Enslin early on the 14th, to find that Lord Roberts' last Division had marched the day before on its journey towards Pretoria.

Headlam, R.H.A., and I, with servants, having detrained, tried to do our duty by a very nasty "bully-beef" breakfast on the sandy veldt by the railway, after which we went and reported our arrival to Count Gleichen, the Camp Commandant, and then to my sorrow I learned that, though a battle was expected next day, he

---

[1] Now commanding the 1st Battalion Royal Garrison Regiment.—Ed.

could not mount me and enable me to join the Regiment, which was already toiling along 25 miles off.

There was a fair amount of life outside the camp; in one direction, Modder camp, heavy guns were being fired into Kimberley, and a large war balloon hovering over Methuen's forces; eastward, dense columns of sand rose heavily in the air, denoting the march of Infantry Columns and lines of wagons some 20 miles off; we also noticed, some miles away, a mule wagon coming slowly towards camp, which on arrival proved to be a wagon

TABLE BAY.

carrying sick officers, among them Ruck Keene, looking very seedy and worn out. I may mention that this wagon and its mules formed part of my convoy, which was to start later.

Gleichen now rode up, and said he had just received a most pressing telegram from Lord Roberts, ordering him to send by convoy boots, kit, etc., for the Highland Light Infantry and Highland Brigade; and as some remounts for the Duke of Cornwall's Light Infantry and mules had come in, he would mount me if I would take charge, or rather *tactical* charge, of the convoy.

This offer I jumped at, as I was anxious to be with the Regiment in time for the fight.

At 7 p.m. that evening I was warned that the small convoy was ready to start, and at once joined it, to find the carts drawn by thirty odd, tired-looking mules, and an escort consisting of 2nd Lieut.C.P.M.Craigie-Halkett, Highland Light Infantry, Dr. Kelbe, a gallant Colonial doctor, who, having just lost his wife, had come, apparently reckless of life, to rejoin the Highland Brigade, six mounted scouts of Kitchener's Horse, lent by Colonel Legge, and sixteen convalescent casuals of Infantry; and also, at the last moment, another half-dozen convalescents, but these last were unarmed, and took advantage of our escort and joined us by order.

My instructions were, as there were no drifts marked on our maps of South Africa, to follow the field telegraph wire through Ramdam, cross the Riet River at Waterval Drift, and catch up Lord Roberts' army on the other side. We had not much difficulty in following the tracks, as many dead horses and mules lay about; but the occasional unloading and lifting carts out of holes by my none too strong men, made an hour or two's rest by the water at Ramdam a necessity; we, therefore, out-spanned and waited for daylight, the men lying down to sleep without a thought of food. I looked up a doctor in charge of sick at the only house within sight, who casually remarked, " Begad, there's not a Boer within forty mile of ye!" I here noticed that my servant had lost himself, and fancy he joined a convoy of sick, which passed us on its way back to Enslin, just as a furious thunder shower made us turn our heads for a minute the wrong way; at any rate, I have not since seen him; but a month or so after I received a letter from him, asking me to let him have his kit, as he had been drugged (by the Boers?), who had left him at Orange

River, miles behind us, without even his horse, boots, or "britches," and with only a belt on; and he added insult to injury by asking me if I knew anything of the horse that had carried him.

At 10 a.m., on February 15th, the convoy passed through a ridge of kopjes; we found the Riet a mile in front,[1] and a battle going on as far as the eye could reach on the other side. I have since learned that 2,000 Boers, with guns, under De Wet, had fallen on the rear-guard, which was not strong enough to put him to rout, and it therefore had been obliged to retire slowly.

I further saw my advanced scouts galloping back, one wounded through the thigh, the bullets flicking up the sand about them as they came along; and when they arrived the convoy had then a fairly heavy fire opened on it from a distant kopje. We were moving down hill, so I at once directed the head of the convoy towards a small plateau, where there appeared to be a chance of cover on my right, and then turned to try and find out what was meant, and saw, about a mile away, two sections of about 30 Boers each galloping for us, and a fairly dense cloud of sand, evidently raised by a larger body moving fast to my right.

My first idea was to retire my convoy back through the kopjes and hold the enemy there, but a second's consideration told me that my mules could not get the carts up the hill in time, as I had already outspanned several to die, and, therefore, that we must fight all we knew where we stood. I at once ordered a low parapet of all available boxes, bales of hay, and clothing to be made.

Just then four East Lancashire Mounted Infantry, who had been bringing along some cattle, rode up, so I sent them with three mounted scouts to hold a shoulder

---

[1] Waterval Drift, where the 6th Division had bivouacked on the 13th Feb. *Vide* Map, page 86.

which looked down on us some 300 yards off, and the two remaining to a Company of Mounted Infantry, which was retiring under fire a mile on my left, to ask its Commander for assistance.

In the moment or so before firing was opened on us, I could not help noticing that, although all knew they were in for a hot time of it, the men exhibited the greatest calmness, as they sat on boxes carefully examining their bolts and sights; yet all were tired out and parched with thirst, the heat being intense, and the well we had just passed had had a dead horse in it, and the water therefore undrinkable.

I may here say that four men out of my 16 Infantry reported broken rifles to me, and a Kitchener's Horse scout had anxiously asked me to instruct him how to get his cartridges from the magazine to the barrel.

A heavy fire now began from the enemy, under cover, about 400 yards in front, and my mounted scouts were at once driven from their hill by a body which turned out to be 100 strong.

As the Boers were impossible to see, I at first reserved my fire; but on "independent" commencing, we all found that our helmets and pouches prevented us firing under cover lying down, and the sun being too fierce to take our helmets off, it became necessary to expose ourselves when firing, which, under the circumstances, did not mean deliberate shooting.

The mules and drivers I had sent away, that they might, if possible, escape the fire directed on us; but every horse had now been shot down, as a heavy magazine fire had been opened from at least 150 rifles on to our small patch of ground from three different quarters; that from the shoulder was the most searching. Now a Company on my left flank worked up to within 80 yards. I was on that flank, and had now, with the assistance of the men about me, to draw back the left-hand boxes and bales so as to face that attack, and also to save the remainder from enfilade fire.

We now began to suffer most severely. Private W. Buckle, West Riding Regiment, sharing the left side of my bale, received three bullets in his temple and cheek bone, his blood spurting over me. At the same moment Dr. Kelbe, behind the box next on my right, was shot through the windpipe; and then, having fired several shots, I turned round and shouted to Craigie-Halkett, who commanded the right flank, to ask how he was getting on, but received no answer—he, poor boy, having been shot through the heart and stomach. I saw only wounded men writhing, the bullets, which were pouring in, simply knocking our boxes and bales to pieces. I noticed rows of brown boots or shoes and tartan plaids, and after a minute or so our poor doctor, black in the face, and waving his handkerchief as a flag of truce, evidently determined before his death to save our lives, and undoubtedly two minutes more would have seen the last of us.

His action, however, placed me in a most awkward position; but, recognising that the situation was hopeless, and that a further continuance of the fight meant a useless expenditure of life, I was therefore obliged to accept the signal, and hold up my red handkerchief, which I tied to my carbine. At first this was taken as defiance; but as I, who had the only effective rifle on that flank did not fire, the Boer leader rode in from his men, shouted to me to surrender, and I surrendered. Our loss was 2nd Lieut. Craigie-Halkett and Private Buckle killed; Dr. Kelbe mortally and six privates wounded. About half our small force.

We had, with about 20 effective rifles on an untenable position, to face 150 of the enemy, holding on our left flank a kopje which thoroughly commanded the inside of our small defence.

I must say, that I was surprised at the generous behaviour of the Boers when once we had stopped fighting, each man offering his water-bottle and bread eagerly to our parched men.

They ordered us to move on at once, and towards the river, so that we might drink, and poisonous stagnant water it appeared to be. I was allowed to leave behind two excellent fellows, Private Clark, of Kitchener's Horse, and Private Finucane, of the Hampshire Regiment, to bury our dead and bring on the wounded in ambulances brought up by the Boers. We then walked some eight miles to a farm—Winterspruit—where we were joined by Lieut. Horne and some 30 other prisoners taken between Waterval Drift and Jacobsdal. The enemy meant to cram us into two rooms for the night, but on my word being given that we would not attempt to escape, we were allowed to lie on the ground outside. I held up poor Kelbe for some hours, but thanks to an urgent remonstrance, Dr. Tubner, a German surgeon and an excellent fellow, was sent for, and in time arrived, and drove poor Kelbe to the Koffyfontein hospital.

The next morning, having breakfasted off a supply of our own biscuit, we marched into Koffyfontein, where we filed into the gaol, and in ten minutes I was all but asleep, face on haversack, but was then told that I was wanted. Horne and I were led through a door in the gaol, and found ourselves in a comfortable little parlour, where the Town Provost was. He most civilly had a bottle of beer for each of us, and then handed us over to the gaoler, Mr. Bailey, an old K.D.G., who, with his good wife, gave us a comfortable lunch.

The next day or so we heard a good deal of heavy firing, and were accordingly hurried on, in the most cruel of wagons, and always over rough ground, the next night being spent at Fauresmith, where another gaol awaited us ; but after a short time Horne and I were put into a house, which was being built for the gaoler. Here we were indeed refreshed by a large basket of grapes, brought to us by an English girl, whose brother had to fight on commando, but whose old father saved himself from fighting against us by offering himself as an escort for prisoners. The next night we were hustled on again, and in passing through Jagersfontein were allowed to be entertained by the diamond miners for half an hour with biscuits and whisky and soda, and excellent they were !

A great deal of heavy firing could be heard, and we hoped our Cavalry might appear on the scene, but no such luck, and, on the other hand, we were not allowed to stop till we got to Edenburg, a station on the railway south of Bloemfontein. Hence in a couple of hours we were sent on by train to Bloemfontein, where we arrived in the evening, 19th February, the men being sent to gaol, but Horne and I were driven to Grey College, where we were placed on parole, and lived in luxury in the house of the kind Dr. and Mrs. Leith, he being the head professor there, and a real good Scotchman. As I had not undressed for eight days, the delights of a warm bath, clean night shirt, and a spring bed is not to be easily forgotten.

The next evening we were forwarded by train to Pretoria, and arrived the following day at 8 p.m., our men prisoners having increased to at least 100. Here also our escort were right good fellows. One, Elfers, a Swede, whose brother was a bookseller, gave me half-a-dozen first-class novels, which I and my fellow prisoners enjoyed much. I may mention that at Fauresmith Dr. Keyes, a real nice fellow, gave me a razor, and Dawson, who had been an officer in our service, a toothbrush.

At Pretoria, Horne and I had to walk from the train through a dense crowd of fashionable Pretorians, while our trainful of prisoners in loud tones sang, to the greatest annoyance of the assembly, " God Save the Queen." The train took the men on to Waterval, twelve miles out; we had a walk of a mile to the Staats Model School, and Horne did not forget to carry a bottle of whisky in his great-coat pocket, which had been given

BLOEMFONTEIN RAILWAY STATION.

us with many cigarettes by the Mining Superintendents as we passed Vereeniging.

The Model School, a rectangular one-storied red brick building, about 70 yards long, was surrounded by an iron paling, outside which at every 20 yards a fully-armed Zarp or policeman stood. He was always spoken of as a Zarp, although the letters on his shoulder only stood for

Zud African Republiek Polis. The School contained about 100 officers, mostly brought in from Stormberg, Nicholson's Nek, Tugela, and some civilians, among whom were the Rev. Hoffmeyer, and the defender of Kuruman, the Magistrate Hilliard, both very able and excellent fellows. And now began a life of weary despondency, which was to last me 3½ months. The climate was distinctly hot at this time, so most of the day was spent on chairs in the front and back verandahs reading books. Some of us managed to get exercise by playing fives, otherwise we usually waited till after tea, and then there was a continuous stream of walkers round the building—nine times round to the mile. The building was divided into about 20 rooms, the largest being used as a dining room, the remainder as dormitories, the school gymnasium being used as a storeroom. The room next to mine had 14 fellows in it, mine eight, and at one time for 17 days we had Haldane of the Gordons, Le Mesurier of the Dublin Fusiliers, and Brockie, Imperial Light Horse, lying under the boards of the floor previous to their escape, and many were the loaves of bread and candles sneaked under my coat to pass down to them during the quietness of the meal time. Only six former inhabitants of our room knew their whereabouts, as the greatest secrecy was necessary with these Zarps everlastingly listening and staring into the building a few yards off. The account of their escape I have seen in a book written by Haldane. We at this time daily read accounts of hastily-left food being found in empty houses, and eventually of the escaped men being re-captured and shot. Some men spent the hot days illustrating the walls, and most perfect maps, 20 feet by 10 feet, were painted by Holford, a gunner, on his room walls. These were afterwards varnished over and carefully preserved by the Boers, but they expended whitewash. bought at our expense, on excellent caricatures painted by Frankland, Dublin Fusiliers; one being " Oom Paul going to Restore Courage to his Burghers," when he went Bloemfontein way, and another, " Oom Paul's Return." The old man, running hard, trousers halfway up to his knees, Bible, umbrella, top hat, flying loose, and, after him, an excellent picture of Lord Roberts, with drawn sword, in his usual kit of khaki, and moving 40 miles an hour.

They allowed us as food daily, $\frac{1}{2}$ lb. of trek ox, 1 lb. of bread, and a small quantity of coffee, sugar and salt, but we did very fairly, as a certain shopman, Bosscher, was allowed to attend to our wants, and his foreman, Bennett, an Englishman, obtained anything we put down for, but naturally at three times the value. We had a mess committee, and a hard and thankless job they had of it, especially as it entailed keeping a shop. We suffered from no internal rules beyond roll call at 10 a.m. and 5 p.m., and were not allowed outside the building after 8 p.m., and at the afternoon hour were allowed to buy, at a " tikky " per copy, the *Volkstem*, or daily liar, half Dutch and half English, the latter side certainly containing the daily depressing news of English slaughter and defeat. About this hour the inhabitants of Pretoria made our two bounding roads their fashionable walk, just to get a sniff of British prisoner air.

We could afford to smile at the news the *Volkstem* contained, as we knew regularly by Kruger's private telegrams the very latest news, the receipt of them meaning health and refreshment to these hundred odd men longing for better days. I may add that we were allowed about 20 privates from Waterval to act as servants.

When word was passed that the " Dog " man had walked past, we did not rest till in possession of the latest news. The "Dog" man was a Mr. Pattison, the head of the Telegraph Department, and I need hardly say an Englishman, who was always accompanied by a large mastiff. His friend, a Mr. Cullingworth, also an elderly Britisher, lived in a house opposite the end of the school. Besides his wife there were two Miss Cullingworths, and also a little girl and two boys. The two elder daughters had been taught to flag-wag most correctly, and on receipt of the latest messages these girls got in touch with our look-out man, usually Bonham, Essex Regiment, when, stationed about 15 feet back in their own hall, the small children acting as scouts in front, they sent over the usual two or three messages. This was a dangerous operation, as they were suspected though never caught by the police, but poor old Pattison and Cullingworth were in the end commandeered, and equipped and sent to Kroonstad, where in attempting to escape they were caught by an outlying picquet and sentenced to be shot, but were saved by Joubert and sent to prison at Pretoria, where they were released on June 4th, and where they afterwards were employed in a civil capacity and spent their time arresting old friends. Men who fell sick went into Bourke's hospital next door. Bourke is an Irishman of means, and was forced to find and keep up this hospital or go on commando and fight his countrymen. The hospital was an excellent one, some of the Boer Generals' wives and daughters acting as the kindest of Sisters. Of the doctors, however, Dr. Veale behaved very badly to our men at Waterval, and was forced to leave the country after June 4th.

The prisoners were under the jurisdiction of a committee, Reitz, Kruger's private secretary, being the chief, but we were immediately under the control of Commandant Oppeman, a thorough scoundrel, who usually walked about with a sjambock, so that he might look, to outsiders, as if he used it pretty freely when amongst us. His assistant, Dr. Gunning, was a fairly decent little fellow, who, I fancy to suit his feelings, ran with the hare and hunted with the hounds.

Of course there were rumours of conspiracy amongst us to break out, and, with the assistance of British towns-people, to seize arms and plant ourselves in one of the forts, or take a train and run to Lorenzo Marques ; but the plans when submitted to a board of senior officers were invariably found to be worthless, and some of us did not like the idea of giving the Waterval prisoners the slip. However, when Churchill escaped, good care was taken of us by increased sentries, with an outer line of Kaffir police ; at length, what with the supposed escape of Haldane and Co., and the rumour of towns-people assisting in a conspiracy, the order came for us to be moved to the " Bird Cage," a long, corrugated iron shed situated on the slope of a kopje north of the town, which had been built to hold the officers of the Lady-smith garrison when it should have fallen !

Our Sunday service was originally held by a disgrace-to-the-Church, the Rev. Godfrey, who seized the oppor-tunity of Churchill's escape to write and tell us that he could not hold service for the companions of men who broke their parole. I must say that had we been given parole to walk up and down outside our palings it would have been much valued, but no offer of parole had ever been suggested by the Boers. About March 14th, to the delight of the poor fellows under the floor, who succeeded in making good their escape that night, we were told to turn out and move off to the Bird Cage ; so some marched in fours and were well guarded, while the remainder of us drove in victorias, the cab of the country, accompanied by a strong escort. The Bird Cage stands well above the town, and from it there is a good view of the valley in which Pretoria lies. The view stretches some ten miles west, Mafeking way, and includes three of the fairly-modern forts which defend Pretoria. The Cage itself is a corrugated iron house, 100 yards long, of one story, and consists of an unboarded sleeping-room, which held 140 of us, a bed being provided for each, these beds being placed in four long rows, with a space of half a yard between each, or rather the breadth of the chair each of us was allowed. At this end of the building, but outside, were the four fairly good bath-rooms we were allowed ; at the other side of the bedroom was an equally large dining-room, containing four long rows of plank tables and forms, and beyond a small kitchen and office of the mess committee.

Fifty yards clear round the house was a barbed wire entanglement, five yards broad, and six feet high, and outside again a sentry at every thirty yards. Just inside, and twenty feet high, was a row of electric lights, and inside again, after a space of two yards, was a wall of chicken-run wire, about twelve feet high, and hooked to wooden beams underground. The entrance was by double gates, over a space six feet broad, and held by two sentries.

The Commandant here was Westerling, a businesslike man, who was very fair in his treatment of us throughout.

The weather was still fairly hot, and the dense swarms of locusts sometimes blackened the sky for miles and quite obstructed our view. We most of us sat on particular spots and read, when a book or paper was obtainable. My particular spot faced Mafeking way, whither I always had a longing gaze for B.P.'s troops. Each day had its cricket match—Eton *v.* the World, or Mounted *v.* Unmounted, played with a pickaxe handle and soft ball, the space not being large enough for anything else. Once we had some excellent sports, which were made amusing by our bookey, Haig of the Inniskillings. At 4.30 p.m., immediately after tea, everyone walked round the path we had made for the general lounge until dinner, or till our daily *Volkstem* arrived.

Chess also was much played, and Duhan, of Kitchener's Horse, acquired great fame, as he could beat the next two best on different games when blindfolded, or else six unblindfolded; but then he had made a dead heat of it in the English Midland Counties Chess Tournament. After dinner many took to " patience " or whist, bridge, etc.; but one long table was crowded with six roulette tables, worked by one roulette board in the centre, stakes unlimited, and this naturally was not quite pleasant to the senior men, if only for the noise it caused. However, at 9 o'clock the electric house light went out, but only to be replaced by the candle each man produced.

At first snakes were plentiful, and at the sight of one there was usually a crowded rush to see him end his days.

One attempt to escape was made by four men; each one lay in a selected spot by the chicken-run wire about 11 o'clock one night. But the moment the wire connecting the surrounding lights was cut by their accomplice, a heavy fire was opened by the sentries, which was the signal for every guard who was comfortably in bed to jump out and rush with lamps to different stations round the enclosure. This attempt to escape was unsuccessful, and no further attempt was made, as it was quite recognised as hopeless. We all knew that a combined effort would make us masters of the guard, but the outlying distant commandos and the distance of our forces rendered that way of escape impossible.

Once or twice bullets whistled by our heads, just playful games of odd Boers returning to the town after a little rifle practice at a kopje near us; but this became rather warm one day, when the bullets came unpleasantly close to their own sentries, and afterwards nothing of this sort was allowed on our kopje. This meant also no more telegrams. The Sunday before, the two Miss Cullingworths had climbed up to the top of a near kopje, and as the weather was hot, it was natural that their handkerchiefs should be pulled out to fan themselves. We apparently looked anywhere but in their direction, but our look-out men read to our delight, "Mafeking relieved. Giving them fits at Kroonstad."

About this time Mr. Hoffmeyer was released, and an excellent Wesleyan clergyman undertook our services; we were naturally anxious to get information, and therefore the latter was afterwards accompanied to the gates, he and each of his guards being surrounded by at least half a dozen of us. Much interesting conversation was carried on with the guards, so that the latest news unwound from the parson might be emitted unheard by them.

One Sunday shortly afterwards, great was the attention paid to his sermon, when in it he imparted the pleasant news that Lord Roberts was coming along fast. The time at length came when someone heard a distant explosion. Of course it was one of our guns, and the informant was told to keep such nonsense to himself; but on May 29th a steady cannonade was carried on all day, and pleasant was the sound thereof. We imagined the fighting to be a few miles off, but it afterwards proved to be at Elandsfontein, nearly forty miles away. However, it was enough for old Kruger, for whilst at dinner that evening the American Consul, and Leigh

Wood, the manager of the Bank of Natal, came up and told us that the town was in a state of disorder, that looting was rife everywhere, that a mob was carrying goods from the Government stores, and that Kruger was at the station, and was just about to bolt eastwards, and that he had sacks of gold with him, which were lying about in the most unsafe way on the platform. It appears that he had commandeered all loose gold in the National Bank, and had then paid his officials by worthless cheques on the same bank. We were all most excited, cheered heartily, and sang our National Anthem, feeling that the good time was soon coming. The Consul and Mr. Leigh Wood then told our senior, Colonel Hunt, R.A., who had been badly wounded at the Tugela, that our men at Waterval could scarcely be restrained, as they were in such an excited state, and that the consequences might be very serious, and requested that we would send over twenty officers to steady them. This was agreed to, and twenty officers, whose Regiments were well represented there, went off to them at once, but with the agreement that neither officers or men were to be removed from their present quarters in the event of Lord Roberts taking Pretoria.

The following day anxiously was every pass and road watched for a sign of our advanced patrols, but day after day passed without encouragement, and our spirits rapidly fell. Then a Column was seen coming in Mafeking way, and this was the first of several strong Boer Columns which retreated into Pretoria after B. P. had been relieved.

However, it occurred to many of us that Roberts would not let the 4th of June go by without a fight, and delightfully were we aroused that morning by an undoubted cannonade. We found that a fieldwork had been thrown up during the night; that it was firing rapidly, and that shells were bursting over it, and in an hour the range of kopjes in front reminded one of a Crystal Palace firework display. There had been serious meetings in the town to form a ladies commando, one of the principal duties being to guard the prisoners, but from this morning the idea was given up. Now firing was opened on the large fort in front, each lyddite shell struck it, and by the huge volume of smoke [1] and dust which arose, and by the heavy explosion, we thought the fort must have disappeared; but I rode up the following day, and can with a clear conscience say that a four-year-old boy would have scraped a hole with his spade in two minutes similar to any hole on the parapet, and the one shell which we had seen fall in the centre of the fort, and which drew forth our congratulations, had on inspection knocked off the top of a brick gate-post, and had broken one window.

Our shells were now passing over the range of kopjes, some bursting very unpleasantly on the edge of the town, and clearing out the inhabitants pretty fast; they were, however, intended for the station, and luckily just missed two trains full of British prisoners who were being brought in from Waterval and were passing eastwards. Our balloon was now a welcome sight in the sky, and frantic cheers greeted it.

All day and the day previous the town had been full of large columns of mounted men and guns going east, and at five o'clock that evening the supreme moment appeared to have arrived. The Western Valley was full of galloping Boers making north through Dasport, the northern outlet from Pretoria. Hundreds of shells were passing over the kopjes, but were falling

[1] Called by the Kaffirs "Zum Bimeby"—Zum standing for the discharge, Bimeby for what came after.

short of the retreating Boers, and a heavy cannonade was being directed on the main force retiring into Pretoria.

A well-mounted commando now rode past the Bird-cage, and we momentarily expected a shot or so into us as a keepsake; but a pleasant-spoken fellow called out "Your friends are near," and another "The old man is coming along." Towards dusk the fire ceased, and our eyes looked anxiously for our advancing troops, but night came, and we felt at any rate we should be "out" to-morrow. I felt a bit overwrought that night, after the exciting day we had undergone, and we certainly all went to bed feeling that something was wrong; however, the hour came when the usual snoring proclaimed that sleep had conquered, but not for long, for between one and two a.m. we were aroused by the Commandant who, walking past the foot of our beds, called out in a loud tone, "Get up, you have to march at three o'clock." After some five minutes' consideration, I felt it would be no use saying "I won't," so I got up. Many fellows were already up, and the language was a bit boisterous. Outside were half a dozen wagons being packed with our sentries' tents, and a fair-sized commando sitting quietly on their horses, but looking a bit determined. About this time fellows began slipping out of the building to examine a rock, or a shrub or out-house, with a view to hiding till the remainder had marched and daylight had brought up our people, and several went to where there was a hole in the ceiling, but were greeted by jeers from a Colonel and half-a-dozen others, who had got up to it by climbing a plank, and had drawn the plank up afterwards. Yet still 120 remained angrily talking in the building, till McInerny, a huge Australian, threw his weight, both moral and physical, on the side of refusing to go; so it was settled that we should offer a passive resistance.

The Commandant now came in to see that we were all up, but he no sooner got in than he was made a prisoner by McInerny; and shortly afterwards his Adjutant came to seek the Commandant, but he also shared the same fate. The commando outside now began to consider sending an armed party into the building, but by this time some serious conversation had been carried on. The Commandant admitted the promise made on the 29th not to remove us, and eventually he was released on parole to go out and square the matter with the commando leader, our message being, that they might shoot if they liked, but we would not go. This he did, and after some strong language, to our relief the commando moved off; but it afterwards turned out that Hutton's Mounted Infantry and some Cavalry were working north, and the commando feared being cut off. We then to a man turned in, and in the early morning were somewhat surprised to find ourselves still there. As soon as we were up, we occupied ourselves trying to decide whether the distant masses were troops or cattle, when someone exclaimed, "Why, here are two fellows riding up in khaki!" Then followed a cry of "No, they are burghers!" and we gnashed our teeth. Then loud shouts of "Khaki, khaki!" followed by a rush to the fence and frantic cheers, for there was Marlborough and Churchill, attended by the Commissioner of Pretoria police. Then every sentry ran to the guard-house followed by a cheering, frantic mob, and in two minutes a Union Jack was flying, every sentry a prisoner, and shortly after a guard of servants was on duty over our prisoners, and we were off down town to greet Lord Roberts, and see his troops march in; and so ended an experience which no one need wish to share.

At Waterval, the Commandant gave our men to understand that they were to be sent into Pretoria, to be handed over to Lord Roberts, and great was the rush to two empty cattle trains that came in; but the officers sent over from the " Bird Cage " decided that those who had been in longest should be the first released; and, therefore, the men of the Royal Irish Fusiliers and Gloucester Regiments were directed to fill these trains, and off they went to find themselves being hustled eastwards, and our lyddite shells fall pretty adjacent when passing through Pretoria Station. Those poor fellows were afterwards released at Nooitgedacht, but not until three months later.

The following day our Cavalry were in sight of Waterval, and the Greys were soon mixed up and shaking hands heartily with the poor men, but not for long; two Boer shells landed in their enclosure, and, I heard, killed and wounded 15 men; and then a succession of shells began falling among our 4,000 unarmed men, who were forced to leg it, many of them in a deplorable state of weakness, the twelve miles into Pretoria.

We then became the Prisoners' Division under Colonel Hunt, R.A., and in a few days, those who were fit enough, were armed with Martini's and black powder cartridges, and were sent off to guard the railway at certain places. At one of these, named Honing's Spruit, poor Hobbs was killed—rather bad luck after undergoing seven months' imprisonment.

I was Provost Marshal, and therefore remained till the men had left. I now found Ian Hamilton's Division just off to Heidelberg, and he kindly allowed me to apply to leave with him, but the application was refused, so I took up the billet of Registrar, and lived in a commandeered house in Pretoria.

I was doing this work, and acting Crown Prosecutor, when an accident befel me. My cob fell in a gallop, and I was insensible for ten days, coming to myself in a condition necessitating my shortly afterwards being invalided home.

The only other prisoner of the Oxfordshire was Bugler Adams, who on our release acted as servant to me.

LIEUT.-COLONEL F. J. EVELEGH.

CHAPTER XVI.

WITH BOER PRISONERS TO CEYLON.

By Captain W. C. Hunter.

Having obtained permission to go out to South Africa on the express condition that I returned to India by the time my leave expired, I was compelled, about five weeks before that date, reluctantly enough, to send in an application for a passage to India. A reply came in due course, ordering me to report myself at Cape Town in ten days' time. I did so, and was informed that I had been detailed to do duty with a batch of prisoners of war proceeding to Ceylon on board the transport *Ranee*. She was lying at Simonstown and might start any day; I therefore went down by train the same afternoon, arriving there in a storm of wind and rain. I was anxious to get on board at once, but the harbour boatmen declared it was too rough to go out to the ship that evening, and absolutely refused to do so; I was therefore forced to spend the night at an hotel, hoping that the *Ranee* would not sail in the meantime.

Next morning I went on board and found that, after all, there had been no reason for my haste, as there were only 200 prisoners on the ship so far, and the number was to be made up to 600 before we could start.

The escort consisted of 6 officers, including myself, 1 civil surgeon, and 110 N.C.O.'s and men. The latter were representatives of 52 different Corps, and included 4 or 5 men from the 43rd, a Life Guardsman, several Foot Guardsmen and men belonging to the Imperial Yeomanry, various Colonial Corps, etc., rather a mixed lot altogether.

The officers told me they had already been on board a week, and were heartily sick of hanging about and receiving contradictory orders.

They had twice been round to Cape Town, and on arrival had been promptly ordered back to Simon's Bay again. "Doubling" the Cape of Good Hope in stormy weather, they declared, was not a pleasant experience, and loafing in Simon's Bay was rather worse.

The prisoners, whom they had embarked in driblets during the week, were, I think, men who had spent a considerable time in the prisoner camps at Cape Town and Simonstown; in fact, one of them, an Englishman by the way, informed me that he had been taken at Dundee or Glencoe, I forget which, at the very beginning of the war, and had been at Green Point Camp ever since.

The day after my arrival, orders came for us to go round to Cape Town again to embark 400 prisoners. We started as soon as steam was up, arriving the same evening, and the following morning went alongside the docks at Cape Town.

Presently a train came in, crowded with Boers. Their escort detrained first and formed up, lining both sides of the docks between the train and the ship. The prisoners were then got out, and came wandering along looking very bewildered, and reminding one rather of cattle being driven into pens.

These particular men had surrendered with Prinsloo, and had been brought straight down country. They were of all ages, some being quite old men who could hardly get along, loaded up with their roll of bedding and other goods, and others were quite young. In fact, our youngest prisoner was twelve years old. He and his father had wept so bitterly when it was proposed to leave the boy behind, that he was eventually allowed to accompany us. The very old men were subsequently weeded out and kept back, and are probably still at Green Point.

The prisoners, on first arrival, presented an exceedingly ragged appearance, having been in the field, I suppose, for months. Enormous quantities of clothing and games had, however, been sent on board by "Prisoner of War Benevolent Societies" (I do not know what their correct title is), and very soon our Boers turned out looking quite respectable, and as soon as sail baths were rigged, fairly clean.

As they filed on board, the prisoners were told off into messes like soldiers on a troopship; in fact, everything was carried out during the voyage as on a troopship. The escort occupied the aft, and the Boers the forward troop deck, the soldiers not being allowed to mix with the prisoners at all.

We were informed by the Staff at Cape Town that the foreign element among the prisoners included several noted bad characters, and that we might expect some trouble during the voyage. We were also told that in the event of any serious disturbance, the sentries were to have no hesitation in firing on the prisoners. Our commanding officer, Brooke, a captain in the King's Own Yorkshire Light Infantry, issued a ships' order, warning the Boers what their fate would be in case of mutinous behaviour, and this apparently had an excellent effect, as with the exception of a few " minor offences," the behaviour of the prisoners was very good.

After the embarkation was completed, we expected to be allowed to proceed on our voyage, but much to our disgust the ship was again ordered round to Simonstown, where a government clerk of some sort came on board in order to make out elaborate nominal rolls of the prisoners, giving their names, ages, birthplaces, the commandos to which they had belonged when taken, and their places of residence. This occupied a long time, as the genuine old Boer farmer either is or pretends to be a particularly thickheaded individual when any information is required of him.

Our constantly putting into Simon's Bay did not tend to make us popular with the officers of H.M.S. *Doris*, the flagship of the station, as, in addition to keeping the searchlight on us the whole night long, the officer of the watch had to patrol round our ship as a further precaution against the escape of any of the prisoners. Several of the latter had been noted " tunnelers " when in the Boer camps at Green Point and Simonstown. I imagine the naval officers were as thankful as we were when, on August 14th, we finally started for Ceylon.

Luckily the weather during the first week was fine, which gave everybody a chance of settling down, but even so, in spite of there being hardly any motion, some of the Boers were very seasick, and lay about the decks looking supremely miserable, which caused great amusement to those who remained fit.

The escort was divided into two Companies of 55 men each, under an officer, the prisoners being similarly divided into two batches, one officer, two British N.C.O.'s, and an interpreter being told off to each batch. At first I was in charge of one batch, but about four days after starting Brooke had a bad attack of malaria, which lasted practically the rest of the voyage, so I, being the next senior, took over the command from him.

The daily routine was as follows :—Orderly Room at 9.30 a.m., parade at 10 a.m. for the escort, and inspection of the troop and prisoners' decks by the Captain of the ship and C.O., and guard-mounting at 4.30 p.m. Roll call for the prisoners took place at

5 p.m., and they were turned down below at 8 p.m. for the night. An Orderly Officer was detailed daily, who carried out the usual duties and visited the prisoners' decks at the breakfast and dinner hours to find out if they had any complaints.

Orderly Room was rather an amusing function, owing to our very zealous acting Sergeant-Major, who insisted on manœuvring the Boers into the room as if they were soldiers, after carefully looking them up and down and taking possession of their caps. The usual offence was refusing to obey the Sergeants in charge of the prisoners' decks when they ordered the floors and tables to be scrubbed for inspection; three or four days' cells were generally awarded for this crime. Occasionally one of the foreigners and a Boer had a quarrel which they insisted on having settled in Orderly Room, and as it was seldom possible to get to the bottom of the matter, the only thing to be done was to warn both parties that if such a thing occurred again they would find themselves in the cells.

The prisoners' decks were kept wonderfully clean, principally owing to the exertions of the British Sergeants in charge, who kept the orderly men of the different messes hard at work scrubbing between the breakfast hour and inspection at 10 a.m. If the Boers had been left to themselves, I do not suppose they would have taken the trouble to clean their decks the whole voyage.

Guard-mounting was rather more of an imposing function than is usual on a troopship. The men paraded in drill order, 18 strong, and were marched off to their guard with fixed bayonets and magazines charged. When at sea, there were six sentries on duty at a time; and I imagine the Boers looked upon the formal relieving of the sentries with arms at the " port," etc., with a certain amount of contempt. " If any prisoner tries to escape, shoot him," was one of the orders which no sentry ever omitted to give over correctly.

A number of the burghers were in a very bad state of health, suffering continually from malaria and other kinds of fever; in fact, some of them were admitted into hospital as soon as they came on board, where they spent the whole voyage. About ten days after leaving Simonstown one of them died and was buried at sea. The old burgher, who conducted the daily services, officiated at the funeral. The Captain of the ship duly ordered the engines to be stopped, when he considered it probable that the body would be sent overboard, calculating the time in accordance with the English burial service. Unfortunately the minister was a very eloquent man and began an extempore prayer after closing his book, which continued at least 20 minutes. All this time the ship was motionless, and the Captain fuming on the bridge lamenting his spoilt day's run. We buried another man a few days later, but this time the ship was not stopped till the prayer was actually ended.

There were about 50 foreigners among the prisoners, including four or five Englishmen, any number of Germans, Austrians, and French, and also a couple of Americans. It was curious to note how entirely apart the Boers and Freestaters kept themselves from these foreigners. They never seemed to associate in any way, and the foreigners appeared to find much amusement in chaffing the Boers, whilst the latter simply ignored them. The foreigners were extraordinary linguists. They spoke to each other in English, French, German and Dutch, and there was a regular scramble for the English magazines, which we gave them from time to time. We should have had a dull voyage had it not been for these men. They played all kinds of games in the afternoons, some of which were most amusing to watch, and every evening, after they had been counted down, they collected together and sang till "lights out" at 8 p.m. English and French music-hall songs, German Volkslieder and airs out of operas, all seemed familiar to them, and they sang them wonderfully well. We used to sit and listen to them before dinner almost every evening, and frequently asked for some particular song, which they always seemed to know, and started at once. The only lady on board, the wife of one of the officers, on one occasion asked for "Soldiers of the Queen" and "Rule Britannia," but an English prisoner, called Glen, who took the lead in everything, answered quite seriously that none of them knew those songs.

Some of the Germans were most unsoldierly-looking people, being more like German professors than anything else; but we were informed that they were great artillerists, and one man in particular was popularly believed to have an intimate knowledge of every form of gun in use at the present time. If that was really the case, it was about time to deport him to Ceylon.

The younger Boers and Freestaters had their games in the afternoons also, which consisted of wrestling and various feats of strength. The older men sat apart, smoking, and looking surly and bored with the whole proceedings.

The real burghers were very pious, holding daily services, morning and evening; and during the rest of the day many of them might be seen with Bibles in their hands. Eventually we had to allow them the use of the forecastle deck for their devotions, as the foreigners apparently scoffed at their religion, and continued their games and singing during the services, which the older men resented deeply. As the whole 600 were on one deck, it was impossible to order the majority to remain quiet for an hour or so whilst the few prayed, so the only thing to be done was to find another place for the services. We heard from our interpreters that the two deaths on board had seriously alarmed the Boers, and served to recall to their minds all the tales of British atrocities they had ever heard. Some of the very ignorant ones actually believed that our excellent and hardworking doctor had received a hint from a brutal government to kill off prisoners of war, as being useless and expensive articles.

We had an inspection of the Boers' kits a few days after starting, and found a large number of articles captured from the British among them. Soldiers' belts, great-coats, straps, " coats warm British," and two large mail bags, labelled London to Pretoria, were some of the things, all of which we confiscated. One man was in possession of a complete Field Artilleryman's kit.

The only time that the prisoners could really have given trouble was at night. If a few of them had combined and rushed the three sentries nearest to their quarters, the remainder could have run aft and easily overpowered the sleeping guard and seized their rifles. To avoid this, we had a strong electric light on the prisoners' part of the ship all night, so that the sentries could see any attempt at collecting together on their part, which, of course, they had orders to stop at once. As an additional precaution, our interpreters kept constantly moving about among the prisoners during the day, listening to their conversation, and breaking up any suspicious-looking groups. On the Queen of Holland's birthday several Boers and Freestaters tried to make inflammatory speeches, but were promptly stopped by the interpreters, and the offenders duly appeared in Orderly Room next morning.

When nearing the Equator, our friend Mr. Glen and his clique asked leave for Father Neptune and his Court to board the ship and celebrate the occasion in the usual manner, by shaving and baptizing those who had never previously crossed the Line. Permission was given, and they certainly got up a very good entertainment. The ship's purser provided the regulation costumes, and a large sail-bath was prepared. Glen represented Neptune, and the part of his wife was taken by a little Frenchman. Most of the younger men took the shaving and ducking in good part, but the older ones did not appear to appreciate the joke. After about an hour or so, seeing that the relations between the burghers and foreigners were becoming rather strained, we thought it more prudent to stop the entertainment.

Everybody on board was very thankful when, on the 17th day after leaving Simonstown, we steamed into Colombo Harbour. The officers and men of the escort had nothing to complain of during the voyage in the way of accommodation, but the Boers were very crowded. It was almost impossible to thread one's way through them when they were all on deck; but after all, they could hardly expect to travel luxuriously.

The disembarking Staff Officer came off shortly after we had anchored, and informed us that the first 300 prisoners were to disembark the following morning at 4 a.m., and the remainder the morning after at the same hour. We were thus tied to the ship for three more days; but, luckily, there was no prisoners' correspondence to be waded through and censored, as there had been during the days we stayed at Cape Town and Simonstown. Some of those letters by-the-bye were rather amusing reading. We officers took over the English, French, and German ones, and letters in any other language—such as Italian, Spanish, or Russian—had to be sent to the Intelligence Department at Cape Town. Nearly all the letters I read contained some flattering allusion to the kindness of the officers; hoping in this way, I presume, to ensure the writers having an easy time during the voyage. One of the letters I read was an exceedingly long one from a German to his ladylove, and was nearly all in poetry. It must have taken him days to compose.

Whilst we were lying in Colombo Harbour, waiting to disembark the prisoners, the sentries were doubled, and two harbour police boats patrolled round the ship night and day. This latter would appear to have been a very necessary precaution, as when the next ship carrying prisoners of war arrived, one of the prisoners, an Englishman, succeeded in evading the sentries' vigilance and jumped overboard during the night. He made for the first boat he saw, not being able to swim as far as the shore, which, unfortunately for him, turned out to be one of the police boats. He told some story about being a sailor and wishing to get on shore for the night; the police, however, had seen the whole occurrence and took him straight back to his ship. Luckily there was no excitement of that description on board the *Ranee*.

At 3.15 a.m., on September 12th, the escort fell in for the disembarkation of the first batch of 300. Four lighters were alongside, and an officer with a few men were placed in each as a guard. The prisoners were then called up on deck one by one, and passed over the side, each man's name being checked on a nominal roll as he stepped out on to the ladder. It was a pitch dark night, and we were anxious to get them on shore and handed over without losing any on the way. If by any chance a prisoner became separated from his father or brother or particular friend there was great lamentation, and we found it difficult to make him believe that he would meet his relative again on shore. A detachment of the 60th Rifles, lately arrived from South Africa, was waiting on the landing-stage, which was lighted by flaring torches placed every few yards.

The disembarkation occupied about two hours, as the lighters had to make several journeys each; but by 6 a.m. all the prisoners were entrained and their rations for the day served out, and shortly afterwards we saw our first 300 Boers steam away from the docks with an escort of the 60th Rifles on the train, *en route* for Diyatelawa.

The disembarkation of the remainder was carried out in the same manner the following night, and I think we were all very glad and somewhat relieved to hand over our 598 prisoners (two having died at sea), and to feel that our responsibility was now ended.

Some of the prisoners seemed to be quite sorry to see the last of us, and bade us good-bye in Dutch as they went down the ladder, and thanked us for the treatment they had received. One polite Frenchman went so far as to write to one of the officers from Diyatelawa camp. After going into ecstasies over the beauty of the scenery on the way up country, he ended by saying that "if ever you find yourself in the same predicament that I have had the misfortune to be in, you may be sure that I will do my best to make your captivity as little irksome as possible, in return for your kindness during our voyage on the *Ranee*."

CHAPTER XVII.

WITH A MOUNTED INFANTRY BATTALION IN SOUTH AFRICA.

BY CAPTAIN H. L. RUCK KEENE.

RUMOURS of war in South Africa were rife when the Regiment, having finished its Irish tour (to the regret, I fancy, of most of us), moved across to Devonport, early in September, 1899. Little did we think that the event was to come off so soon, and hardly had I settled down to a quiet life on detachment at Bull Point, when, on October 4th, matters came to a head as far as I was concerned, a War Office letter arriving on that day informing me that I had been selected for the post of Adjutant of Mounted Infantry, in the event of a Cavalry Division being sent to South Africa. This " in the event of " sounds funny to us now, but the same wise folk who thought that 30,000 odd troops would be sufficient to quell all trouble in that country, were also apparently of opinion that it was quite an off-chance whether a Cavalry Division would ever be required—and then, two Battalions of Mounted Infantry were considered, with the addition of the small number already in South Africa, enough to meet any contingencies! We learnt better afterwards, to our cost—but of this it is neither my business nor desire to speak. Anyhow, I had got my billet; just the billet I should have chosen of all others, and was the envy of the whole Regiment, for at that time there was supposed to be little, if any, chance of the 43rd being wanted. I had

—

very little opportunity of getting the necessary kit together, for on October 8th, the 1st and 2nd Battalions of Mounted Infantry mobilized at Aldershot; the former under Lieut.-Colonel Alderson, the latter under Lieut.-Colonel Tudway.

The 2nd Battalion, of which I was Adjutant, consisted of the Northern Company, commanded by Captain Hart, East Surrey Regiment; the Western Company under Captain Brooke, Yorkshire Light Infantry; the Scottish Company under Captain De Lisle, Durham Light Infantry; and the Eastern Company under Captain Atkins, Wiltshire Regiment. Each Company was composed of four different sections, belonging to four different Regiments, and commanded by Subalterns belonging to these Regiments; thus the Battalion represented sixteen different Regiments. In addition to the above there were two machine-gun detachments, each having two Maxims, and commanded by a Subaltern. These Maxims were worked on tripods, and the whole gear carried on pack animals—a system useful for Infantry but entirely unsuited for M. I. work, as the pack-horses were quite unable to keep up with the rest of us when we were doing rapid movements. Consequently it can be imagined that, at first, confusion reigned supreme; and I was nearly driven mad by the preparation of documents, issuing of mobilization stores, etc., etc. However, I was extremely lucky in having two Riflemen as Sergeant-Major and Quartermaster-Sergeant — both belonging to the 4th Rifle Brigade; and it would be impossible to speak too highly of the way in which they worked throughout. Mansfield Clarke, also of the Rifle Brigade, came to act as Quartermaster, but most unfortunately was laid up, with scarlet fever, I think, just before we sailed, and so was unable to accompany us.

In addition to my other troubles, ponies began to arrive from Ireland in great numbers and at all times of the day and night, and arrangements had to be made for sending for them, and then for finding accommodation; this was particularly hard lines on us, as we were not to have the benefit of them in South Africa.

Another very real grievance was that when the Battalion was complete, more than half of the men were untrained; and of those who had, at one time or another, gone through a Mounted Infantry course, a great many were Reservists, and had forgotten all about their work. This was, of course, owing to the impossible system of training Mounted Infantry as at present laid down.

On October 22nd, the Staff and Northern and Western Companies embarked at Tilbury, on the good ship *Orient*, which also carried the Black Watch—a right good lot of fellows—many of them, alas! to be soon mowed down at Magersfontein. We had an excellent voyage out, but I began rather badly by getting my head broken against a sky-light while playing "Rugby football" with poor Freddie Tait, the celebrated golf champion (killed at Koodoosberg, after being badly wounded at Magersfontein). The ship was most comfortable, and the officers a capital lot; unfortunately, we had to have the yellow-flag flying all the way owing to some cases of scarlet-fever on board, and so could not land at St. Vincent, where we coaled and got news of the unfortunate affair of Nicholson's Nek. Cricket, concerts, and dinners, varied by inoculation, passed the time away until at 4 p.m., on November 13th, we made Table Bay.

The next day we got alongside the quay, and it seems funny now to think what a hurry we were in to disembark, a great many of us thinking, even at that time, that we should be too late for "the fun." All that night we were busy unloading the ship, and sleeping where and when we could. Half a Battalion of the Black Watch left for De Aar at 10 p.m., and the other half at 3 a.m. the following morning. We entrained at 8 a.m., also *en route* for De Aar, which place we reached at 8 p.m. on the following day. Here there were immense quantities of stores, guarded only by the 2nd Yorkshire Light Infantry, the Black Watch, and two old 7-pr. M.L. guns —the whole commanded by General Wauchope; subsequently this garrison was reduced, and why the Boers never made a raid

IN THE HORSE LINES.

on the place no one could understand. The following morning we turned out of the train at 4 a.m., in a most ghastly dust storm, and then had a very busy morning moving up stores, pitching camp, etc. In the afternoon we drew 100 country-bred ponies from the Remount Department, and had terrible work with the little beggars, which were very timid, but, contrary to our expectations, showed little, if any, vice; these ponies were divided equally between the two Companies.

Next day we were up at 3.30 a.m., and had a mounted parade, which turned out a most discouraging affair—ponies all over the place, and half the men unable to ride. In the course of the show two ponies got loose and dashed off over the veldt; I pursued them for miles, and succeeded in catching one, the other, for all I know, is still at large. Later on we were moving our camp nearer to that of the Black Watch, when the General rode up and gave us orders to be ready to entrain at 12.30 p.m. for Hanover Road, where we were to hold an important bridge over the Seacow River. General Wauchope came in the same train, and went on to Naauwpoort, which he re-occupied with half a Battalion of Black Watch and half a Battalion 2nd Berkshire Regiment, not forgetting the two ancient guns, under an unfortunate Gunner 2nd Lieutenant. We reached our destination very late at night, and were met by Captain Ottley and Lieut. Shepherd, of the 2nd Yorkshire Light Infantry, who had been guarding (?) the bridge over the Seacow with 40 men and about half that number of horses for the last fortnight.

Here again considerable thanks were due to the un-enterprising nature of the average Boer; anybody else could have annihilated this small force and blown up the bridge with a very small amount of trouble. We detrained and bivouacked close to the station, sleeping in our great-coats—our first night of real discomfort.

The following morning we were up at 4 a.m., and shifted our bivouac to a farm about a mile off, inhabited by an old Dutchman, who I believe was loyal, though we had doubts about his son. Our bivouac was quite a nice one, plenty of good water, and some shady gum-trees, under which we slept in our Wolseley " flea-bags," and were fairly comfortable; we were also able to get fresh milk and eggs at the farm, while near the station an excellent Jew, Levigne, kept a store, where one could buy varieties of useful articles.

To-day the Colonel and Ottley went out on a long reconnaissance, while I rode over to the Yorkshire camp at the bridge, and went out a long way in company with a Rimington's Tiger; we saw no Boers, but about 14 springbok, which were wonderfully tame, and I longed to have a shot at them. The weather was extremely hot all day, but at night it blew a hurricane and rained in torrents, so that we rather sighed for a tent, our valises being very poor protection against weather of this sort.

The next day was taken up by more patrolling and reconnoitring work on the part of the Colonel, Ottley and Hart, and in the afternoon the Colonel was sent for to De Aar for a consultation, leaving me in command, being senior officer. It blew very hard again to-night, rained in torrents, and there was a tremendous thunderstorm, with most vivid flashes of lightning, while, to add to all these delights, at 12.15 a.m. a boy turned up from the station with a wire from the G.O.C. De Aar, saying that he had heard on reliable authority that 2,000 Boers with 2 guns were advancing with a view to destroy the bridge ! Cheerful news this ! Sent down to Ottley at the bridge, and slept very little for the remainder of the night.

In the early morning we had coffee with the Dutch family at the farm, the old man very agreeable, but unable to speak a word of English. I was pleased to notice pictures of the Queen and the Prince and Princess of Wales hanging up in his parlour.

This morning I was all ready to do a bolt, though I meant to have a shot or two first, but the 2,000 Boers fortunately did not turn up, and I sent Brooke out reconnoitring towards Colesberg. Later on I went down to the station and had a short talk with General French, who had just come round from Natal, and was on his way to Naauwpoort, and soon after this I received orders to entrain in the afternoon for Naauwpoort, our C.O. coming along with more ponies. We left poor Ottley and his Subaltern behind, bitterly bemoaning their fate, and reached Naauwpoort at 7.30 p.m., in pitch darkness. General French met us on the platform, and informed us that he wanted us out on reconnaissance at 3.30 a.m. next morning; our C.O. (not unnaturally) struck, and I am afraid the General was rather disgusted with us, still more so next day when he saw our men on parade, and realised how utterly unfit they were as yet for fighting. After unloading our ponies we blundered up in the dark to the place told off to us next to the Berkshires, who looked after us most kindly, and we slept as we were.

On Wednesday, November 22nd (the following day), we were busy unloading and getting things ship-shape, and later I went down to the General's for orders, and had an excellent lunch with him and his Staff.

At 3 a.m. the following morning Hart went out with a reconnoitring party towards Arundel, where the Boers had a position, and at 4 o'clock the Colonel went with about sixty of our men by train in the same direction, the General with twenty-five of the 5th Lancers and half a Battalion Black Watch going in the same train; about thirty N.S. Wales Lancers, under Captain Cox, preceded Hart. I was left behind in command, and at 11 a.m. we got an alarm and turned out very quick, made the best of our way to a line of kopjes about five miles out on the Colesberg railway, and there took up a position to cover the retirement of the force which had gone out. After a long wait the train returned, and later our people, they having come into action at

Arundel, with the result that two men were wounded, one, Corporal Thomas, in four places. As no ambulances had been taken, the wounded had to be left out, but later a hospital train was sent out, and the Doctor found that the Boers had treated our men most kindly. He had an interview with the Boer General Grobelaar, who allowed him to bring the wounded men back, but was very indignant at being told there were only two wounded, and pointed out several other places where he had seen men fall. I should add that a Cape policeman was also shot in the leg, but pluckily rode the whole way back to Naauwpoort. Corporal Thomas was subsequently sent home, recovering rapidly.

On the 24th we got our tents and were quite comfortable ; Ottley's people joined us, and were attached to us. The following day we had another " cheap excursion " to Arundel; this time the N.S. Wales Lancers and a few 5th Lancers went on early, while about 100 of us, with Ottley's men, some police and scouts, together with Captains Lawrence and Laycock of General French's Staff, went later by train, Colonel Tudway in command of the whole force. The scouts were sent out a long way and got fired on, but there were no casualties, and having sent the train home early, we had a long hack home of about fourteen miles. Extract from my diary: " Pretty useless day—hate these railway excursions." After this quite a quiet time ensued.

On the 28th the 12th Lancers, under Lord Airlie, arrived, together with a Battery of R.H.A.; this day we also sent out some of our people, and Cox, with his N.S. Wales Lancers, reconnoitring, but nothing resulted.

About this time things began to look serious, as far as our ponies were concerned, no fewer than 35 being in sick lines; poor brutes, they had been brought up from getting a scanty living on the veldt, and then put to hard work, with a lumping Infantryman sitting on an uncouth "howdah," hung round like a Christmas-tree with nose-bags, shoe-cases, wallets, etc., etc. Several died of paralysis of the spinal muscles, but the great majority of strangles.

On November 29th the New Zealand Mounted Rifles arrived, a most useful-looking body of men, and excellently mounted; the Suffolk Regiment also came to-day. Another patrol under the C.O. went out next day at 3 a.m., and returned at dusk, having done nothing, men and ponies quite tired out. Got orders for a similar show on the morrow, but mercifully it was counter-ordered.

November 28th.—The C.O., with 150 of our men, was sent off to-day to Rosmead to guard the line. I was left behind, and in the evening got orders to send 25 men and an officer at 3 a.m. the following morning to Hart's Kopjes, on the way to Colesberg, while the General and Staff, with the N.S. Wales Lancers and two Companies of the Berkshire Regiment, were to follow by train at 4 a.m. The 12th Lancers had gone out this morning, and finding the country as far as Arundel clear of Boers, bivouacked there for the night. The proposed reconnaissance in force did not, however, come off, as the 12th Lancers were recalled and despatched to Orange River.

On Monday, December 4th, the Colonel and his party returned from Rosmead, not having come into contact with any of the enemy, though scares had been frequent.

December 5th.—The whole of our force, including the New Zealand Mounted Rifles, N.S. Wales Lancers, one Battery R.H.A., two Companies 2nd Berkshire Regiment, and the Suffolk Regiment, the whole commanded by Col. Watson, went for a route-march to a place called Valschfontein, about eight miles up the Colesberg Railway. We took all our transport, loaded as if for real business, having struck camp before we started. Got back to camp very late—the poor old M.I., always having the dirty jobs to do, had to act as whippers-in; and, as the Suffolks were only just fresh out from home and were still soft, our work was no sinecure. The Carabiniers arrived to-day, and we got orders for a move to Arundel to-morrow.

At 5 a.m. the following morning we started the Regimental Transport off; one wagon per Company, and one water-cart. We paraded at 10.45, strength just 200, and marched down to the station to entrain, but had to wait till 3 p.m. before we could get away.

We detrained at a place called Hartebeestefontein, about five miles short of Arundel, and it was already beginning to get quite dark. However, we were not allowed to water our ponies, and had to advance, Colonel Porter, of the Carabiniers directing the operations. The Carabiniers found patrols in front and on the flanks, while we advanced slowly in an enormous long line—an absurd formation for Mounted Infantry. However, we at last reached Arundel without firing a shot, while one of the Cavalry patrols succeeded in collaring Grobelaar's Adjutant, one Muller, who was out shooting springbok. He expressed himself delighted to be captured, and made a present of the buck which he had shot to Colonel Porter, accompanying the gift with a neat speech. We then bivouacked on the veldt near the station, and had to put out two officers' picquets, the M.I. having to find them, of course; just as we had got our picketing lines down, we were ordered to shift back about a mile to a bridge dynamited by the Boers, where all the transport was stuck and unable to move any further. This was a bit trying, as we had been on the move all day, and it was now about 10 p.m. However, back we had to go, and then found the supplies were not there, so we went another mile further back, and here found we had yet another half mile to go. This was too much, so we stopped where we were, and tied our ponies up to the wire railway-fence. The Sergeant-Major and I then had to blunder back over the veldt in pitch darkness to where the Carabiniers were bivouacking; I woke up Colonel Porter, and received orders to turn out at 2.45 a.m. the following morning (regardless of the fact that at that hour it would be still pitch dark) and reconnoitre kopjes in front, which were known to be occupied by the enemy. As we had to draw our supplies, I managed to beg a little delay, the hour of our starting being altered to 4 a.m., and then blundered back to our bivouac, which I reached at 11.30 p.m., and slept where I could.

By the way, I afterwards saw to-day's operations described in an English paper as "The Taking of Arundel;" the place really consisted of one large kopje, at the base of which were two small farms. I fear that, in spite of the large type in which the account was published, there will be no clasp to my medal for this affair!

I had a poor night of it, as we were up next morning at 2.30 a.m., and going back along the line for some distance we reached the spot where the train had dumped down the supplies the night before. After drawing food and forage we went out beyond Arundel, and reconnoitred various kopjes, taking up a position on our left front, and sending Ottley with some scouts on to a further line of kopjes in front, from which he got heavily fired on and retired. I had to gallop back about four miles to Colonel Porter, who sent the New Zealanders up to reinforce us, and then sent us on to take the kopjes, where the Boers had been who fired at

Ottley. Fortunately for us these gentlemen retired to their main position, and we occupied the line of kopjes at a place called Sannah's Dam, the New Zealanders prolonging the line to the left. We got considerably fired at by the Boers at 2,000 yards, and we returned their fire now and then, once getting some pretty shooting at one of their patrols at about 1,500 yards, causing one of them to dismount hurriedly.

The Carabiniers with General French went out to the front and both flanks, and were fired at a good deal, and shelled, but they had no casualties; though at one time, a squadron retiring on the right flank got hung up by a wire fence, and were for a bit in a decidedly hot corner, the Boer shells dropping right in among them, and it seemed marvellous that no one was hit.

Later on we made our first acquaintance with a " pom-pom," the Boers loosing off as our ponies crossed an open space on their way to water at the Dam; but they made rotten shooting, and no damage was done.

We withdrew to Arundel at 5.30 p.m., having one Company out, which also retired at dark. I was uncommonly glad to get something to eat when we got back, and was not long in going to sleep, being dog-tired.

Next morning we had ample time for a decent wash and breakfast; but at 10 had to go out to our yesterday's position, relieving the New Zealanders. We spent an uninteresting day; the Boers fired at us a good deal with no result, while we held our fire. Watching through glasses, we saw a good many wagons going and coming constantly between Colesberg and the Boer position known as Taaiboschlaagte.

On Monday, December 11th, Brooke was sent out in the afternoon with his Company as escort to two R.H.A. guns, a squadron of Carabiniers also going. A farm was shelled and one Boer killed, while seven more were supposed to be wounded. Our people fired some long-range volleys. No casualties to our side.

December 12th.—Sent Hart out with his Company in the afternoon, escorting two guns; they went out in an easterly direction after a party of Boers, who were lurking about our right flank. Shelled them and cleared them out. Casualties on our side: one Sergeant

KAFFIR KRAAL.

of the Carabiniers wounded and taken prisoner, two horses killed. To-day Vaalkop, an isolated hill about two miles to our left flank, was occupied by a squadron of Carabiniers and two guns, and an advanced post was established there; it was a horribly jumpy place, and, from the shape of the hill, very hard to hold; everybody hated it cordially, though it was the apple of General French's eye.

Next morning at 5 a.m. we had an alarm, and rushed up to our posts on the large kopje, known as Look-out Hill; I stayed below and saw the ponies saddled up, and then brought in close to the base of the kopje, after which I rejoined our people on the top. The Boers were making a determined attempt to get round our right flank and cut the railway between us and Naauw-poort, but they were not " slim " enough, and a very pretty fight ensued, though we had nothing to do but sit still and watch it. Our guns made most excellent prac-tice, throwing shrapnel all over the kopjes; and, though bullets were spitting up the dust all round them, the men worked as coolly as if on parade. (I think I am right in stating that the first shell fired by R.H.A. in S. Africa was fired to-day, and that the Battery was " O.") The Boers retaliated with a " Long Tom," but the third shot from our guns silenced it for the rest of the day; they also played a pom-pom on to our guns. The Cavalry was sent right out on to the plain, and it was exciting to watch the game of " drawing fire " being played by their scouts, who sometimes got right up to a kopje before the Boers fired on them, and then had to ride away like blazes. In the evening the Boers had had enough of it, and scooted back to Taaibosch.

While they were still retreating, I took Brooke and his Company and posted them behind a small kopje close to the position vacated by the enemy, and here they had to remain all night. They relieved some of the Innis-killing Dragoons (which Regiment had joined our force a few days previously), and before coming away I had the satisfaction of seeing a Maxim, directed by Lieut. Neil Haig, bowl over a Boer who was crossing a bit of open in company with some half-dozen others—a fine shot at a range of about 900 yards.

The casualties on our side to-day were one officer of

the Inniskillings, and five men wounded—none of them
seriously. That night (and many subsequent ones) we
slept fully dressed, rose the next morning at 3 a.m. and
saddled up; after which Colonel Tudway and I rode out
to Brooke's picquet, where we found everything quiet,
and the Boers had evidently cleared out. Brooke had
sent an officer out with a patrol over part of the country
where the Boers were yesterday; they found eight dead
Boer horses and the same number wounded, and they
also brought back some clothes, boots, etc., belonging to
one Tynden, with a waterproof sheet stamped O.V.S.
(Orange Free State), on which we were pleased to notice
considerable blood-stains; besides these, the subaltern
picked up some Boer newspapers, one of them, the
Bloemfontein Express, printed half in English half in
Dutch, containing an amusing account of the battles of
Graspan and Belmont, describing a charge of the
"Ghoorkas and Lancers." The picquet brought in one
wounded Boer horse, shot through the neck; but from
the fact that its mane and withers were stiff with blood,
we concluded that the rider had evidently been either
severely wounded or killed. Hart's Company relieved
the picquet in the evening.

In the morning we received orders for the remainder
of the M.I. to reinforce the post of Vaalkop; accordingly, the C.O. went out with Brooke's Company, while
I was left in camp with twelve men and twenty-seven
sick ponies. At 4 p.m. there was an alarm of Boers
on our right flank; the Cavalry went out and scoured
the country round, but found nothing, and evidently
the alarm was a false one. Hart's picquet returned in
the evening, bringing four rifles taken from a farm and
another Boer horse.

On the 15th December we were aroused by heavy
firing in the direction of Vaalkop, and soon after Colonel

Tudway came in bringing the advanced post, consisting of Brooke's Company of our Regiment, a Squadron of the 10th Hussars, and two R.H.A. guns with him. It appeared that early in the morning the Boers had brought a heavy cross-fire on the kopje from two Long Toms and a pom-pom, stampeding mules and rendering the position untenable. General Brabazon, who had arrived a few days previously, went out with the Cavalry, but nothing was done. At 4 p.m. we got an alarm, and the whole force turned out; a patrol of Inniskillings had been heavily fired on at Sannah's Dam, and poor Jackson (7th D.G.'s) was killed. Our guns shelled all the kopjes round about, but not a Boer was to be seen, and I fancy only a few of their snipers were out.

On the 17th December a Cavalry Division was formed, Colonel Porter commanding one Brigade, Colonel Fisher (10th Hussars) the other; Hart's Company told off to the former, Brooke's to the latter; consequently Colonel Tudway, I, and the staff were left as sort of " nobody's children."

December 18th.—General French went out to-day with two guns and the New Zealanders, and shelled a farm called Kraaifontein; unfortunately, it proved to be empty; but several Boers, more enterprising than usual, came down from Taaibosch, and some brisk fighting took place, in the course of which one New Zealander and two horses were killed, and several Boers knocked over.

The following day was uneventful, except that we got the news of General Buller's reverse on the Tugela, which did not tend to brighten our spirits.

Now ensued a period of comparative inactivity, by no means unacceptable; the days being varied by picquets and patrols and springbok shooting. These animals were fairly plentiful, but very hard to get at, and the

Boers were also at the same game, which made it more exciting. One of our subalterns, Geary of the Hampshire Regiment, was successful in shooting one and a steinbok, and right good they were to eat. (Poor Geary was an excellent shot; he was killed later at Thaba'nchu, but not before he had accounted for fifteen Boers to his own rifle).

On Christmas Eve the New Zealanders serenaded the Camp, and sang Christmas carols; very sporting of them, and they were a charming lot to deal with always—all most gentlemanly, excellent riders, and good shots.

Christmas Day was, by tacit consent, observed as a truce by both sides; it was cruelly hot and dusty. In the afternoon there were sports and an officer's race over about five furlongs, in which I competed, but my pony was not fast enough, and Captain Kenna, V.C. (21st Lancers) won easily on an English polo-pony from a field of about twenty-five. We had excellent Christmas dinners, as also did our men, but it was very unlike the real thing.

On Boxing Day, our picquet at Sannah's Dam captured five Boer horses; and on the same day rather a smart "coup" was brought off by a Subaltern of ours in charge of a Detached Post on the Naauwpoort line. Certain of the burghers were allowed, on payment of 5l., to take a little leave at Christmas time, for the purpose of visiting their "vrouws" and families. The wily Subaltern heard of this and made a descent on a farm, bagging four Dutchmen and hauling them away amid the execrations of the ladies and their families. Rather hard luck on the burghers, and a poor wind-up to their short Christmas holiday! Soon after this the Boers, knowing how our force had increased, and fearing to be surrounded, evacuated their position at Taaiboschlaagte and retired to Colesberg, where they established themselves in the kopjes round the town.

On the 29th Colonel Tudway left us, and I found myself in the position of Commanding Officer without, however, anybody to command; so I attached myself to Colonel Fisher's Brigade.

On December 30th, Colonel Porter's Brigade marched out to Rensburg, a place on the railway line about five miles nearer Colesberg, and a little beyond Taaibosch; here they encamped, and established several posts of observation. The next morning at 9 a.m. Colonel Fisher's Brigade followed, Brooke's Company forming the escort to the convoy. We reached Rensburg, and received orders to move on again at 4 p.m. Colonel Fisher had sent on a troop of Inniskillings with a Maxim, and seized Maeder's Farm, about nine miles west of Rensburg. The Brigade marched to Maeder's, and arrived there in the dark; we linked our ponies and lay down as we were on the veldt. I had to go round the place later with a staff officer, as we had to guide the half Battalion of the Berkshire Regiment, who had come on in wagons, in order to be fresh for next day's operations.

On the morning of January 1st, 1900, we fell in again at 1.30 a.m., self very weary after only two hours' sleep. I showed the way to the Berkshire Regiment, who passed through our lines and marched in front; of course, it was still quite dark, though a lovely starlight night. The whole Brigade then moved off in the direction of Coleskop, and blundered along a rough road. Owing to the noise made by the rattling of the chains of the machine guns of the Berkshires and ourselves, they were sent to the rear by a staff officer, and considerable confusion was caused, the Column becoming disjointed; and I think I am right in saying that some, if not all, of the Berkshires lost their bearings and marched in a line which would eventually have brought them into Colesberg, *pace* " our friends in front."

Anyhow, at 3.30 a.m., I found myself opposite a high kopje on the right of the Boer position, with Brooke and his Company, numbering about 60 men; dawn just beginning to break. For a moment confusion reigned supreme; the General could not be found, and I wondered what I ought to do. A staff officer galloped up in a violent state of excitement, and asked me if I knew where the General was, and what had become of the Berkshire, to both of which questions I could only answer "Lord knows." He then gave me an order to advance on the kopje in front, which he knew to have been unoccupied yesterday, and take up as advantageous a position on it as possible. This, thought I, with 60 men against an unknown quantity of Boers, was a "bit thick." However, there was nothing for it but to advance; so I dismounted our boys, and—ran slap into a Boer picquet. What a hullabaloo there was! "Wie is daar?" (Who's there?) they screamed, and bolted like hares; two Companies of the Berkshire suddenly turned up on our right, and were on the point of charging us; orders and counter orders flew about—"Fix bayonets," "Charge," "Retire"—and to crown everything, the high kopje began to ring with the "pip-pop," "pip-pop," of the Mauser; the burghers shooting merrily away for all they were worth, their bullets going harmlessly over our heads, and even over the heads of our horse-holders, whom I had left a long way back.

It was still quite dark, though the day was beginning to break, and this may account for my perhaps missing a burgher at 50 yards, at whom I took a pot-shot as he was bolting; I may have hit him, but at any rate he was a "strong runner," and was not "gathered." We at last got a definite order to retire; but hardly had we gone twenty yards before another order came to fix bayonets, advance, and take the hill. This was done, and we clambered up over huge boulders, the Boers retiring before us; but we never succeeded in clearing them right off the kopje, and they always held the end nearest Colesberg, and from here fired at us at about 600 yards; while from another kopje opposite, afterwards known as Gibraltar, they had our range at about 1,200 yards.

I have always felt a little hurt at the credit of the taking of the kopje being given entirely to the Berkshire Regiment, as our boys had quite as much, if not more, to do in the business; the kopje was afterwards called McCracken's Hill, after the Major commanding this half-battalion of the Berkshire.

However, to go on with my story of the fight. While Brooke was gallantly leading his men up the kopje, my Sergeant-Major came up and told me that he could see some Boers bolting from this hill across the open to another, about 800 yards off, so I took Fargus and his machine-gun section (composed of the 2nd D. C. Light Infantry) to the corner of the kopje, where we could see about 20 Boers running over the open as fast as they could lay legs to the ground. Fargus at once opened fire, but the Maxim, with the usual cussedness of the things, could only fire single shots owing to the fuzee-spring being weak, and was therefore useless. The gun-detachment, however, blazed away, and I succeeded, after three shots, in bowling a burgher over at 600 yards; I always *did* fancy myself at the " running man ! " The Sergeant (Bird) also winged a man, but he carried on. As they now began to shoot at us rather unpleasantly, I withdrew the gun and party, and, climbing up the kopje, found our people out of breath, but very exultant, and a certain amount of firing going on on both sides.

Our R.H.A. guns now began shelling, and drew on

themselves a very hot fire from a pom-pom, though the Boers never used their Long Tom on them, I fancy the reason being that they were also heavily engaged on the Rensburg side, where the New Zealanders and Hart's Company had seized a hill, afterwards called Porter's Hill. Meanwhile our Cavalry, who should have pushed on and seized a kopje commanding the Colesberg road (afterwards called Pink, or Suffolk Hill), through some misunderstanding of orders, remained inactive behind Coleskop, and when they did move out eventually on to the open plain, they could do nothing, and got heavily shelled. Consequently, though the papers always insisted that Colesberg was "surrounded" by us, this was never really the case, nor do I think that the Boers were ever in such straits as to consider a surrender advisable, though there can be no doubt that General French's subsequent harassing tactics did annoy them a great deal, and had a good moral effect.

Perhaps it was as well that we never did get into Colesberg, as Norval's Pont would have been a terribly hard nut to crack, and to turn the Boers out of that country must have entailed great loss of life. The fight went on all day and was very exciting; we sniped and were sniped at constantly. My people, I am thankful to say, had no casualties, but the Berkshire had several, including one officer, 2nd Lieut. West, killed; I should put the total casualties on our side to-day at under five-and-twenty.

We and the Berkshire remained on our captured end of the kopje, where I was fated to stay another seven days; there was no water, and we only had our great-coats to sleep in. The men were posted in reliefs along the top of the kopje, while we bivouacked at the base. I should also add that there were about seventy of the

Inniskilling Dragoons here under Lieut. Neil Haig, of polo fame.

Next morning we were up before dawn and got our ponies right in under the hill, where they were safe from shell-fire. A miserable day followed, no end of sniping going on on both sides, and it was rather "hairy" work going round my sentries. Porter's Brigade shelled the Boer position from the Rensburg side, and two of our guns did likewise from the bottom of Coleskop; the Boers retaliated with a pom-pom and two Long Toms, but did little damage.

It was an exciting ride to and from our kopje, as the Boers shot at anyone going over the open plain, and wasted some hundreds of rounds at the game; their favourite target was our water-carts, but our black drivers were most gallant, and made their mule-teams gallop *ventre-à-terre*; later, however, we had to stop sending for water in the daylight as two native drivers of the Berkshire got hit, though neither of them seemed to mind much. We had just enough water for drinking, but none for washing, which was very disagreeable.

In the course of the afternoon our Sergeant-Major greatly distinguished himself by taking out a volunteer stretcher-party to look for an unfortunate gunner who had been wounded the day before, and was lying at the bottom of Coleskop. The Sergeant-Major walked in front, waving a large Red Cross flag, but, in spite of this, the Boers kept up a constant rifle-fire on the party, the bullets kicking up the dust all round them. The gunner was found, still alive, and the party returned under the same shower of bullets, the Boers only ceasing to fire while the gunner was being placed inside the Berkshire ambulance, which had been sent out to meet the stretcher-party, and then, as the ambulance drove back, firing away as hard as ever. However, the gallant party returned unscathed, amid loud cheers from our men on the hill, mingled with hearty curses for the Boers.

The following day was spent in sniping and being sniped at, shelling and being shelled. De Lisle turned up to-day, having ridden over from Hanover Road, where his Company was guarding the bridge; he had heard the firing while out on patrol, and fearful of being left out of the show, had pushed on by himself; he afterwards sent for his Company and took over command of the Battalion. Haig and his Inniskillings left us this afternoon, having a dashing gallop over the open; the Boers loosed off about twenty rounds at each man as they went singly, but failed to hit anybody. Two men were wounded on our hill to-day.

January 4th was a rather exciting day, and a decidedly unsuccessful one on the part of the Boers. At 5 a.m., just as we were getting our ponies up under the hill, a tremendous rifle-fire burst out on our left rear. The Boers had crept round in the night, surprised a picquet of the Inniskillings, killed all their horses, and then turned their attention to our convoy which had just arrived from Maeder's Farm. Our guns came into action very quickly, and shelled the line of low kopjes gained by the Boers as hard as the guns could fire, and so the fight went on for some time.

From our kopje we had a grand view of the whole show, and could see the Boer reinforcements coming up constantly over the plain, until presently I noticed several burghers making a wide détour, obviously with the intention of getting still further round our flank. To stop this, I sent Brooke off with two sections to seize a kopje in that direction and lie low for the gentlemen; they galloped off under a very hot pom-pom and rifle-fire, but fortunately got across without a casualty, and were complimented by General Brabazon on reaching the other side. The Cavalry meanwhile were making several unsuccessful darts into the plain, trying to get in a charge, but as 'the Boers worked entirely singly, there was never any object for them to charge at, and they came under heavy shell and rifle-fire, suffering a good deal.

De Lisle now turned up from Rensburg, bringing with him Hart's Company, and after our guns had done a good deal more shelling and the Boers had begun to retire, finding themselves under a heavy fire from a troop of the 10th Hussars on one flank and the Suffolk Regiment (who had arrived the night previous) on the other, he made a most successful attack, took the position without loss, and captured twenty-two prisoners, a quantity of horses, and no end of ammunition and rifles.

It was exciting to watch the Boers retreating over the plain, a considerable number of them under cover of their ambulances; the Suffolks shot at them hard, while their Maxim loosed off a whole belt-full of rounds without stopping, and our guns scattered shrapnel all over them. Our Cavalry again vainly tried to get at them, and I believe one party of the Inniskillings did manage to kill a few, but had great difficulty in extricating themselves, and lost several men. Our total casualties were twenty-nine killed and wounded, among the former being Major Harvey, 10th Hussars, while the Boers owned to twenty-two killed, and subsequently admitted that their casualty-list amounted to seventy odd. Altogether it was a very successful day as far as our side was concerned. Besides the Berkshire there were left now on the hill only Fargus and his gun, Clegg Hill with his section, and myself.

To-night, at about 11 p.m., we were roused by a couple of shots, and soon after a ——shire man rushed up to me, *sans* helmet and rifle, and followed by another man in a breathless state of excitement, both yelling, "The Boers are on us!" I asked them what had become of their regiment, and they replied that they were coming down the hill with our fellows. I persuaded them to come with me, and we climbed up the kopje, only to find everything perfectly quiet, and the whole affair a false alarm. This was an unpleasant incident, but it must be remembered what a nerve-wearing time we were having; in the daytime it was like sitting in the old-fashioned mantlets when volleys were being fired with Martini-Henrys, and the splinters were flying about, and this game used to last regularly from dawn till night.

Next day was comparatively quiet, with the exception of the usual sniping and shelling by our guns. Some excitement was caused in the morning by a gentleman on the other side who had come to be known as the "Boss sniper," and had always been particularly offensive, being successfully picked off by one of our men.

This afternoon I placed Fargus with his Maxim at a corner of the kopje, and from here he could reach a road and farm much used by the Boers, and the embrasure from which they worked their pom-pom, and it used to be very amusing to watch the burghers scatter when the gun began to play.

In the evening I had great hopes of relief, a heliograph message coming from De Lisle:—"We fight to-morrow; can you join us?" I obtained permission from Major McCracken, but my hopes were not realised owing to the answering messages becoming mixed up in transmission.

Here I must remark that considerable carelessness was shown on the part of our signallers at this time; no cipher was used, and as messages were constantly being sent by helio, flag, and lamp to and from all parts of our force, I feel sure that the Boers were able to read a great many of them and learn our movements. Whether it was by these means, or by spies, it is pretty certain that they knew all about the proposed attack by the Suffolks the following day, and made the necessary preparations to resist it. Of this dreadful disaster I had rather not speak, except to say that I watched the whole affair with a telescope, and could plainly see the Boers riding up and down quite fearlessly on the top of the hill, and their firing-line ducking down below their " schanzes " as our guns sent showers of shrapnel over them. We saw the Boer ambulance come out, the survivors of the Suffolks disarmed and led off, and later could hear the Boers singing a hymn as they buried poor Colonel Watson and his Adjutant. Eleven officers and two hundred men were killed, wounded, and missing. Our guns shelled over our heads to-day, being directed by signals on our kopje, but I doubt if they did much harm to the enemy.

To-night I again fondly hoped for relief, but again none came. At 12.15 a.m., however, to my great joy two sections arrived, and after posting them up in all matters connected with sentries, etc., I at last left the hill with Clegg Hill, leaving Fargus and his gun behind, and reached our camp, about half-a-mile further back, at about 2.30 a.m. At 4 a.m. I was up again, and rode out with the Sergeant-Major to De Lisle's kopjes, the position captured by our men on the 4th, where we found picquets of about sixty men all told. On reaching camp again I collapsed for the rest of the day, but in the evening was able to have my long-prayed-for shave, wash, and change of clothes, and managed to put in plenty of sleep. For close on eight days I had not had a wash of any sort, nor once changed a single article of dress, besides which I had had nothing but bully beef and biscuits to live on, and uncommonly little sleep, so perhaps it was not to be wondered at that I was utterly done up at the end of it all.

In the morning I was quite fit again, and at 5.15 a.m. rode out with the Sergeant-Major to the picquets; returned to breakfast (oh, the joy of tea and Quaker Oats!), after which I did a lot of orderly-room work, which was sadly in arrears. At 12 I went out to the picquets, and remained till 7 p.m., when I was relieved by Brooke.

Our camp here (known as Kloof Camp) would have been by no means an unpleasant one but for two things —one being the sad scarcity of water, and the other the constant dropping of Boer bullets in the lines; we had several horses shot in this manner, and one man while washing. There were here three Companies of ourselves and a machine-gun, half a Battalion of the Essex Regiment, under Colonel (afterwards Brigadier-General) Stephenson, a Company of the Berkshire, and a few details.

On January 10th, a field-gun (15-pr.) was hauled up to the top of Coleskop by 180 of the Essex Regiment—a grand feat; later, another gun was also got up, and the Boers were fairly astonished, such a feat having been regarded by them as an utter impossibility.

Next day De Lisle went out with six sections, with Hart and Brooke, to a rebel farm belonging to one Du Plessis, situated at the end of a long ridge, through which ran the road to Colesberg wagon-bridge, and at the far end of which the Boers had a position at a place called Rietfontein. Under cover of their men, De Lisle and Hart (both Staff College men) made some most useful sketches which proved the maps served out to us to be hopelessly wrong! The party returned at 1 p.m.

all safe and sound. Sniping and shelling continued all day and every day.

On the 13th De Lisle rode over to Rensburg for a "Council of War." At 4 in the afternoon I received a wire from him to have 240 M.I. ready to move out at 6.30 p.m. This I arranged, and we marched off at that hour to Windmill Camp, a place about two miles behind Coleskop, where there was a well and a pump, and a Squadron of Inniskilling Dragoons. Here we were joined by two R.H.A. guns, a mounted section of Royal Engineers, half a Squadron Inniskillings, half a Squadron 10th Hussars, and two Companies of the Yorkshire Regiment; the whole force commanded by Major Allenby, Inniskillings, De Lisle being staff officer, and running the whole show. The idea was that we should go round the back of the Boer position at Rietfontein, and, if possible, blow up Colesberg wagon-road bridge. We left Windmill Camp at 8 p.m., and after a nine-mile march in the dark, reached Du Plessis' farm, and bivouacked in a stubble-field, the Yorkshire Regiment finding the outposts; we arrived at our bivouac at 11.30 p.m.

On the 14th we were up at 3 a.m., and, leaving the Yorkshire Regiment behind to guard the pass, moved off at 4 a.m. A long and very "hairy" march then ensued; at one place we had to go through a narrow pass where ten men could have stopped a Brigade, finally emerging on to a flat and open plain beyond; a Company from our lot was left behind here to hold the pass and cover our retirement. At a farm a little further on we halted, watered and fed, and had breakfast, and then marched on for miles in broiling heat. After some time we met a native shepherd, who told us that some way on there was a Boer laager, the inhabitants of which were chiefly women. We found the place—a nice-looking farm—and after surrounding it, carefully advanced and captured four Boers. The place was crowded with women, and there was a quantity of wagons; a wounded Boer was also found in an outhouse. Leaving an escort with the prisoners, we pushed on to within about two miles of the wagon-bridge.

As we had marched a very long way, and the horses and ponies were very tired, it was decided not to attempt to blow the bridge up, and so, after firing about ten shells in that direction (drawing the fire of a pom-pom from a kopje a long way in front) we " up-sticks and hooked it " as fast as we could, taking our prisoners and their Cape-cart and a pair of ponies with us. This Cape-cart and ponies were afterwards given to us by General French, and were of the greatest use to us. The Boers were now coming down from their position like bees out of a hive, and Hart's Company and Brooke's were sent out to our left flank; about 600 Boers made a dash to cut us off, but Brooke raced to a hill with a Maxim and twelve men, blazed away and frightened them off. We got through the dangerous path safely, and at last reached Du Plessis' farm, all dog-tired, and my two ponies both ridden to a stand-still; here the force bivouacked again. To-day's affair, in the opinion of most of us was a very risky undertaking, and hardly worth the candle.

Next morning we were up at 5, and leaving our bivouac at 6.30 marched back to Kloof Camp without being fired on. Our yesterday's casualties were two ponies mysteriously shot, and three dead of exhaustion.

On the 17th we sent out a foraging party to Du Plessis' Farm—a risky business; they went out at 8.30 p.m., and returned next day all safe, and bringing back a splendid lot of wheat and barley, though not much oat-hay. The wheat and barley were afterwards sold to the

Commissariat, and the result—25*l.*—was placed to the credit of our C.O.'s fund—a very useful little haul.

This morning I climbed up Coleskop, an awful grind, which took fully 25 minutes; in return for the contents of my water-bottle, two shots were fired at a Boer Cape-cart, the shell burst a little too high, but it was most amusing to see the burghers scoot for all they were worth. A grand view of the surrounding country could be obtained from here, and one could see all the Boer laagers and positions most clearly.

January 18th our two 5-inch howitzers arrived, and most of us went out to see them shell Pink Hill; the effects of the lyddite bursting was grand; huge boulders (frequently described by our men as parts of Boers) being hurled into the air; our Coleskop guns also fired like blazes; so altogether the burghers must have had a poor day of it. As a result of this, a vast "trek" from Colesberg began next morning before dawn and continued till 11; we supposed the wives and families were clearing out, one or two of the lyddite shells having burst in the streets of the town. On the 23rd, De Lisle rode into Rensburg for a Council of War—a sure fore-runner of an approaching fight.

January 24th.—De Lisle returned this morning, and at 12 we all marched out, the Essex Regiment relieving our picquets. We marched to a farm belonging to one Hobkirk, a good old Scotchman; and here were joined by the Wiltshire Regiment, four Companies Essex Regiment, and two Companies Yorkshire Regiment. General Brabazon, with the Cavalry and a Battery R.H.A. went to a farm called Ketelfontein, about five miles further on. Our bivouac at the farm was a very nice one, and we were able to get some fresh milk and a chicken or two; at night we slept in Hobkirk's coach-house and were very comfortable; the farm was about seven miles from Kloof Camp, at the extreme end of the Rietfontein ridge and on the way to Du Plessis' Farm.

Next morning we started at 6.45 a.m., and De Lisle being Staff Officer, I was in command of the M.I. We first marched in a N.E. direction, my object being to collect our picquets; Hart's and Brooke's Companies having been posted out over night, and then to join the Cavalry Brigade. However, on our way there, a Staff Officer rode up with orders to occupy a long, flat hill in front of us, which I did successfully with the Scottish Company, Hart and Brooke joining us there. It appeared that the Wiltshire Regiment was to have been on this hill by 7 a.m., but they waited behind at the pass through which I had come for their water-cart, and their non-arrival at the appointed time rather upset the show. We held the hill and fired long-range volleys at 2,200 yards at the Boers, who had a laager and a large convoy behind a conical-shaped hill, and were also lining part of the high ridge behind.

At 9 the Wiltshire at last arrived, quite done-up from their march, the Regiment being then only just out from home, and consequently soft; we retired and joined the Cavalry Brigade down below. Four R.H.A. guns shelled the Boers all day, while two 15-prs. did likewise from the other side of the ridge; we skirmished about all over the country, finding Boers in unexpected places, and once getting into rather a hot corner. Hearing heavy firing going on, we galloped back quickly to our original hill, and found that General French, who had arrived in the course of the afternoon, had sent the Wiltshire across the flat ground at the bottom, with orders not to get within less than 500 yards of the Boer position, while the Yorkshire Regiment attacked on the flank along the high ridge.

Had the attack been pushed home, I believe the Boers would have been ousted, but for some reason—possibly on account of the lateness of the hour, the order to retire was given. The Wiltshire lost about twenty men killed, wounded, and missing. The Boers had unmasked two guns, and shelled our Cavalry and guns a good deal, but, I fancy, with very little result. The whole of our force now retired, the Boers firing a *feu-de-joie* as we did so.

I went back with the led horses of one of our Companies which had been told off to cover the retirement, and waited at a pass called Bastard's Nek, where the main road from Colesberg to the wagon-bridge passed through, and here had to wait for the whole of our force to pass. We then marched back to Kloof Camp, leaving one section and a Maxim at Hobkirk's Farm, and on reaching Camp found our new C.O., Colonel Martyr, of Uganda fame, arrived. On the whole, to-day's operations can hardly be called successful, and I have no doubt the Boer newspapers described the affair as a "Crushing British Defeat."

The following day the Colonel and I, with the Western and Scottish Companies, went to Hobkirk's Farm, where we bivouacked and made ourselves very comfortable; Hart was left behind with his Company at Kloof Camp. Two Companies of the Wiltshire were also at Hobkirk's. The C.O. and I rode round in the evening and saw to the posting of our picquets, one post being established at Bastard's Nek.

On the 31st we left Hobkirk's Farm (with much regret) and marched to Windmill Camp, where we encamped, relieving some Inniskillings. The Boers about this time began to be very cheeky, and besides sniping into Kloof Camp, they also managed to reach Coleskop with a Long Tom and a pom-pom; no harm was done,

however, and our two field-guns still remained on the
top.   De Lisle left us to-day, having been appointed
to command the 6th M.I. Regiment.

On February 3rd, we received orders to move next
day to Rensburg *en route* for Orange River; "jumps"
abounded considerably, and poor old Hobkirk brought
over his wife and daughter and camped with us.

A BOER FAMILY.

The following day we were relieved by half a Squadron of Inniskillings, and marched to Rensburg in the
afternoon; found very few troops here, and a Boer
attack expected hourly.   We rather felt as if it were
high time to be off, as the Boers knew all about the
withdrawing of such a large portion of our force, and
were getting uncommonly enterprising; in fact, it was
very shortly after our departure that they compelled

the remaining force, under General Clements, to retire hurriedly back to Arundel, suffering considerable loss in doing so; they brought a Long Tom up to Bastard's Nek, and from here shelled Windmill Camp—poor Hobkirk and his family had to flee under heavy fire, while the Boers looted his farm and bagged over 1,000 sheep, besides all the cattle and horses, while the small force supposed to be guarding the farm barely escaped annihilation, and two Companies of the Wiltshire were collared at Kloof Camp. This retirement *may* have been part of the Plan of Campaign, as was stated in the papers, but I have my doubts.

On February 6th, we started in two trains at about 10 a.m. on our way to Orange River, which place we reached at 6 a.m. the following morning. Here there were lots of troops of all kinds, and a Mounted Infantry Division in the process of formation, commanded by Colonel Hannay (afterwards killed on the way to Paardeberg).

The new Mounted Infantry Regiments were then in a terrible state of unpreparedness; very few of their men, and barely half their officers, had ever been trained in M.I. work; in fact, the method of the authorities appeared to be to give a man a pair of putties and a pony and then say to him, "Now you're a Mounted Infantry man." Even this was not done in the case of the Gordon Highland Section, who, poor fellows, had to start in khaki trousers—or trews, as I suppose they would call them. We encamped on a hill well out of the ghastly dust and near the river; and here we found Atkins' Company, and for the first time since leaving Aldershot the Battalion (or Regiment, as it was now called), was complete.

In the evening we all went down to the river and bathed; though the water was warm and very dirty, it was delightful to be able to get a wet all over. I find in my diary the entry—" Slept in pyjamas "—a luxury which I had been unable to enjoy for very many nights.

On the 9th we received orders to move in the evening for a general advance into the Free State, our force being the Carabiniers, New Zealand Mounted Rifles, Rimington's Guides, Kitchener's Horse, and about five Regiments of Mounted Infantry. We paraded at 3.15 p.m., and marched down to the Orange River Bridge; here there was indescribable chaos, owing to all the transport being hopelessly stuck. Orders came that we were to go back and wait for 24 hours; then that we were to go on and bivouac with the baggage on the other side of the river. At last we got over, and having made all our arrangements, settled down for the night. Hardly, however, had we got our lines laid down when another order arrived to go on at once; but as most of our fellows had gone down to the river to bathe it was some time before we could get under weigh again, and it was in pitch darkness that we did at last move off. The heat and dust were terrible, but we pushed on as fast as we could, and eventually caught up Colonel Porter and the Carabiniers. After going about six miles we all halted for about three-quarters-of-an-hour, and then blundered on again; lost the rest of the force, and at last reached Ramah, where the whole force should have bivouacked, but the 2nd M.I. were the only people who managed to reach the place this night. We lay down and slept anyhow and anywhere; it was 2 a.m. Altogether this was a very unpropitious start for our advance into the Free State.

At 5 a.m. next morning we were up again, and later the rest of the Column turned up; we were also joined here by two Squadrons of the 14th Hussars and some

Queensland M.I. from Zoutpan's Drift. Thanks to our transport having all come to grief, we had an unexpected day's rest, which was by no means unwelcome, as the heat now had become terrible.

On February 11th we were up before dawn, and paraded in pitch darkness. The confusion was awful; we could get no orders and nobody apparently had any idea where to go; we eventually moved off and blindly followed some of the other M.I. Regiments, passing over a glorious collection of articles dropped by them, such as picketing-pegs, head-ropes, nose-bags, etc., which we longed to pick up, but had no time to do so. A commando of Boers, whose strength was estimated variously as 200 and 2,000, had taken up a position on the only respectably-sized kopje within miles of us; it had been deemed necessary to stir these people up, and for this purpose De Lisle (now Colonel) with his M.I., some Colonials and some 14th Hussars, had started out earlier than the rest of the Column to work round their flank, and, if possible, turn them out. After a lot of aimless wandering about on our part, during which we saw huge herds of springbok, the order came for us to send a Company up to the kopje, so Atkins was despatched with his Company.

In the meantime De Lisle's lot had become seriously involved, and though he "commandeered" some of Henry's M.I. to help, matters looked very ugly for him. The Boers had unmasked two guns and heavily shelled the 14th Hussars' horses; our force had not a single gun to reply (neither had we a single ambulance with the Column). Atkins' Company fired long-range volleys whenever they could see anything to fire at, which was not often, and eventually received the order to withdraw, leaving De Lisle to extricate himself as best he could, which he did under cover of darkness, with a casualty list of about 40 killed, wounded, and missing.

This affair, though by no means a success, was at any rate useful in drawing the Boers' attention off our long line of transport, which was able to pass without molestation; but I think I am not far wrong in surmising that it was this same commando of Boers who followed us up, and afterwards made such a haul by capturing the huge convoy belonging to Lord Roberts' force.

On the way to our next bivouac we halted at a pass to water, and here the Boers, with a little enterprise, could have made a fine bag. The heat had been grilling all day, and horses and men were mad with thirst; the former were beyond control, and many of them, rushing into the pass, were hopelessly bogged, while a deep ditch, over which we had to jump to get back on to the sound plain, added to the confusion.

Several other M.I. Regiments and Kitchener's Horse came crowding in, and if the Boers could have brought a gun to bear on the struggling mass from the kopje we had just left, the results to our Column must have been disastrous. After a long and terribly hot march we reached our next bivouac, Roodepoort, very late at night; De Lisle's people arrived at about midnight.

I went to headquarters for orders at 5 a.m. next morning, and found everybody rather down in the mouth about yesterday's business. I had been very seedy on and off now for three weeks, and to-day was so bad that I drove in our Cape-cart with our mess-cook; it was a dreary business passing dead and dying horses all over the place, and the heat was terrible.

We reached Ramdam in the dark, and here found lots

of troops, Lords Roberts and Kitchener, and the 6th Division, in which were the 43rd ; I longed to see them again, but was so bad that I collapsed on getting out of the cart, and was quite done for. Another fellow of ours, Haire-Forster, who had had one of our Machine-gun Detachments, also went sick to-day with what turned out afterwards to be enteric.

The following morning the troops all moved off at 4 a.m., and Haire-Forster and I were left to our own resources ; we fortunately secured a buckwagon and team of mules, and in this were carried over to an old farmhouse, in which there were quantities of sick from all sorts of troops, including several officers, and, luckily for us, the P.M.O. who commandeered the buckwagon and team for our use. In this farmhouse we spent a most

BOER SHELTER AT MAGERSFONTEIN.

wretched day, sleeping on the bare mud floor, and without any hospital arrangements, and with very little food.

On February 14th, after a miserable night, Forster and I, with about seven other sick and the P.M.O., started at 4 a.m. in the buck-wagon, and had a ghastly jolting ride of ten miles across country to Enslin, where, to my joy, I met Evelegh just preparing for the unfortunate march which eventually landed him a prisoner at Pretoria. That afternoon I reached Orange River, and after a horrible night in a crowded ward, with no clothes on my bed and nothing to eat, was sent off next morning *en route* for Wynberg.

At Cape Town I stayed till March 6th, and then, feeling quite fit, I was discharged from the hospital

M.I. MESS AT BLOEMFONTEIN.

and started north again, travelling with the Hampshire Yeomanry.

On the 9th, after having a look at Magersfontein on the way, I reached Kimberley, and was fated to remain there till the 17th, as all the convoys had been stopped going across country to Lord Roberts' force. It was pretty sickening work to have to stay and hear all about the successful march to Bloemfontein without being able to take any part in it, and I felt fairly miserable at missing such a lot.

On the 17th I started from Kimberley, and reached Bloemfontein at 6 a.m. on the 21st. Here I was rejoiced at finding the 43rd; it was good to see one's old pals again after such a long separation, but very sad to note the gaps in the Regiment caused by Klip Kraal, Paardeberg, and disease. The next day I rejoined my Mounted Infantry at a place called Waterval, some eight miles from the town. Here, though very seedy again, I had a quiet time, and even went so far as to buy an old gun in Bloemfontein for 12*l.* 10*s.*, with which I shot quail, hares, koran, plover. etc., and varied this with fishing in the Bloemspruit, in which we used to catch some capital yellow fish and " berber," which made excellent additions to our larder. I found our men showing every sign of hard work, and their clothing in rags, but all pretty fit, and our casualties had been wonderfully few. Of the officers, poor young Courtenay had been killed at Paardeberg, and Hart slightly wounded; while among the men the total casualties did not exceed a dozen. What few ponies we had left were nothing but skin and bone, and dreadful to look at. I also found a new C.O., Brevet-Major Dobell, he making the fifth C.O. the Battalion had had since leaving home. I was not destined to see much more of the Regiment, as I became very ill again, and on the 29th was sent to hospital at Bloemfontein, from which place I was sent down to Cape Town on April 1st, and subsequently invalided home for six months by a Medical Board.

So end my experiences of the first part of the Boer war, and I hope I have not been too garrulous in " fighting my battles o'er again "; it was hard luck for me, having gone through most of the dirty work at the beginning of the campaign, to miss the real successes which now followed, and the brilliant march to

Pretoria; but when I think of the numbers of old friends who have fallen, I can only consider myself fortunate in having got out of the country with a whole skin.

RONDEBOSCH HOSPITAL, NEAR CAPE TOWN.

CHAPTER XVIII.

EVENTS IN 1901.

Regimental Diary :—

January 1st, 1901.—The Headquarters of the Battalion were at Heilbron, Orange River Colony ; Lieut.-Colonel Hon. A. E. Dalzell was in command of the Battalion, as well as of the Station and the lines of communication between Heilbron and Woolvehoek; Major R. W. Porter, Assistant Provost-Marshal, Heilbron ; and Captain and Adjutant C. H. Cobb, Station Staff-Officer. The Battalion furnished the following detachments : (1) Leeuwpoort Halt (about four miles up the line towards Woolvehoek, where a deep spruit is crossed by a long bridge), A Company, consisting of Lieut. Hon. G. W. F. S. Foljambe (commanding), Lieut. J. F. C. Fuller, and 65 N.C.O.'s and men ; (2) Gottenburg (further up the line and about 14 miles from Heilbron), Major G. F. Mockler (commanding), Lieut. H. L. Wood, 2nd Lieut. F. J. Scott-Murray, and 165 N.C.O.'s and men.

Heilbron is situated about 50 miles north-east of Kroonstad, and is the terminus of a branch line which joins the main line at Woolvehoek, 30 miles to the north-west. There is telegraphic communication with Woolvehoek, heliographic with Vredefort Road (a station on the main line about 22 miles to the west), and by heliograph and lamp with Gottenburg and Leeuwpoort Halt. Two trains run per week (Tuesdays and Fridays), arriving at 9 a.m., and leaving again at 1 p.m.

Boers are always to be seen on the hills round the town, especially to the east, where they take up a position watching the road to Frankfort, 30 miles east of Heilbron. Communication with Frankfort is maintained by means of native runners, who manage to get through by travelling at night across the veldt and away from the road.

January 2nd.—Information having been received that a gun was buried on the farm of a man named Schoeman at Bronkhorstslaaifontein, about 12 miles south-east of Heilbron, the following force paraded at 5 a.m., under the command of Lieut.-Colonel Hon. A. E. Dalzell: 2 Companies, 1st Oxfordshire Light Infantry (Captain Childers' and Captain Lathy's, each 100 strong); 2 guns, 17th Battery R.F.A. ; 30 men, 77th Company Imperial Yeomanry ; 10 mounted men, 1st Oxfordshire Light Infantry ; 1 Maxim gun.

The morning was dark and cloudy, and at about 7 a.m. a heavy downpour of rain set in, accompanied by thunder and lightning, which lasted up to 11.30 a.m., and made the going very heavy.   On approaching the farm, many Boers were seen on the farms around, and they opposed our advance considerably.   Bringing the guns into action, and sending the mounted men forward, the main kopje overlooking the farm was taken, and the other hills round were also soon in our possession. The farm itself was then occupied.   Mrs. Schoeman and her two daughters were on the premises, but denied all knowledge as to the

BOER SURRENDERING TO MAJOR PORTER.

whereabouts of the owner of the farm, or of there being guns or anything of the kind buried in the vicinity.   A search was then instituted, and several likely spots were dug out, but without result.   Then four natives were sent into the dam, to feel about in the mud at the deep end, when, after a little time, a gun-wheel was located.   The search was now prosecuted thoroughly, and the following were found, with great difficulty dragged to land, and placed on wagons : 1 Krupp gun-carriage, 1 ammunition wagon, 2 limbers, 5 wheels, 16 metal shell boxes, 16 leather cartridge cases, 2 long rammer brushes, and a great quantity of shells, rifle ammunition, and other articles. During the time that the things were being collected, the enemy kept up a continuous fire on our posts on the surrounding hills. Though the gun itself had not been found, it was deemed advisable, owing to the time it had taken to get together what we had found, not to delay any longer, especially as we knew that the enemy were being reinforced, with a view to opposing us on the march back. Accordingly, at 2 p.m., a start was made on the return journey, and we had not proceeded far when a heavy fire was opened on us from Spitz Kop, a hill on our left which was strongly held, the fire soon becoming general from all sides. In this manner we were opposed the whole way home until within three miles of Heilbron, the casualties being as follows : *Wounded*, Trooper Chesworth, 77th Company Imperial Yeomanry, severe ; Privates Harvey, Douglas, and Gilder, Oxfordshire Light Infantry, all severe ; one horse and one mule *killed ;* one R.A. horse *wounded* in two places ; one mule *wounded.*

Troops reached camp at 6 p.m. Our scouts afterwards reported that the Boers brought two ambulances on to the field, and were busy loading them, Commandant Welman being severely wounded.

January 5th.—About 3 p.m. a convoy of wagons was seen coming over the hills to the east. This turned out to be a sick convoy, with 30 wounded officers and men of the Commander-in-Chief's Body Guard. The action had taken place at Spytfontein (near Lindley), where 700 Boers, under Philip Botha, had captured 120 of the Body Guard. All the wounded were placed in the Court House, and a special train was sent for.

January 6th.—Two of the Body Guard died of their wounds during the night. At 9 a.m. the remainder of them except two (Captain Butters and Sergeant-Major Ramsay) left by train for Kroonstad. Captain Butters and Sergeant-Major Ramsay died of their wounds during the afternoon ; the latter had eight wounds.

January 7th.—Captain Butters and Sergeant-Major Ramsay were buried in Heilbron Cemetery with full military honours. The escort consisted of 100 men 1st Oxfordshire Light Infantry, under Captain Childers ; the band and buglers were also present, and as many officers of the garrison as could be spared off duty.

January 8th.—Firing was heard at dawn from the direction of Vecht Kop, south-east. General C. Knox was expected to arrive soon from that direction.

January 9th.—Big guns were heard at 6 a.m. to the south-east, and in the same direction again in the evening.

Scouts brought in word that a large British Column was advancing from the Lindley direction, and another was moving towards Reitz.

January 11th.—This morning at Leeuwpoort Halt at 3.25 a.m. one of the sentries (Private Venn, 1st Oxfordshire Light Infantry) was sniped. Two shots were fired at him, one bullet passing through his helmet, the other through the sleeve of his coat. This man had previously been sniped when on sentry at Leeuwpoort one night about two months ago, and on that occasion had two bullets through his clothes ; he also had two more through his clothing at the battle of Paardeberg on February 18th, 1900.

At 4.40 a.m. Lieutenant Hon. G. Foljambe went out with a mounted

HON. G. W. F. S. FOLJAMBE.

patrol in the direction of Gottenburg. When the patrol had reached the high ground above Steyn's Halt, and were just going down the other side, Lieutenant Foljambe looked to his left to see what Private Appleby was doing, and saw about 20 Boers to his left rear. He immediately gave the signal to retire, and all got away under a heavy fire, except Private Appleby, 1st Oxfordshire Light Infantry, who was shot through the head and killed.

January 19th.—A terrific storm struck the camp at 2 p.m., doing considerable damage. The roof of the Officer's Mess was blown off.

The Mess was composed of railway sleepers, with a roof of sheets of corrugated iron. The roof contained 32 sheets of corrugated iron, held down on each side by a 30-foot steel railway rail weighing over 500 lbs. The whole roof was blown away in one piece, and fell 30 yards from the Mess, where it broke up and scattered, one piece of corrugated iron being picked up 132 yards away. The rail on the side on which the storm struck was blown over the building, and fell 30 yards away behind the Quartermaster's tent. Terrific rain and hail lasted till 3.30 p.m.

January 24th.—A convoy of 53 wagons arrived at Heilbron escorted by 200 Mounted Infantry, under command of Lieut.-Colonel Williams (the Buffs). During the afternoon 300 men and a Maxim Royal Sussex Regiment and 50 Yeomanry arrived by train to join his Column.

January 25th.—Lieut.-Colonel Williams left Heilbron at 5 a.m. with the above-named force (plus one 15-pounder field-gun lent from the Heilbron garrison) *en route* for Frankfort.

January 30th.—Guns were heard this morning in the Frankfort direction about 11.30 a.m., probably Lieut.-Colonel Williams engaging the enemy on his return from Frankfort.

February 1st.—Frankfort having been evacuated, the garrison, consisting of the following, came into Heilbron : 2nd Battalion Royal West Kent Regiment ; two guns, 2nd Battery R.F.A. ; 33rd Company Imperial Yeomanry. They also brought in 490 refugees, 250 natives, 664 cattle, 2,337 sheep, and 150 goats.

February 4th.—Lieut.-Colonel Williams moved off with his Column at 4.30 a.m., taking with him also 6 officers, 271 men, 1st Oxfordshire Light Infantry ; 5 officers, 186 men, 2nd Royal West Kent Regiment ; 2 guns, 2nd Battery, R.F.A. The officers of the Battalion accompanying Colonel Williams' Column were : Captains Lamotte, Childers, and Lathy, Lieuts. Sullivan, Hawkins, and Barron. They moved in a south-easterly direction towards Spitzkop, the intention being to clear the country to the south and south-west of Heilbron of all stock, food-stuff, and women and children.

February 6th.—Guns heard in the direction of Spitzkop; probably Williams' Column.

February 7th.—Williams' guns again heard to the south.

February 9th.—Heard from Colonel Williams, at Rhenoster Drift, near Zwavel Krans, saying that he had handed over to a Column, which had met him from Rhenoster Station, 15 ox-wagons, containing 171 Dutch people and one prisoner of war, and a quantity of sheep and cattle, and that he had burned immense quantities of mealies, forage, and food supplies. He intended crossing the river at Slootkraal, then moving north and crossing Elands Spruit, and clearing Spitzkop (this is another one not to be confused with the one mentioned on February 4th. That one is south-east of Heilbron ; this one is west of it).

February 10th.—We saw Colonel Williams' Column at 9 a.m. moving north, about seven miles west of Heilbron. Enemy were following him, and fighting was going on.

February 13th.—Colonel Williams arrived at Berlin, south-west of Gottenburg, and north-west of Heilbron. He sent into Gottenburg 64 Dutch and 31 Kaffirs, also 2,000 sheep and 200 cattle.

February 14th.—Colonel Williams to-day moved on to Elandskop, north-east of Heilbron, always a favourite resort of the Boers. A Column moved out from Heilbron (under Major Western, 2nd Royal West Kent Regiment) to demonstrate to the east.

February 15th.—Colonel Williams arrived at Leeuwpoort to get supplies. A force of 110 Infantry, 24 Yeomanry, under command of Captain E. A. Lethbridge, moved out to Kalkfontein Farm (north), and brought in a quantity of mealies.

February 16th.—Colonel Williams' Column left Leeuwpoort, moving south.

February 17th.—Colonel Williams was at Paardekraal North, south of Heilbron, on the Kroonstad road.

February 26th.—Captain R. E. Watt, with 50 men of the Regiment, 25 men 77th Company I. Y., and five wagons, moved out at 4 a.m. to a Kaffir kraal two miles east of camp, and brought in 67 sacks of mealies.

About 3 p.m. two Boer refugees, whom we had armed and sent out on cattle guard to protect the refugees' cattle, were surrounded about two miles out to the north. Captain E. A. Lethbridge, with 40 men and the 77th Company I. Y., went out and rescued the two men, both of whom had had their horses shot. One of the refugees had killed a Boer.

March 2nd.—The detachment at Gottenburg, under command of Major G. F. Mockler, rejoined headquarters, being relieved by the 2nd R. W. Kent Regiment. The detachment marched into Heilbron, arriving at midnight. Twenty men proceeded to Elandsfontein to join the M. I. Company.

March 8th.—Guns were heard to westward at 7 a.m.

March 9th.—Guns were heard to south-west at 9 a.m.

March 13th.—A farm called " Jamaica," about one mile from our outposts on the west side, had been used for some time by us as an isolation farm for lung-sick cattle. Whenever any died and had to be dragged out, the Boers always collected on the ridge beyond (about 4,000 yards from our outpost line) and sniped from some old kraals there. To-day a party was organized to drive some lung-sick cattle out beyond the farm. The 77th Company I. Y. found the escort for the party. The 5-in. gun was hidden below the crest of our hill, and with it an escort of 50 men of B Company 1st Oxfordshire Light Infantry, under command of Captain L. F. Scott. As soon as the party moved out the enemy collected in the kraals and commenced sniping. The Yeomanry replied and kept them busy, while the gun was got ready. Then the kraals were shelled, and the Yeomanry pushed forward and seized the ridge. The lung-sick cattle were then driven into the kraals on the ridge and there slaughtered, thus rendering the kraals untenable in future for the Boers. Our loss was nil ; the enemy's loss unknown, but one Boer had his head blown off by a lyddite shell.

March 15th.—At 2 a.m. Lieut. Hon. G. Foljambe signalled from Leeuwpoort that loud explosions were taking place up the line beyond him. Directly after several more loud explosions were plainly heard at Heilbron. Lieut. Foljambe then signalled that heavy firing was taking place at the next post up the line. Reinforcements were at once sent out to Leeuwpoort. In the morning it was found the Boers had blown up three culverts, four telegraph poles, and damaged two miles of the permanent way. A construction train was sent for to mend the break.

Telegraphic communication was stopped at 2 a.m., but messages were got through by signal to Gottenburg, and thence by wire on.

By 4 p.m. telegraphic communication was re-established, and the line repaired by 9 a.m. the following morning.

March 18th.—A force of 150 Infantry and 50 Yeomanry paraded at 3 a.m., and proceeded to a place known as Pierce's Trees, about four miles out to the east, the object being to seize the high ground there before daybreak and hold it all day, in order to give the large amount of cattle a good day's grazing. Sniping went on all day ; result, one Boer killed and three wounded, our casualties nil.

With the force were 100 men 1st Oxfordshire Light Infantry, under command of Lieut. C. F. Henley and 2nd Lieut. F. J. Scott-Murray.

In the evening a flag of truce came in from Christian De Wet bringing two letters, one for Lord Kitchener, and the other addressed to the O.C., Heilbron, asking him to forward the letter to Lord Kitchener.

At 9.45 p.m. a special troop train arrived from Virginia Siding bringing two officers (Captain Lathy and Lieut. Barron) and 93 N.C.O.'s and men from Lieut.-Colonel Williams' Column.

March 19th.—2nd Lieut. F. J. Scott-Murray proceeded to Pretoria by the train to-day, to convey C. De Wet's letter to Lord Kitchener.

March 27th.—At 1 p.m. to-day a force moved out from Heilbron with eight days' forage and rations, under command of Major Western, 2nd

Royal West Kent Regiment, to operate in conjunction with Lieut.-Colonel Williams' Column. With the force were 150 men 1st Oxfordshire Light Infantry, under command of Lieut. H. L. Wood and Lieut. C. A. Barron.

STATE OF THE 1st OXFORDSHIRE LIGHT INFANTRY.

HEILBRON, ORANGE RIVER COLONY, 1st *April*, 1901.

Station.	No. of Companies.	Lieut.-Colonel.	Majors.	Captains.	Lieutenants.	2nd Lieutenants.	Staff.	Sergeants.	Buglers.	Corporals.	Privates.	Public Horses and Mules.		
												Riding.	Draught.	Pack.
At Headquarters	4	1	2	4	2	4	2	29	14	20	444	7	42	7
With M.I. Company	1	—	—	—	2	1	—	2	1	5	160	—	—	—
At Leeuwpoort	1	—	—	—	1	1	—	3	—	3	57	—	—	—
At other places	—	—	—	3	1	1	—	5	—	4	47	—	—	—
With Col. Williams' column	2	—	—	1	1	1	—	3	—	4	133	—	—	—
With Major Western's do.	1	—	—	—	2	—	—	6	—	3	128	—	—	—
In hospital, &c...	—	—	1	—	1	—	—	7	—	5	107	—	—	—
In military prison	—	—	—	—	—	—	—	—	—	—	3	—	—	—
Servants to officers	—	—	—	—	—	—	—	—	—	—	7	—	—	—
Total..	9	1	3	8	10	8	2	55	15	44	1086	7	42	7

NEWS FROM HOME.

CHAPTER XIX.

DESPATCHES AND GAZETTES.

THE following are extracts from the South Africa Despatches[1] :—

No. 1.

From Field-Marshal Lord Roberts to the Secretary of State for War.

Army Headquarters, South Africa,
Cape Town, 6th February, 1900.

*   *   *   *   *   *   *

Shortly after my arrival, the troops of the 6th Division, under Lieut.-General Kelly-Kenny, reached Cape Town, and were despatched to Naauwpoort, one of the Brigades being temporarily detached for employment under Lieut.-General French. The duty assigned to Lieut.-General Kelly-Kenny was to allay unrest and check disaffection among the Colonial population, and to open up the railway line as far as possible from Middleburg in the direction of Stormberg.

*   *   *   *   *   *   *

In order to carry out the concentration north of the Orange River, I shall have to make use of the whole of the 6th and 7th Divisions, and am obliged to postpone the reinforcement of Lieut.-General Gatacre's force, although it is barely sufficient effectively to control a civil population, which contains many disturbing elements, or to regain possession of the territory which the enemy has invaded. I am compelled also to withdraw the greater part of the force under Lieut.-General Kelly-Kenny from Naauwpoort and its neighbourhood, in spite of the importance of restoring railway communication between Middleburg and Stormberg.

*   *   *   *   *   *   *

No. 2.

From Field-Marshal Lord Roberts to the Secretary of State for War.

Army Headquarters, South Africa,
Camp Jacobsdal, 16th February, 1900.

I expressed the opinion that the military requirements of the case demanded an early advance into the enemy's country, that such an

---

[1] Presented to both Houses of Parliament by command of His Majesty, February 1901.

advance, if successful, would lessen the hostile pressure both on the northern frontier of the Colony and in Natal, that the relief of Kimberley had to be effected before the end of February,[1] and would set free most of the troops encamped on the Modder River, and that the arrival of considerable reinforcements from home, especially of Field Artillery, by the 19th February, would enable those points along the frontier, which were weakly held, to be materially strengthened.   *   *   *   *

No doubt a certain amount of risk had to be run, but protracted inaction seemed to me to involve more serious dangers than the bolder course which I have decided to adopt.

      *   *   *   *   *   *   *

I received reports on the 2nd February that parties of the enemy had been observed some eight miles to the west of the railway between the Orange and Modder Rivers, their object apparently being either to injure the line or to get grazing for their horses and oxen. I therefore gave orders on the 3rd February for Major-General MacDonald, with the Highland Brigade, two squadrons of the 9th Lancers, the 62nd Field Battery, and No. 7 Field Company Royal Engineers, to move from the Modder camp down the left bank of the Modder River, and make a show of constructing a small field redoubt commanding the Koodoosberg Drift, distant about 17 miles from the camp. The object I had in view was to threaten the enemy's line of communication from the west of the railway to their position at Magersfontein, and also to lead the Boers to believe that I intended to turn their entrenchments from the left of the Modder River camp.

The troops marched early on the 4th, bivouacked for the night at Fraser's Drift, and reached Koodoosberg Drift at 2 p.m. on the 5th, the enemy's scouts being met with as soon as the Cavalry approached the drift. The position was reconnoitred that afternoon, and on the morning of the 6th February work was begun on the redoubt, a site for which was chosen on the north or right bank of the stream, in close proximity to the drift. The enemy, however, had now occupied in some strength a kopje to the north of the drift, whence the site of the redoubt was within artillery range, and it became necessary to dislodge them. After some desultory fighting, the southern portion of the kopje was occupied by the Highland Brigade, and fighting continued throughout the day, both on the summit of the hill and between it and the river. As the number of the enemy was manifestly increasing, Major-General Mac-Donald thought it desirable to ask for the reinforcement, which had

---

[1] I had inquired by heliograph, and been informed by Lieut.-Colonel Kekewich that Kimberley could not hold out longer than the end of February.

been held in readiness to support him. This, consisting of two Batteries of Horse Artillery and a Brigade of Cavalry, under Major-General Babington, marched from the camp at Modder to Koodoosberg, along the northern bank of the river, and arrived at about 3 p.m. on the 7th. The fight, which had recommenced at daybreak, continued until night-fall, the enemy gradually falling back, and being followed up by the Horse Artillery and Cavalry.

It being evident that permanently to hold the Koodoosberg Drift would require a larger force than could be spared, and the troops employed there being by this time required elsewhere, the Cavalry and Infantry Brigades were ordered to return to the Modder River Camp, which they did on the 8th without molestation, the Boers having previously fallen back from the position.

I will now briefly describe the operations for the relief of Kimberley.

*   *   *   *   *   *   *

On the 11th February the Cavalry Division, under Lieut.-General French, with seven Batteries of Horse Artillery and three Field Batte-ries, proceeded from Modder River Camp direct to Ramdam, the 7th Infantry Division, under Lieut.-General Tucker, proceeding to the same point from the railway stations of Enslin and Graspan. On the 12th February I moved to Ramdam ; the Cavalry Division marched to the Riet River, occupied with slight opposition the Dekiel and Waterval Drifts, and reconnoitred across the river ; the 7th Division proceeded to the Dekiel Drift ; and the 6th Division, under Lieut.-General Kelly-Kenny, which had moved by rail to Enslin and Graspan, replaced the 7th at Ramdam. On the 13th February the Cavalry Division advanced to the Modder River, seizing the Ronddavel and Klip Drifts, while the 6th Division moved from Ramdam to the Waterval Drift on the Riet River. The 9th Division, under Lieut.-General Sir Henry Colvile, proceeded on this day to Ramdam, while the 7th Division was occupied in getting supply wagons across the Dekiel Drift, where I established my Headquarters. On the 14th February the Cavalry Division reconnoitred to the north of the Modder River ; the 6th Division moved down the Riet River from the Waterval to the Wegdraai Drift ; the 7th Division from the Dekiel Drift to the Waterval Drift ; and the 9th Division from Ramdam to the Waterval Drift. My Headquarters were at the Waterval Drift.

For some time previous to this I had been moving troops to the east of the Orange River Station, in order to attract the enemy's attention to that quarter, and, if possible, to give rise to the idea that my intention was to make for Bloemfontein *viâ* Fauresmith.

A considerable force of Cavalry and Mounted Infantry was collected at Zoutpan's Drift, under the command of Colonel Hannay, and that officer was ordered to proceed on the 11th February towards the Riet River, to act in conjunction with the Cavalry Division. Near Wolve Kraal Colonel Hannay came in contact with the Boers, who held the hills on his right flank. He handled his troops with ability, and while he contained the enemy with a portion of his force, he pushed his baggage and main body through to Ramdam.

Late in the evening of the 14th February the 6th Division marched to Ronddavel Drift, on the Modder, and the 7th Division to the Wegdraai Drift, on the Riet. On this date troops from the 6th Division entered Jacobsdal, and found it deserted by the enemy, though the houses were still occupied by their women and children. The troops were fired on when returning to camp, and a further encounter took place on a stronger detachment being sent out to drive off the Boers. This detachment fell back before nightfall with the loss of eight killed and wounded. On the 15th February I proceeded from the Waterval Drift to Wegdraai, accompanied by the 9th Division.

During the day of the 14th I informed Lieut.-General Kelly-Kenny how essential it was that he should join hands with Lieut.-General French, in order to free the Cavalry for a further advance ; and, notwithstanding the long and fatiguing march of the previous day, the 6th Division pushed on that night across the veldt, and reached Klip Drift before daybreak on the 15th February.

Being thus free to act, Lieut.-General French at 9.30 a.m. proceeded on his journey towards Kimberley. The enemy's suspicions had by this time been aroused, and they had been able to occupy two lines of kopjes, a few miles north of the Modder River, and through which the road to Kimberley _viâ_ Abons Dam and Olifantsfontein runs. Bringing a fire to bear upon these kopjes by the Brigade Divisions of Horse Artillery, under command of Lieut.-Colonels Eustace and Rochfort, and escorted by the 1st Cavalry Brigade, under Colonel Porter, Lieut.-General French, with the 2nd and 3rd Brigades, under Brigadier-Generals Broadwood and Gordon, and the Brigade Division Horse Artillery, under Colonel Davidson, galloped through the defile in extended order until he reached some low hills, from which he was able to cover the advance of the rear troops. Casualties : One officer (Lieut. A. E. Hesketh, 16th Lancers) killed, and 20 of all ranks wounded.

At Kimberley the inhabitants were found to be in good health and spirits. On the 16th the 6th Division marched to Klip Drift, and was opposed by the enemy, who were driven off with loss. The 9th Division joined the 7th at Wegdraai, 200 Mounted Infantry, under Colonel Ridley, being left behind at Waterval to escort a Supply Column of ox-wagons thence to Wegdraai. Shortly after the departure of the 9th Division from Waterval, a Boer force with several guns, which must have come up during the night, attacked Colonel Ridley's detachment, and did a good deal of injury to the oxen and wagons of the Supply Column. On hearing of this I sent back a reinforcement, consisting of one Field Battery, one Battalion, and 300 Mounted Infantry at 10 a.m., and subsequently despatched a second Battery and Battalion, on the arrival of which the enemy disappeared.

The native ox-drivers had, however, taken to flight, so that it was impossible to inspan the ox-teams. The wagons contained a quantity of supplies of groceries for the troops and of grain for animals, and I felt that to abandon them meant a considerable loss to the stores, on which we had to depend. In view, however, of the absolute necessity of pushing on the advance, and realising, as I did, that to leave troops at Waterval Drift until such time as the convoy could again be set in motion would weaken my force and probably cause it to be delayed, I decided to abandon the supplies, wagons, and oxen, and to order the troops to withdraw to Wegdraai Drift during the night, which operation was carried out unmolested by the enemy.

At 11 a.m. on this day I directed Major-General Wavell's Brigade, of the 7th Division, to occupy Jacobsdal, which was done with very slight opposition. The officers and men who had been wounded and taken prisoners the previous day were found in the hospital at this place, as well as several other wounded men, both British and Boer. All had been taken the greatest care of by the German Ambulance.

On the 16th February I moved my Headquarters to Jacobsdal, replenished my supplies from Honey Nest Kloof and the Modder Camp, and established telegraphic communication between the latter place and Jacobsdal. The Cavalry Division has been following up the enemy to the north of Kimberley, and the 6th Division, which has marched to the east of Klip Drift, has been similarly occupied. By mid-day I received information from Lord Methuen that the Magersfontein intrenchments had been abandoned, and the latest reports point to a general retreat of the Boers in the direction of Bloemfontein. It is my intention to follow them up as rapidly as possible, and by taking full advantage of the shock which they have sustained, to break up their organisation as a fighting force. Lord Methuen has been ordered to proceed to Kimberley, after restoring the railway line, for the purpose of putting affairs in order, arranging for the military control of the town and district, and taking steps to re-open communication with Mafeking.

* * * * * * *

One of the most pressing needs in South African warfare is the supply of a sufficient quantity of drinking-water to the troops when marching, especially in the daytime, the climate being an extremely dry one, and the sun's heat very trying. The number of water-carts at present available is inadequate. Moreover, these carts cannot follow the troops over stony or broken ground, and I have therefore asked for 2,000 bheesties, with a due proportion of mussaks and pakhals, to be sent here from India.

*   *   *   *   *   *   *

No. 3.

From Field-Marshal Lord Roberts to the Secretary of State for War.

Army Headquarters, South Africa,
Camp Paardeberg, 28th February, 1900.

My Lord,—In my letter No. 2, dated the 16th February, 1900, the narrative of the operations in the Orange Free State was carried up to the occupation of Jacobsdal, and the pursuit of the enemy in an easterly direction to Klip Drift, on the Modder River. On the above date 78 ox-wagons loaded with stores, and two wagons containing Mauser rifles, explosives, and ammunition, were captured at Klip Drift by the 6th Division. On the evening of that day I ordered the 9th Division, consisting of the 3rd and 19th Brigades under Lieut.-General Sir Henry Colvile, to Klip Kraal Drift. Early the next morning Lieut.-General Tucker, commanding the 7th Division, with the 14th Brigade, marched from Wegdraai Drift to Jacobsdal, which the other Brigade of the Division, the 15th, under Major-General Wavell, had occupied since the 15th February.

On the 17th February arrangements were made for the military administration of Kimberley, and the protection of the railway line between that place and the Orange River. The command was entrusted to Lieut.-General Lord Methuen, who was directed to move his Head-quarters to Kimberley as soon as the railway had been repaired. The following troops were placed at his disposal :—1,000 Imperial Yeomanry ; 20th and 38th Batteries, Royal Field Artillery ; 2 Canadian Field Batteries ; 1 New South Wales Field Battery ; the 9th Infantry Brigade, consisting of 1st Battalion Northumberland Fusiliers, 1st Battalion Loyal North Lancashire Regiment, 2nd Battalion Northamptonshire Regiment, 2nd Battalion Yorkshire Light Infantry ; a second Infantry Brigade, consisting of 1st Battalion Highland Light Infantry, 3 Militia Battalions, leaving England on the 15th February, and due at Cape Town about the 10th March.

On the arrival of the Militia Battalions, the 2nd Battalion Royal Warwickshire Regiment is to join the 18th Brigade, and the 1st Battalion Munster Fusiliers the 19th Brigade.

The 1st or Guards Brigade was thus set free to join the force operating in the Orange Free State.

While leaving it to Lord Methuen to employ the troops under his command as he might think best, I impressed on him the desirability of holding the Modder Railway Bridge with a Battalion of Infantry in an intrenched position, and of guarding other important points along the line. I also desired him gradually to break up the Field Hospital at Modder River by the transfer of the sick and wounded to Cape Town.

On the 17th and 18th February my Headquarters remained at Jacobsdal with the 7th Division. On the former date the pursuing troops came into contact with the enemy under Cronje below Paardeberg Drift. Throughout the day a series of rearguard actions took place, the enemy skilfully seizing one defensible position after another and delaying our advance. The Boers continued their retreat, and on the morning of the 18th were found to be holding a position in the bed and on the north bank of the Modder, three miles above Paardeberg Drift, where the river makes a curve to the north. In this position they had begun to intrench themselves during the previous night. As soon as our troops came up, the 6th Division occupied the ground to the south of the stream opposite the Boer laager, with Mounted Infantry in its front to the east. The Highland Brigade was also on the south side of the Modder, while the 19th Brigade of the same Division, under Major-General Smith-Dorrien, advanced along the north side, of which also two Brigades of Cavalry, under Lieut.-General French, were converging from the direction of Kimberley. Early in the afternoon it seemed likely that the laager would be captured; but the Boers held their ground so obstinately, and it was so difficult to force a passage through the trees and undergrowth fringing the river on both banks, that the troops had to be drawn off. Heavy loss was inflicted on the enemy, while our own loss was hardly less serious, the casualties being as follows :—Officers (Duke of Cornwall's Light Infantry.—Lieut.-Colonel W. Aldworth, D.S.O.; Captain E. B. Wardlaw; Captain B. A. Newbury. Seaforth Highlanders.—2nd Lieut. R. H. McClure. Argyll and Sutherland Highlanders.—Lieut. G. E. Courtenay. West Riding Regiment.— Lieut. F. J. Siordet. 1st Battalion Yorkshire Regiment.—2nd Lieut. A. C. Neave. Oxfordshire Light Infantry.—Lieut. A. R. Bright; 2nd Lieut. V. A. Ball-Acton. King's Royal Rifles.—Captain J. Dewar; Lieut. E. Percival. Norfolk Regiment.—Lieut. J. C. Hylton-Joliffe.

Seaforth Highlanders.—2nd Lieut. D. P. Monypenny. Mounted Infantry Staff.—Colonel O. C. Hannay. Welsh Regiment.—Lieut. Angell) killed, 15; wounded, 54; missing, 8; prisoners, 3. Men—killed, 183; wounded, 851; missing, 88; prisoners, 9.

The officers and men shown as missing must, I am afraid, have been killed, as the enemy could not have sent prisoners to the rear, while only the numbers shown above as prisoners have been released by the eventual capture of the laager.

A kopje to the south-east of the position, commanding the Boer intrenchments and the whole course of the stream from the Paardeberg Drift upwards, was captured during the afternoon of the 18th, but retaken by the enemy after nightfall, owing to the Mounted Infantry, who held it, having gone down to the river to water their horses.

On the evening of this day I directed the Brigade of Guards to march from their camp at Modder along the north bank of the river to Klip Drift. I also ordered the 14th Brigade of the 7th Division, under Major-General Sir Herbert Chermside, to proceed from Jacobsdal to the Paardeberg Camp, distant about 30 miles, which was reached on the evening of the 19th.

Leaving Jacobsdal at 4 a.m. on the 19th, I reached Paardeberg at 10 a.m. When I arrived on the scene I learnt that an armistice of 24 hours had been granted to General Cronje, who had asked for it on the plea that he desired to bury his dead. This armistice I immediately revoked, and ordered a vigorous bombardment of the enemy's position. General Cronje knew, as we knew, that considerable reinforcements were hastening to his assistance from Natal and from the south, and his request was obviously only an expedient to gain time.

I found the troops in camp were much exhausted by their previous marching and fighting, and I therefore decided not to make a second assault on the laager, the capture of which by a " coup-de-main " would have entailed a further loss of life, which did not appear to me to be warranted by the military exigencies of the situation. During the morning of the 20th February the kopje on the south-east, which I have already mentioned, was recaptured, the enemy abandoning their defences on being threatened in rear by the Cavalry and Mounted Infantry. In the afternoon the Boer laager and the intrenchments surrounding it were bombarded for several hours with Naval guns, 5-inch howitzers and field guns, much damage being done to the enemy's wagons, trek oxen and horses. On the 21st and 22nd the bombardment was continued, and trenches were gradually pushed forward on both flanks of the river, but chiefly on the north, in view of an eventual assault, should such an alternative be forced upon me.

After his force had been surrounded, Cronje contrived to open helio-graphic communication with Bloemfontein, and doubtless asked for assistance, as reinforcements began to come up in scattered parties of varying strength from the east and south-east. Each commando was composed. of men belonging to different districts, some of them having been withdrawn from Ladysmith, and others from the northern frontier of the Cape Colony. On the morning of 23rd February the 1st Battalion Yorkshire Regiment engaged one of these parties, about 2,000 strong, at the eastern end of the position south of the river, and drove off the enemy with heavy loss, losing themselves three officers and 17 men wounded. Later in the day the 2nd Battalion of the Buffs, which had come up in support of the Yorkshire Regiment, captured 80 Boer prisoners. Similar parties of the enemy appeared in other directions, but were beaten back without difficulty by our troops. After being repulsed the Boers seem in most cases to have dispersed, whether to their homes or to join other commandos it is impossible to say.

On this day a balloon reconnaissance was made of the Boer laager and entrenchments, which showed that much injury had been done to the enemy's wagons and stores by shell fire. On the 24th February 40 more prisoners were taken, and a considerable number of natives came in from the enemy's camp both on this day and on the previous days, having managed to escape during the night-time. The services of these Kaffir refugees are being utilised to look after trek oxen and slaughter cattle, about 800 of which were captured in the vicinity of the Boer laager. Our casualties from the 19th to the 24th February inclusive, were as follows:—Officers—wounded, 12. Men—killed, 9; wounded, 102; missing, 8.

Nothing calling for special notice occurred on the 25th February, except that heavy rain caused the Modder River to rise over three feet, and thus delayed the movement of convoys from and to the advanced base at the Modder Station, as well as from and to Kimberley, where a Supplementary Commissariat Depôt had been established. I may here mention that the railway to Kimberley was re-opened on the 18th, and that Lord Methuen established his Headquarters there on the same day.

Early on the 26th four 6-inch howitzers arrived at this camp from Modder, and the Boer laager was again shelled during the afternoon.

At 3 a.m. on the 27th the Royal Canadian Regiment and No. 7 Company, Royal Engineers, commanded respectively by Lieut.-Colonel W. D. Otter and Lieut.-Colonel W. F. Kincaid, supported by the 1st Battalion Gordon Highlanders, advanced under a heavy rifle fire to within 80 yards of the enemy's defences, and succeeded in intrenching themselves, with the loss of 2 officers wounded, 7 men killed, and 27 wounded. A gallant deed, creditable to all who took part in it.

At 6 a.m. I received a letter from General P. A. Cronje making an unconditional surrender and throwing himself and his troops on Her Majesty's clemency. The following is a translation :—

> Headquarter Laager, Modder River,
> 27th February, 1900.

HONOURED SIR,—Herewith I have the honour to inform you that the Council of War, which was held here last evening, resolved to surrender unconditionally with the forces here, being compelled to do so under existing circumstances. They therefore throw themselves on the clemency of Her Britannic Majesty.

As a sign of surrender a white flag will be hoisted from 6 a.m. to-day. The Council of War requests that you will give immediate orders for all further hostilities to be stopped, in order that more loss of life may be prevented.

> I have the honour to be, Sir,
> Your most obedient servant,
> (Signed) P. A. CRONJE, General.

To FIELD-MARSHAL LORD ROBERTS.

P.S.—Messrs. G. R. Keizer, my secretary, and H. C. Penzhorn are authorised to arrange all details with your Lordship.

Cronje was received by me in camp at 8 a.m., and he with the other prisoners, numbering 3,919 men, exclusive of 150 wounded, were despatched in the afternoon to Cape Town.

In addition to the prisoners' rifles and a large quantity of Mauser ammunition, three 7·5-centimetre Krupp field guns, one old pattern 12-pounder quick-firing gun, and one Vickers-Maxim automatic 3·7-centimetre quick-firing gun have been taken, as well as many ox and mule wagons.

A very large area has to be occupied in a country like this, consisting of flat plains with isolated hills or kopjes, to prevent the enemy from seizing one or more of the latter, and thence by long-range gun and rifle fire rendering the interior of the position untenable. The perimeter of the Paardeberg encampment surrounding the Boer laager was about 24 miles, and the distances from one point to another added greatly to the labours of the troops.

I also enclose a list of prisoners taken on 27th February.

I am sanguine enough to hope that the complete defeat and surrender of Cronje will materially improve the prospects of the campaign. For over two months he held us in check at Magersfontein, and his following included many influential men, both from the Orange Free State and from the South African Republic. The despatch of these men, with nearly 4,000 other prisoners, to Cape Town, cannot fail to encourage the loyal inhabitants of the Cape Colony and Natal, and to dishearten the disaffected, while the capture of one of their ablest and most determined commanders must inflict a severe blow on the Boer cause.

It is my present intention to halt here for about a week longer, in order to get the Cavalry and Artillery horses into better condition, replenish my supplies of food and ammunition, and prepare my transport train for a further advance. On reaching Bloemfontein I propose to re-open railway communication between that place and the Midland railway line, and to transfer my advanced base from the Modder River Station and Kimberley to Colesberg or Naauwpoort. In anticipation of this transfer, and to relieve the congested state of the docks at Cape Town, I have directed a number of vessels carrying stores and supplies to proceed to East London.

*   *   *   *   *   *   *

Apart from the progress of the war, there are two matters affecting the force under my command, to which a brief reference seems desirable. On the 25th February I telegraphed to your Lordship requesting that 100,000 khaki warm coats of the Indian pattern might be sent to the Cape Colony and Natal from India. These coats proved very serviceable during the expeditions on the North-west Frontier in 1897–98, and will greatly conduce to the health and comfort of the troops in South Africa as soon as the cold season sets in. On 26th February, in reply to a telegram from your Lordship, I asked for the 8th Infantry Division to be despatched to South Africa as quickly as possible, more troops being needed in my opinion to enable me to operate in sufficient strength in the Orange Free State and Transvaal.

No. 4.

From Field-Marshal Lord Roberts to the Secretary of State for War.

Army Headquarters, South Africa,
Government House, Bloemfontein,
15th March 1900.

My Lord,—In my letter No. 3, dated the 28th February 1900, I continued my narrative of the operations in the Orange Free State and elsewhere up to the end of the month.

On the 1st March I proceeded to Kimberley from my camp at Paardeberg, for the purpose of discussing with Lieut.-General Lord Methuen the measures to be taken for the relief of Mafeking. I returned the next day to Osfontein, about five miles east of Paardeberg, where I established my Headquarters.

The troops at Paardeberg marched to Osfontein on the 1st, on which day the following movements were ordered :—

The Mounted Infantry at the Modder Camp to leave on the 4th March and arrive at Osfontein in three marches ; the three Batteries of Field Artillery at Jacobsdal, under Lieut.-Colonel Flint, to proceed to Osfontein, arriving there on the 6th ; the 1st, or Guards Brigade, at Klip Drift and Klip Kraal, similarly to arrive at Osfontein on the 6th ; and the 15th Brigade at Jacobsdal, under Major-General Wavell, to accompany the last convoy from the Modder Camp, and to reach Osfontein on the 7th. On these movements being completed, I directed the line of communication with the Modder Camp to be abandoned, that with Kimberley being maintained for a few days longer until I was ready to advance on Bloemfontein.

As there had been considerable additions to the strength of the Mounted Infantry, I redistributed this branch of the Service into the following commands :—

1st Brigade.

Lieut.-Colonel E. A. H. Alderson, Commanding.

1st Regiment Mounted Infantry.
3rd Regiment Mounted Infantry.
Roberts's Horse.
New Zealand Mounted Infantry.
Rimington's Guides.

2nd Brigade.

Lieut.-Colonel P. W. J. Le Gallais, Commanding.

6th Regiment Mounted Infantry.
8th Regiment Mounted Infantry.
City Imperial Volunteers.
Kitchener's Horse.
Nesbitt's Horse.
New South Wales Mounted Infantry.

3rd Brigade.

Lieut.-Colonel C. G. Martyr, Commanding.

2nd Regiment Mounted Infantry.
4th Regiment Mounted Infantry.
2nd Battalion Durham Mounted Infantry.
2nd Battalion Essex Mounted Infantry.
2nd Battalion West Riding Mounted Infantry.
1st Queensland Mounted Infantry.
2nd Queensland Mounted Infantry

4TH BRIGADE.

Colonel C. P. Ridley, Commanding.

5th Regiment Mounted Infantry.
7th Regiment Mounted Infantry.
1st City of Grahamstown Volunteers.
Ceylon Mounted Infantry.

Heavy rain fell daily up to the 6th, greatly impeding the march of the troops, and delaying the convoys of provisions and stores, the drifts across the Modder River becoming almost unfordable.

It had been my original intention to move towards Bloemfontein as soon as the enemy's force under Cronje had been obliged to surrender, but the Cavalry and Artillery horses were so exhausted by their rapid march to Kimberley and back, and so weakened by the scarcity of forage, that I found it absolutely necessary to give them a week's rest.

Meanwhile reports came in that the enemy were collecting in considerable strength to the east of Osfontein, and were intrenching themselves along a line of kopjes, running north and south, about eight miles distant from the camp at Osfontein. The northernmost or Leeuw Kopje was to the north of, and two miles distant from, the river; and the southernmost cluster of kopjes, to which the name of "The Seven Kopjes" was given, was eight miles to the south of the river. The front of the Boer position extended, therefore, for $10\frac{1}{2}$ miles.

It was noticed that several gun emplacements were being constructed on the summit of a flat-topped kopje (called "Table Mountain"), which formed a salient in the centre of the alignment, and guns were also mounted on the Leeuw Kopje at the northern end, and on "The Seven Kopjes" at the southern end.

On the 6th March I gave orders for an attack on the enemy's position early the following morning. The Cavalry Division, with Alderson's and Ridley's Brigades of Mounted Infantry and seven Batteries of Horse Artillery, was directed to march at 2 a.m., its object being to circle round the left flank of the Boers, to take their line of entrenchments in reverse, and moving eventually to the river near Poplar Grove to cut off their line of retreat. The 6th Division, under Lieut.-General Kelly-Kenny, with its Brigade Division of Field Artillery, one Howitzer Battery, and Martyr's Mounted Infantry, was to follow the route taken by the Cavalry until reaching a point south-east of "The Seven Kopjes." It was then to drive the enemy from these kopjes, and afterwards move to the north in the direction of "Table Mountain."

In the attack on "Table Mountain" the 6th Division was to be assisted by Flint's Brigade Division of Field Artillery, four 4·7-inch Naval guns, Le Gallais' Brigade of Mounted Infantry, and the Guards Brigade. This latter force was to concentrate at daybreak near a small kopje and farm distant two miles to the east of Osfontein Farm, where my Headquarters had been established. "Table Mountain" being the key of the enemy's position, I anticipated that the Boers would retire to the river as soon as it was occupied by our troops.

The 14th Brigade of the 7th Division, with its Brigade Division of Field Artillery, Nesbitt's Horse, and the New South Wales and Queensland Mounted Infantry, was ordered to march eastward along the south bank of the river, for the purpose of threatening the enemy, distracting attention from the main attack on "Table Mountain," and assisting the Cavalry in preventing the Boers from crossing the river at the Poplar Grove Drift. The 9th Division, with three Naval 12-pounders, and Mounted Infantry, under Lieut.-Colonels De Lisle and Henry, was instructed to act in a similar manner on the north bank of the river, and to drive the enemy from the Leeuw Kopje, which formed the northern extremity of their defensive position.

On the 7th March the operations were carried out in accordance with the above scheme, but the 6th Division made too wide a detour to the south, the result being that, before it approached "The Seven Kopjes," the Boers had been dislodged by the Horse Artillery fire in reverse, coupled with the well-aimed shell-fire of the 4·7-inch Naval guns in front, while the turning movement of the Cavalry and Horse Artillery, in conjunction with the advance of the 9th Division and 1st and 14th Brigades, caused the enemy to evacuate "Table Mountain" and Leeuw Kopje without offering any serious opposition. Long distances had, however, to be traversed by the troops, the ground was heavy owing to the recent rain, and the Cavalry and Artillery horses were in very poor condition. Moreover the Boers displayed such skill in delaying the pursuit of the Cavalry Division, that they succeeded in taking away with them almost all their guns and wagons, and it was not until the evening that the main body of the force reached Poplar Grove, to which I had ordered the baggage to be transferred as soon as I perceived that the enemy were in full retreat.

Had the Cavalry, Horse Artillery, and Mounted Infantry been able to move more rapidly, they would undoubtedly have intercepted the enemy's line of retreat, and I should have had the satisfaction of capturing their guns, wagons, and supplies, as well as a large number of prisoners. The failure to effect this object was the more mortifying when I learnt the next day on good authority that the Presidents of the

Orange Free State and South African Republics had been present during the engagement, and had strongly urged the Boers to continue their resistance. Their appeals to the burghers were, however, unavailing, as the Boer forces were quite broken, and refused to fight any longer.

In the course of the afternoon the Russian and Dutch Military Attachés with the Transvaal Government, Lieut.-Colonel Gourko, and Lieut. Thomson, who were accompanying the enemy, claimed our protection, the horses in the cart in which they were travelling having been killed by shell-fire.

One Krupp gun and six ox-wagons were captured during the day, and a large quantity of rifle ammunition was afterwards found in the deserted trenches. The casualties during the day were not heavy, and were confined almost entirely to the Cavalry Division. They consisted of 2 officers (Lieut. Keswick, 12th Lancers, Lieut. Frieslich, 1st Grahamstown Volunteers) and 2 men killed, 3 officers and 46 men wounded, and 1 man missing.

On the 8th and 9th of March the force halted at Poplar Grove, but on the latter date the 1st Cavalry Brigade and the 6th Infantry Division moved eight miles eastward to Waaihoek, on the road to Abraham's Kraal.

On the 9th I issued orders for the advance of the force in three Columns on Bloemfontein. The left Column, under Lieut.-General French, consisted of the 1st Cavalry Brigade, Alderson's Mounted Infantry, and the 6th Division. The centre Column, which I accompanied, comprised the 9th Division, the Brigade of Guards, the 2nd Cavalry Brigade, Martyr's and Le Gallais' Mounted Infantry, the 65th Howitzer Battery, four 6-inch howitzers, the Naval Brigade, the ammunition reserve, the Supply Park, and the 7th Field Company, Royal Engineers. The right Column, under Lieut.-General Tucker, included the 7th Division, the 3rd Cavalry Brigade, and Ridley's Brigade of Mounted Infantry. The left Column was to march by the northern road, through Baberspan, Doornboom, and Venter's Vlei, to Leeuwberg, on the railway line, about 15 miles south of Bloemfontein ; the centre by the middle road, through Driefontein, Assvogel Kop, and Venter's Vlei to Leeuwberg ; and the right Column through Petrusburg, Driekop, and Panfontein or Weltevrade to Venter's Vlei, the distance being, in each case, covered in four marches, with halts at the places mentioned.

It should here be explained that my reason for not proposing to use the northern and most direct road beyond Baberspan was that I had good reason to believe that the enemy expected us to advance by that road, and were ready to oppose us in a strong intrenched position, which they had prepared in the vicinity of Bainsvlei.

On the 10th the movement was begun as ordered, and the right Column occupied Petrusburg without opposition. The left Column found the enemy holding several kopjes behind Abraham's Kraal, and endeavoured to turn their left flank by moving to the south. The Boers, however, anticipated this manœuvre by a rapid march southward, and took up a fresh position on a ridge about four miles long, running north and south across the road two miles east of Driefontein. Lieut.-General French followed up the enemy with the 1st Cavalry Brigade and the 6th Division, and came into contact with them at 11 a.m.

Meanwhile the 2nd Cavalry Brigade had reached Driefontein, and endeavoured, in conjunction with the 1st Cavalry Brigade, to turn the rear of the Boers, by operating in the plain behind the ridge which they were holding. The enemy's guns, however, had a longer range than our field guns, which were the only ones immediately available, and some time elapsed before the former could be silenced, especially a Creusot gun, which had been placed in a commanding position on an isolated kopje, two-and-a-half miles east of the northern end of the ridge. The Infantry of the 6th Division reached this end of the ridge about 2 p.m., having been under the enemy's shell fire, which did but little damage, for more than an hour. The Boers were gradually pushed back towards the centre of the ridge, where they made an obstinate stand.

The 9th Division came up at 5 p.m. and I at once ordered the Guards' Brigade and the 19th Brigade to the assistance of the 6th Division; but before these reinforcements could reach the ridge, the enemy's position was stormed in the most gallant manner by the 1st Battalions of the Essex and Welsh Regiments, supported by the 2nd Battalion of the Buffs. The bodies of 102 Boers were afterwards found along the ridge, mainly in the position which they held to the last. Many of their horses were killed.

I regret to say that our casualties were heavy, aggregating 4 officers (The Buffs.—Captain Eustace. Welsh Regiment.—Captain Lomax. Essex Regiment.—Lieut. F. N. Parsons, 2nd Lieut. A. B. Coddington) killed, and 20 wounded; and 60 men killed, 314 wounded, and 16 missing. The Cavalry, Artillery, and Mounted Infantry suffered comparatively slight loss, 1 officer (Mr. McCartie, a retired Indian civilian) being killed, and 4 wounded; and 4 men killed, 25 wounded, and 2 missing.

A flagrant breach of the recognised usages of war was the cause of most of the casualties in the Infantry. The enemy held up their hands and hoisted a white flag in sign of surrender, but when our troops approached they were fired on at close quarters by a number of Boers posted under cover in rear of their front line, and had to retire until re-inforced, when the position was carried at the point of the bayonet. The holding up of their hands on the part of the Boers was observed by me and by several officers of my Staff through telescopes, and it, as well as the persistent use by the enemy of flat-nosed expanding bullets, has been brought to the notice of the Presidents of the Orange Free State and South African Republic in a telegram, dated 11th March, a copy of which was forwarded for your Lordship's information, with a request that its contents might be communicated to the neutral Powers.

On the evening of the 10th the left and centre Columns bivouacked together in the vicinity of Driefontein. On this date I directed Lieut.-General Tucker to halt the 7th Division and 3rd Cavalry Brigade at Driekop, until he was joined by the 2nd Battalions of the Hampshire and Warwickshire Regiments. These corps had been left behind, together with Lieut.-Colonels De Lisle and Henry's Battalions of Mounted Infantry, at Osfontein and Poplar Grove respectively, for the purpose of keeping open communication with Kimberley, until certain convoys, which were being despatched from that place, had arrived, and until the sick and wounded, who were being sent back from Poplar Grove and Osfontein, had crossed the Modder River.

I may here mention that the Russian and Dutch Military Attachés, who had given themselves up on 7th March at Poplar Grove, were sent to Kimberley *en route* to Cape Town with this convoy of sick and wounded.

On the 11th March the combined left and centre Columns marched to Assvogel Kop, no opposition being met with. This day I ordered the 3rd Cavalry Brigade with two Batteries of Horse Artillery to proceed from Driekop to Venter's Vlei. On 12th March my Headquarters, together with the 6th and 9th Divisions, moved to Venter's Vlei, while the 1st and 2nd Cavalry Brigades, under Lieut.-General French, pushed on to Brand Dam Kop, seven miles to the south-west of Bloemfontein. I diverted the Cavalry from Leeuwberg, which was their original objec-tive, to a point much nearer Bloemfontein for two reasons :—

First, it was reported that reinforcements from the north were hourly expected at Bloemfontein, and it thus became imperatively necessary to forestall the enemy's movements. This report has subsequently been substantiated by a telegram from President Kruger to General Joubert, which has fallen into my hands.

Secondly, if any delay occurred, the Boers would have had time to remove the locomotives and rolling stock, which I understood to be still in the railway station at Bloemfontein.

Some slight resistance was met with by the Cavalry, but no serious fighting took place, and the only casualties that occurred were on the side of the Boers.

Early the next morning I proceeded to Brand Dam Kop, accompanied by the 3rd Cavalry Brigade, and found that the hills commanding the town had already been occupied by the 1st and 2nd Cavalry Brigades. At noon several of the leading citizens of Bloemfontein, including Mr. Frazer, drove out to the kopje which I had just reached, about a mile from the town and tendered its submission to the British Government. I entered Bloemfontein at 1 p.m., meeting with a cordial reception from the inhabitants, a number of whom accompanied the troops singing " God Save the Queen," " Rule Britannia," &c. I established my Headquarters in the official residence of the State President, which Mr. Steyn had vacated at 6 o'clock on the previous evening. The 1st Infantry Brigade marched this day from Venter's Vlei to Bloemfontein, and the 6th and 9th Divisions from the same place to Brand Dam Kop. On the morning of the 14th the 6th Division advanced to Bloemfontein, being joined there in the course of the day by the 9th Division. As soon as the troops occupied the town I appointed Major-General G. T. Pretyman, C.B., to be Military Governor of Bloemfontein, granting him, subject to your Lordship's approval, the rank and pay of a Major-General on the Staff while so employed.

It may here be noted that under my orders the railway north and south of Bloemfontein was broken up for a sufficient distance on the evening of the 12th by Major Hunter-Weston, R.E., attached to the Cavalry Division, and this enterprising officer also succeeded in cutting the enemy's telegraph and telephone wires in both directions. Eleven locomotives, 20 carriages, and 140 trucks were captured at the Bloemfontein Railway Station, the Boers not having had time to remove them. The acquisition of this amount of rolling stock will greatly facilitate the re-opening of railway communication with Cape Colony, in spite of the fact that the bridges at Norval's Pont and Bethulie were blown up by the enemy when they withdrew to the north side of the Orange River.

Yesterday I issued an Army Order thanking the troops under my command for their conduct during the operations which resulted in the relief of Kimberley and Ladysmith, the surrender of Cronje, the capture of a large number of prisoners, and the occupation of Bloemfontein. A copy of this Order is appended,[1] and I trust that your Lordship will agree with me in thinking that, by their spirit and endurance, the soldiers and sailors serving in South Africa have worthily upheld the traditions of Her Majesty's Forces.

---

[1] Vide page 86 of this book.—ED.

No. 5.

From Field-Marshal Lord Roberts to the Secretary of State for War.

War Office, 31st March, 1900.

SIR,—In the foregoing despatches, Nos. 1, 2, 3, and 4, dated respectively 6th February, 16th February, 28th February, and 15th March, 1900, I have drawn attention to the conduct of the troops during the operations therein described.

*   *   *   *   *   *   *

It is now my pleasing duty to bring to your Lordship's notice the names of the following officers, non-commissioned officers, and men, on account of the services they have rendered during the recent operations :—

*   *   *   *   *   *   *

6th Regiment Mounted Infantry.

*   *   *   *   *   *   *

Captain R. Fanshawe, Oxfordshire Mounted Infantry.

*   *   *   *   *   *   *

1st Battalion Oxfordshire Light Infantry.
Lieut.-Colonel the Hon. A. E. Dalzell.
Captain E. A. E. Lethbridge.
Captain F. J. Henley.

*   *   *   *   *   *   *

I confidently recommend those I have named to the favourable consideration of Her Majesty's Government.

I have the honour to be, my Lord,

Your most obedient servant,

ROBERTS, Field-Marshal.

Mentioned in Lord Roberts' Despatches.

Lieut.-Colonel the Hon. A. E. Dalzell.

Major J. Hanbury-Williams, C.M.G.

Major R. Fanshawe.

Captain E. A. E. Lethbridge.

Captain F. J. Henley.

Captain K. R. Hamilton.

Honours and Promotions.

(From the *London Gazette*, April 19th, 1901.)

To be Ordinary Members of the Military Division of the Third Class, or Companions of the Most Honourable Order of the Bath :—

*   *   *   *   *   *

Lieut.-Colonel the Hon. Arthur Edward Dalzell, Oxfordshire Light Infantry.

To be Companions of the Distinguished Service Order :—

*   *   *   *   *   *

Major Robert Fanshawe, Oxfordshire Light Infantry.

*   *   *   *   *   *

Captain Henry Lancelot Ruck Keene, Oxfordshire Light Infantry.

Half-pay.   To be Lieut-Colonels :—

*   *   *   *   *   *

Major John Hanbury-Williams, from the Oxfordshire Light Infantry.

[NOTE.—The following was prefixed to the List of Honours in the *Gazette :* " The rewards given below are for services in South Africa up to the 29th November, 1900, the day on which Field-Marshal Lord Roberts handed over the command, and which date (except where otherwise stated) they bear. Owing to the multitude of recommendations forwarded to the Commander-in-Chief, it has not yet been possible to examine those for regimental service, or those relating to the Militia, Yeomanry, Volunteers, and certain other services. Further distinctions will be notified later. These will bear the same date as those now given, viz., the 29th November, 1900, except where otherwise stated."]

PROMOTIONS FROM THE RANKS.

Prince of Wales's Volunteers (South Lancashire Regiment :—Sergeant Frank Hudson, from Oxfordshire Light Infantry, to be 2nd Lieutenant. (*Gazette*, 22nd May, 1900.)

The Leicestershire Regiment :—Lance - Sergeant Frederick Colquhoun, from the Oxfordshire Light Infantry, to be 2nd Lieutenant, on augmentation. (*Gazette*, 13th July, 1900.)

SOUTH AFRICA MEDAL.

Army Order 94 of 1901 :—

1. His Majesty the King has been graciously pleased to confirm the order given by Her late Majesty Queen Victoria that a medal be struck to commemorate the military operations in South Africa.

2. The medal in silver, will, provided the claims are approved by the Commander-in-Chief, be granted to all officers, warrant officers, non-commissioned officers and men of the British, Indian, and Colonial Forces, and to all Nurses and Nursing Sisters who actually served in South Africa between 11th October, 1899, and a date to be hereafter fixed : to all troops stationed in Cape Colony and Natal at the outbreak of hostilities ; and to troops stationed in St. Helena between the 14th April, 1900, and a date to be hereafter fixed.

3. A clasp inscribed " Belmont" will be granted to all troops under Lieut.-General Lord Methuen's command who were north of Witteputs (exclusive) on 23rd November, 1899.

S 1300.

T

4. A clasp inscribed " Modder River " will be granted to all troops under Lieut.-General Lord Methuen's command who were north of Honey Nest Kloof (exclusive), and south of the Magersfontein ridge (exclusive) on 28th November, 1899.

5. A clasp inscribed " Paardeberg " will be granted to all troops within 7,000 yards of General Cronje's final laager, between midnight of the 17th and midnight of the 26th February, 1900, and to all troops within 7,000 yards of Koodoe's Rand Drift between those dates.

6. A clasp inscribed " Dreifontein " will be granted to all troops with Army Headquarters, and Lieut.-General French's column, *i.e.*, the left and centre columns, which advanced from Poplar Grove on 10th March, 1900.

7. A clasp inscribed " Wepener " will be granted to all troops engaged in the defence of that place between 9th April, 1900, and 25th April, 1900, both days inclusive.

8. A clasp inscribed " Johannesburg " will be granted to all troops who, on 29th May, 1900, were north of an east and west line through Klip River Station (exclusive), and east of a north and south line through Krugersdorp Station (inclusive).

9. A clasp inscribed " Diamond Hill " will be granted to all troops who, on 11th or 12th June, 1900, were east of a north and south line drawn through Silverton Siding and north of an east and west line through Vlakfont.

10. A clasp inscribed " Belfast " will be granted to all troops who, on 26th or 27th August, 1900, were east of a north and south line drawn through Wonderfontein (the garrison and troops quartered at Wonderfontein on those dates will not receive this clasp), and west of a north and south line through Dalmanutha Station, and north of an east and west line through Dalmanutha Station.

11. A clasp inscribed " Wittebergen " will be granted to all troops who were inside a line drawn from Harrismith to Bethlehem, thence to Senekal and Clocolan, along the Basuto border, and back to Harrismith, between 1st and 29th July, 1900, both dates inclusive.

12. A clasp inscribed " Defence of Kimberley " will be granted to all troops in the garrison of Kimberley between 14th October, 1899, and 15th February, 1900, both dates inclusive.

13. A clasp inscribed " Relief of Kimberley " will be granted to all troops in the relief column under Lieut.-General French, who marched from Klip Drift on 15th February, 1900, and all the 6th Division under Lieut.-General Kelly-Kenny who were within 7,000 yards of Klip Drift on 15th February, 1900.

14. A clasp inscribed " Defence of Mafeking " will be granted to all troops in the garrison of Mafeking between 13th October, 1899, and 17th May, 1900, both days inclusive.

15. A clasp inscribed " Relief of Mafeking " will be granted to all troops under the command of Colonel Mahon who marched from Barkly West on 4th May, 1900, and to all troops who were under Colonel Plumer's command between 11th October, 1899, and 17th May 1900, both dates inclusive, and who were south of an east and west line drawn through Palachwe.

16. A clasp inscribed " Cape Colony " will be granted to all troops in Cape Colony at any time between 11th October, 1899, and a date to be hereafter fixed, who receive no clasp for an action already specified in the Cape Colony, nor the " Natal " clasp.

17. A clasp inscribed " Orange Free State " will be granted to all troops in Orange River Colony at any time between 28th February, 1900, and a date to be hereafter fixed, who receive no clasp which has been already specified for an action in the Orange River Colony.

18. A clasp inscribed " Transvaal " will be granted to all troops in the Transvaal at any time between 24th May, 1900, and a date to be hereafter fixed, who receive no clasp for an action in the Transvaal which has been already specified.

19. A clasp inscribed " Rhodesia " will be granted to all troops under the command of Lieut.-General Sir F. Carrington and Colonel Plumer in Rhodesia, between 11th October, 1899, and 17th May, 1900, both dates inclusive, who receive no clasp for the relief of Mafeking.

20. A clasp inscribed " Talana " will be granted to all troops under Lieut.-General Sir W. Penn Symons' command on 20th October, 1899, who were north of an east and west line drawn through Waschbank Station.

21. A clasp inscribed " Elandslaagte " wil be granted to all troops at Elandslaagte on 21st October, 1899, who were on the right bank of the Sunday river and north of an east and west line through Buy's farm.

22. A clasp inscribed " Defence of Ladysmith " will be granted to all troops in Ladysmith between 3rd November, 1899, and 28th February, 1900, both dates inclusive.

23. A clasp inscribed " Tugela Heights " will be granted to all troops of the Natal Field Force, exclusive of the Ladysmith Garrison employed in the operations north of an east and west line through Chieveley Station, between the 14th and 27th February, 1900, both dates inclusive.

24. A clasp inscribed " Relief of Ladysmith " will be granted to all troops in Natal north of and including Estcourt between 15th December, 1899, and 28th February, 1900, both dates inclusive.

25. A clasp inscribed " Laing's Nek " will be granted to all troops of the Natal Field Force employed in the operations, and north of an east and west line through Newcastle between the 2nd and 9th June, 1900, both dates inclusive.

26. A clasp inscribed " Natal " will be granted to all troops in Natal at any time between 11th October, 1899, and 11th June, 1900, both dates inclusive, who receive no clasp for an action in Natal nor the Cape Colony clasp as already specified.

27. No individual can have both the defence and relief clasps for either Kimberley, Mafeking, or Ladysmith.

28. The medal in silver, with clasps, will be granted to any native soldiers specially employed within the sphere of operations, who fulfil the necessary conditions.

29. Non-enlisted men of whatever nationality, who drew military pay, will receive bronze medals, without clasps.

30. Commanding officers and heads of departments will prepare nominal rolls, in triplicate, of the individuals entitled to the medal and clasps, and forward them, as early as practicable, to the Under Secretary of State, War Office, London, S.W. A supply of printed forms of rolls will be sent to each unit concerned, and a supply will also be kept at the head-quarters of each Regimental district for the use of individuals detached from their Regiments.

31. The names of officers and warrant officers will be entered in order of rank and those of non-commissioned officers and men in alphabetical order.

32. The names of officers and soldiers, except staff officers, will be entered on the roll of the unit to which they actually belong when the roll is prepared. In the event of inquiries having to be made regarding any individual claims which cannot be certified by the officer commanding the unit, the roll should not be delayed pending the result of the inquiries, but these names should be excluded, and a supplementary roll rendered later.

33. In cases where it is known that individuals have served with more than one unit during the campaign, a note should be made in the column of " Remarks " on the roll showing the unit with which they previously served, and their rank and regimental number therein.

34. The names of individuals who, under Articles 613, 737, 1255, 1256, and 1258, Royal Warrant for Pay, &c., have forfeited the medal are to be included in the rolls, their names being entered in red ink, and the cause of forfeiture stated in the last column. The names of individuals who have become non-effective by death, transfer, discharge, &c., should also be similarly entered in red ink.

CHAPTER XX.

OBITUARY AND STATISTICS.

MAJOR CHARLES RUSSELL DAY died of wounds received at Paardeberg on the 18th February. He was the only son of the Rev. Russell Day, Rector of Horstead, Norfolk, and Maria Isabella, eldest daughter of T. J. Knowlys, Esq., of Heysham Tower, Lancashire, and was born on the 19th April, 1860. Educated at Cheam School and Eton; joined 3rd Royal Lancashire Militia 1880, and gazetted Lieutenant, Oxfordshire Light Infantry, 28th January, 1882. He served for a few months with the 2nd Battalion in Ireland, and was then transferred to the 1st Battalion in India. Captain, 27th July, 1889; Major, 23rd October, 1899. Adjutant of Volunteers, 1892–97.

Photograph by]   [*Mayall & Co., Piccadilly, W.*

MAJOR C. R. DAY.

In 1884–85 he took part with his Company of the 1st Battalion in the operations for the suppression of the Moplah Riots, Southern India, and was severely wounded by a bullet in the chest. Received the thanks of the Madras Government.

In December, 1900, Major Day proceeded to South Africa with the 1st Battalion, being present at all the engagements up to the time of receiving the wounds to which he unfortunately succumbed. In the action at

Klip Kraal, on the 16th February, he was exposed to the full fury of the Boer fire, as evidenced by the fact that whilst lying on the ground his field-glasses were broken to pieces by a bullet. At Paardeberg, on the 18th, he was wounded severely though not dangerously, and there would have been every prospect of his recovery, but in being carried from the field by the stretcher-party he was wounded a second time by an explosive bullet. He died two days afterwards, and his funeral was described by the Chaplain as the most impressive one at which he had ever officiated. Major-General Knox, himself severely wounded, attended, and though the Regiment, being at the time in action, was unable to be present, twenty or thirty wounded men in hospital managed to find their way to the graveside, to show their respect for their officer. The *Church Times* of April 6th, 1900, published a letter from the Rev. J. Blackburn, Chaplain to the Forces, from which the following is an extract :—

On February 21st, I buried Major Day, of the Oxfordshire Light Infantry. It was a most pathetic funeral. About 30 wounded men of his Regiment and General Knox followed. These men were wounded in every conceivable part of the body ; they made a sad picture as we wended our way to the grave. Not many of us returned with dry eyes.

The *Daily Mail* in describing the fighting at Paardeberg said :—

A wounded Corporal[1] gives a pathetic account of Major Day's death at Paardeberg. That cultured and brilliant officer left cover to help the wounded man, and had just reached him when he was shot. When both had been taken under cover, his first inquiry was how the Corporal was getting on. "Never mind me," he said.

Major Day, who was a Fellow of the Society of Antiquaries, was well known in the musical world as an

---

[1] Corporal Knowles, West Riding Regiment. He was invalided home, and, with reference to the above paragraph in the *Daily Mail*, stated that Major Day had saved his life, going to his assistance through a hail of bullets.—Ed.

enthusiast, more especially in the matter of musical instruments and their history. He was an indefatigable worker, and whilst on service in India he formed a large collection of native instruments and copious notes on native airs, which he afterwards published in a magnificent volume entitled " Music and Musical Instruments of Southern India and the Deccan." In 1890 he published another valuable work of reference, " Descriptive Catalogue of Musical Instruments Exhibited at the Royal Military Exhibition," and he contributed numerous scientific papers to musical journals, etc. The Regimental Chronicle also has been indebted to him for interesting articles on Military Music and Bugle Calls, and it is needless to say that the band of the Regiment benefited considerably by the knowledge that he was able to bring to bear on its instruction.

In 1885, when only 25 years of age, he was appointed a member of the University Committee for investigating the Music of India ; 1890, employed on the Musical Committee of the Royal Military Exhibition, London ; 1893, Member of the English Committee, International Exhibition, Vienna ; and previous to his departure for South Africa he had been appointed to a similar post for the Paris Exhibition of 1900. The *Spectator*, of March 17, 1900, in an article headed " Soldier Musicians," paid a tribute to his work as well as to his memory. From this article we extract the following :—

The other side of the question, what soldiers have done for music and how they have availed themselves of their opportunities when upon foreign service for broadening the borders of the art, is, however, more in need of recognition, and a fitting occasion is furnished by the regretted death of an officer who died of wounds received in action at Paardeberg —Major C. R. Day, of the Oxfordshire Light Infantry. While stationed in India Major Day made a special study of Oriental music, and embodied the results in an elaborate and scholarly monograph on the music of Southern India, handsomely illustrated with coloured drawings of the various native instruments, and containing a careful scientific analysis of the melodic and rhythmic bases of this school of Eastern music. Major Day's studies, though they tended somewhat in an archæological direction, were not incompatible with a keen interest in modern music and modern instruments, and the present writer well remembers, on the occasion of a visit in his company to the collection at the Military Exhibition in 1890, how, *à propos* of the saxophone, he referred to the effective use made of that music in Massenet's *Esclarmonde.* "He was not," writes "A. J. H.," to whom we are indebted for some interesting reminiscences of this accomplished and charming officer, "an executive musician, except for a delightful way he had of preludising in a kind of Indian strain on the piano. He was seriously attracted to Indian music between 1882–87, when his Regiment, the old 43rd, was in the Peninsula, as his *magnus opus* shows. He collected a few rare specimens of Indian musical instruments, one a vina, two hundred years old, of rare beauty, all of which I have taken care of for him while he had no settled home. He got together a great deal of serviceable knowledge about the military instruments, and welcomed, with that gentle enthusiasm which was so characteristic of him, the chance of cataloguing the remarkable collection of the Military Exhibition, Chelsea, 1890, to which we owe the admirable volume which Eyre and Spottiswoode published. His ambition was to become the Commandant of Kneller Hall. I believe he would have retired from the Army ere this, being married and having a little daughter, but that he felt promotion was gradually bringing him nearer to the rank essential for the post. Duty called him to Africa, with the sad result which those of us who knew and loved him mourn." [1]

The *Times, Athenæum, Daily News,* and many other journals contained long obituary notices, and the *Musical News* deplored Major Day's loss in a leading article of very considerable length. We will quote only the last few lines :—

The bright example he displayed of industry, thoroughness, and devotion to duty remains for our emulation ; the staff of this journal mourns the loss of a gifted comrade, and—the writer of these lines ventures to add—a courteous English gentleman and a true friend. We tender our heartfelt sympathies to his father and his wife, the daughter of Mr. Scott-Chad, of Thursford, Norfolk, whom the deceased officer married only a few years ago.

---

[1] The writer was evidently Mr. Alfred James Hipkins, F.S.A., a well-known musical critic and authority.—Ed.

LIEUTENANT ASHLEY ROWLAND BRIGHT was born on the 3rd November 1872, and entered the Oxfordshire Light Infantry (from the Militia) as 2nd Lieutenant on the 12th December 1894; promoted Lieutenant, 17th November 1897; appointed Assistant-Adjutant 1st Battalion, 18th February 1898.

In the autumn of 1899 he proceeded to South Africa with the Durham Light Infantry, to which he was attached, in order to take command of the Maxim gun detachment. With them he was actively engaged until the arrival of his own Regiment, to which he was then transferred for duty, taking part in the invasion of the Orange Free State and the subsequent engagements, in command of a Company. He was shot dead through the heart on the 18th February at the battle of Paardeberg, a description of which we

LIEUT. A. R. BRIGHT.

have given elsewhere, and his loss was deeply felt by the whole Regiment.

He was an officer of great ability and much promise, and his Commanding Officer wrote of his death in the following words :—" Poor Bright—I deeply regret his death, for he was an excellent officer, and a cheery, intelligent companion. How he escaped being shot two days earlier, at Klip Kraal, I cannot think, for throughout the day he was exposed to a perfect hail of lead."

2ND LIEUTENANT VERE ANNESLEY BALL-ACTON was born on the 22nd April 1879, entered Sandhurst September 1897, and passed out in December 1898. Gazetted to the 1st Battalion as 2nd Lieutenant, on the 11th February 1899, he proceeded with it on active service, as one of the junior subalterns, at the end of the year. He was present at the attack on Cronje's rear-guard at Klip Kraal on the 16th February, and was shot through the head at the battle of Paardeberg on the 18th, when within a few hundred yards of Cronje's laager. Like his two brother officers, he found a soldier's grave by the side of the Modder River, being buried by a funeral party of Canadians, near whose shelter-trenches he had fallen.

Photograph by]   *[Mr. Charles Knight, Aldershot.*
2ND LIEUT. V. A. BALL-ACTON.

SERGEANT M. MEGGS.
Killed at Klip Kraal.

SERGEANT F. C. WALKER.
Severely wounded at Klip Kraal.

CORPORAL J. GRANT.
Died of Enteric.

PRIVATE W. BAKER.
Killed at Gottenburg.

PRIVATE G. FLEXNER.
Wounded at Kroonstad.

LANCE-CORPORAL J. BATSTONE.
Killed at Paardeberg.

PRIVATE JONES.
Wounded.

CASUALTIES IN SOUTH AFRICA, 1900.

CASUALTIES IN SOUTH AFRICA, 1900.

1st Oxfordshire Light Infantry.

I.—KILLED AND DIED OF DISEASE.

Regimental Number.	Rank.	Name.	Date of Death.	Place of Death.	Remarks.
		KILLED IN ACTION.			
—	Lieut.	A. R. Bright	18-2-00	Paardeberg.	
—	2nd Lieut.	V. A. Ball-Acton	„		
4240	L.-Sergeant	M. Meggs	16-2-00	Klip Kraal.	
5686	L.-Corporal	W. Coleman	„	„	
3743	Private	A. Davis	„	„	
785	„	C. Woodley	„	„	
4791	„	J. Quelch	„	„	
3719	„	J. Comber	„	„	
3027	„	T. A. Cripps	„	„	
1460	„	J. Steward	„	„	
5878	„	C. Cripps	„	„	
5455	L.-Corporal	J. Batstone	18-2-00	Paardeberg.	
3301	Private	J. Goldswain	„	„	
3538	„	F. Yerby	„	„	
5939	„	W. Rudge	„	„	
2994	„	R. Page	„	„	
5634	„	G. Browning	6-6-00	Pretoria.	
5445	„	P. Lawrence	26-7-00	Welegund.	
3934	„	W. Baker	1-12-00	Gottenburg.	
		DIED OF WOUNDS RECEIVED IN ACTION.			
—	Major	C. R. Day	21-2-00	Paardeberg.	Wounded, 18-2-00.
3529	Private	G. Crouch	16-2-00	Klip Kraal.	
3205	„	J. Broom	17-2-00	Klip Drift.	
3360	„	C. Floyd	„	„	
3561	„	W. Ward	21-2-00	Paardeberg.	Wounded, 18-2-00.
5540	„	A. J. Say	18-3-00	De Aar.	
5661	„	H. Boomer	16-6-00	Johannesburg.	Wounded, 29-5-00, at Elandsfontein.
		DIED OF DISEASE.			
2903	Corporal	H. Ward	27-1-00	Cape Town.	
4471	Private	T. Wade	13-3-00	Wynberg.	Dysentery.
3414	„	F. Cook	17-3-00	Bloemfontein.	„
3469	„	W. Quarterman	„	„	„
4629	„	F. Rickson	23-3-00	Not stated.	Enteric.
2963	„	W. Sawbridge	24-3-00	Kimberley.	Dysentery.
3351	„	F. Horwood	27-3-00	Bloemfontein.	Enteric.
2939	„	H. Bateman	30-3-00		„
3499	„	C. Warner	„	Cape Town.	Tetanus.
3380	„	H. Buck	1-4-00	Rondesboch.	Typhlitis.
2645	Sergeant	C. Clarke	4-4-00	Bloemfontein.	Enteric.
5604	Private	G. Townsend	6-4-00	Naauwpoort.	
2916	L.-Corporal	F. Rymell	10-4-00	Bloemfontein.	Dysentery.
5142	Bugler	H. Wyld	11-4-00	Wynberg.	„
4329	„	R. Lester	13-4-00	Cape Town.	Enteric.
2137	Private	F. Coleman	18-4-00	Woodstock.	
4246	L.-Corporal	P. Mason	24-4-00	Bloemfontein.	„
3631	Private	E. Hunt	„	„	„
7303	„	J. Gould	29-4-00	Sterkstroom.	Dysentery.
3603	„	W. Lidgley	7-5-00	Bloemfontein.	Enteric.
5918	„	J. Churm	10-5-00	„	„
3230	„	R. Wilson	14-5-00	„	Dysentery.
5388	Corporal	A. Whall	12-5-00	„	Enteric.
3951	Private	A. Huckins	19-5-00	Springfontein.	„
2369	„	G. King	20-5-00	Bloemfontein.	„
3828	„	A. Edwards	21-5-00	„	„
4452	„	J. Beckley	„	„	„
5697	„	F. Penny	25-5-00	„	„
2455	„	B. Edwards	23-5-00	„	„

COLOUR-SERGEANT C. BALDWIN.
Severely wounded at Paardeberg.

SERGEANT W. PARRY.

BUGLER T. WILLIAMS.

PRIVATE J. MONKS.
Severely wounded at Paardeberg.

PRIVATE T. H. PAYNE.

PRIVATE H. BOOMER.
Killed at Elandsfontein.

PRIVATE J. STEWARD.
Killed at Klip Kraal.

KILLED AND WOUNDED IN SOUTH AFRICA, 1900.

Regimental Number.	Rank.	Name.	Date of Death.	Place of Death.	Remarks.
3240	Private - -	H. Smith - -	2–6–00	Bloemfontein.	Enteric.
5464	,, - -	W. Wakefield -	5–6–00	,,	,,
3136	,, - -	J. Warner - -	7–6–00	,,	,,
3782	,, - -	J. Devoisey -	6–6–00	,,	,,
1494	,, - -	T. Baker - -	9–6–00	,,	,,
2155	,, - -	H. Inder - -	11–6–00	Kroonstad.	Pneumonia.
4610	,, - -	G. Archer - -	14–6–00	Bloemfontein.	Enteric.
2129	Col.-Sergeant	T. Turnbull -	16–6–00	,,	,,
3701	Private -	W. Heydon -	18–6–00	,,	,,
2781	,, - -	W. Barton -	19–6–00	,,	,,
4195	Sergeant	J. Larden -	,,	,,	,,
83	L.-Corporal -	W. Boon -	20–6–00	Kroonstad.	Pneumonia.
6284	Private - -	G. Jones -	21–6–00	Germeston.	Enteric.
5976	,, - -	A. Stonton -	27–6–00	Springfontein.	,,
1857	,, - -	T. Harwood -	2–7–00	Kroonstad.	,,
4371	,, - -	J. Simmonds -	30–6–00	,,	,,
3190	,, - -	A. Brown -	6–7–00	Wynberg.	Pericarditis.
3036	,, - -	C. Burgess -	3–7–00	Kroonstad.	Enteric.
7233	,, - -	C. Hobbs -	4–7–00	Norval's Pont.	,,
5497	,, - -	H. Ockleford -	5–7–00	Bloemfontein.	,,
2834	,, - -	W. Brooks -	10–7–00	Kroonstad.	,,
3423	,, - -	A. Macefield -	18–7–00	,,	,,
5736	,, - -	H. Horton -	22–7–00	,,	,,
1966	Sergeant	W. Dudley -	24–7–00	,,	Pneumonia.
2485	,,	T. Hearn -	13–8–00	,,	Enteric.
4427	Private -	A. Hockins -	31–8–00	,,	Pneumonia.
3497	,, -	J. Chitty -	18–9–00	,,	Enteric.
3117	,, -	J. Faulkner -	23–9–00	,,	Pneumonia.
5989	,, -	A. Wilks -	2–11–00	Bloemfontein.	Meningitis.
3982	Corporal	G. Grove -	25–9–00	Kroonstad.	Enteric.
4098	Private -	J. Cole -	21–11–00	Heilbron.	,,
5997	,,	T. Merry -	18–12–00	,,	,,
6069	L.-Corporal -	F. Stopp -	10–12–00	,,	,,
3645	Corporal	J. Grant -	17–12–00	Norval's Pont.	,,
3745	Private -	F. Morris -	26–12–00	Kroonstad.	,,

ACCIDENTAL DEATHS.

4747	Private - -	S. Turner - -	5–2–00	Modder River.	Drowned.
5357	,, -	E. Trinder -	27–3–00	Norval's Pont.	Gun-shot.

II.—WOUNDED.

Regimental Number.	Rank.	Name.	Particulars of Wound. Date.	Particulars of Wound. Place.	Particulars of Wound. Degree.	Remarks.
	Lieut. -	F. H. Stapleton -	16–2–00	Klip Kraal -	Severely -	Returned to duty in S. Africa.
	Capt. -	R. E. Watt -	18–2–00	Paardeberg -	Slightly -	,,
	Lieut. -	S. F. Hammick -	18–2–00	,,	,,	,,
	Capt. -	R. Fanshawe }		Not reported.		
	,,	K. R. Hamilton }				
	Lieut. -	C. E. Forrest -	,,	Elandsfontein	Severely -	Invalided home.
	Capt. -	G. N. Colvile -	6–11–00	Bothaville -	,,	Returned to duty in S. Africa.
5988	L.-Cor. -	R. Caudrey -	16–2–00	Klip Kraal -		
3909	Serg. -	F. C. Walker -	,,	,,		
3261	Pte. -	J. Dickenson -	,,	,,		
3539	,,	J. Gilder -	,,	,,	Degree of wounds not reported.	
3493	,,	J. Piddington -	,,	,,		
5414	Bugler	C. Cooke -	,,	,,		
3177	Cor. -	F. R. James -	,,	,,		
5426	L.-Cor. -	G. A. Parmeter -	,,	,,		
3484	Pte. -	A. Mundy -	,,	,,		
3089	,, -	W. Gibbard -	,,	,,		
3233	,, -	H. Taylor -	,,	,,		

Regimental Number.	Rank.	Name.	Particulars of wound.			Remarks.
			Date.	Place.	Degree.	
2997	Serg.	W. Barker	18-2-00	Paardeberg	Severely.	
3425	L.-Cor.	A. Harrison	„	„	„	
5637	Pte.	T. H. Payne	„	„	„	
2001	C.-Serg.	C. Baldwin	„	„	„	
5504	Pte.	T. Payne	„	„	„	
2611	„	E. Lovick	„	„	„	
3582	„	E. Stratford	„	„	„	
4511	„	E. Whitbread	„	„	„	Dischgd. 6-11-00.
5573	Serg.	F. Colquhoun	„	„	„	Promoted 2nd Lt. Leicestershire Regiment.
257	„	E. Ludlow	„	„	Slightly.	
5921	Pte.	F. Watkins	„	„	„	
2923	„	A. Manders	„	„	„	
3441	„	C. Ridgley	„	„	„	
5591	„	H. Jones	„	„	„	
5471	„	E. Hazell	„	„	„	
5528	„	F. Golds	„	„	„	
2010	Serg.	W. Parry	„	„	„	
3329	Pte.	T. R. Harwood	„	„	„	
3523	„	E. W. Hambridge	„	„	„	
3046	„	A. Darrington	„	„	„	
5932	„	W. Harman	„	„	Severely.	
5351	Bugler	T. Williams	„	„	„	
2130	Pte.	G. Lingwood	„	„	„	
3398	„	C. H. Vernall	„	„	„	
3300	„	F. Gardiner	„	„	„	
5808	„	J. Monks	„	„	„	
5010	„	E. Birch	„	„	„	
3363	L.-Cor.	R. Henessy	„	„	„	
4151	Serg.	A. J. Dunn	„	„	„	Dischgd. 14-11-00.
4336	Pte.	R. G. Cox	„	„	Dangerously.	
3671	„	W. Lewis	16-2-00	Klip Kraal	„	
3641	„	J. Kearley	„	„	„	Dischgd. 30-11-00.
5740	„	G. Bridger	„	„	Severely.	
2954	„	W. Grace	„	„	„	
3396	„	F. Crawford	„	„	„	Dischgd. 30-11-00.
3352	„	A. Reeves	„	„	„	
2619	„	T. Boyce	„	„	„	
1245	„	C. Cox	„	„	„	
1088	„	G. Snook	„	„	„	
3372	„	W. Lundie	„	„	„	
3251	„	F. North	„	„	„	
5514	„	C. Cook	„	„	„	
3505	Cor.	S. J. Papfield	„	„	„	
3026	Serg.	J. Turner	„	„	Slightly.	
3348	L.-Cor.	C. Grace	„	„	„	
3232	Pte.	A. Charman	„	„	„	
2930	„	W. Bansley	„	„	„	
3518	„	A. Davis	„	„	„	
3649	„	W. Postle	„	„	„	
3051	„	J. Cox	„	„	„	
3910	„	G. Cripps	„	„	„	
5930	„	A. Emery	„	„	„	
3130	„	W. Folland	„	„	„	
5898	„	C. Valentine	„	„	„	
3516	„	A. Rawlings	„	„	„	
3636	„	F. Harris	„	„	„	
2225	„	F. Barnes	„	„	„	
3589	„	H. Selwood	19-2-00	Not stated	Not stated.	
3134	„	T. Mayne	„	„	„	
2096	Serg.	G. Watson	10-5-00	Kroonstad	Severely	Dischgd. 14-11-00.
2410	L.-Cor.	E. Yates	„	„	Slightly.	
4846	Pte.	G. Fleckner	„	„	„	
5615	„	J. Webb	19-7-00	Bethlehem	Not stated.	
4634	„	W. H. Green	1-12-00	Gottenburg	Severely.	
5982	„	F. Sharman	„	„	Not stated.	
6195	„	T. Mackin	„	„	„	
6107	„	R. Jones	„	„	„	
3646	„	A. Sabatini	26-7-00	Welegund	Slightly.	

SERGEANT G. WATSON.
Severely wounded near Kroonstad.
Discharged as permanently unfit.

SERGEANT F. COLQUHOUN.
Severely wounded at Paardeberg.
Promoted 2nd Lieutenant,
Leicestershire Regiment.

SERGEANT A. J. DUNN.
Severely wounded at Paardeberg.
Discharged as permanently unfit.

THREE WOUNDED SERGEANTS.

CASUALTIES IN 1901.

I.—KILLED AND DIED OF DISEASE.

Regimental Number.	Rank.	Name.	Date of Death.	Place of Death.	Remarks.
		KILLED IN ACTION.			
5751	Private -	T. Appleby - -	11-1-01	Leeuwpoort.	
2568	Col.-Sergeant-	J. Aspey - -	18-3-01	Gredgedacht.	
		MISSING (BELIEVED KILLED).			
5550	Private -	W. Pitman - -	18-3-01	Gredgedacht.	
3407	,, -	E. Webb - -	18-3-01	,,	
		DIED OF DISEASE.			
3271	,, -	J. Kentish - -	5-1-01	Heilbron.	Enteric.
6263	,, -	E. Strong - -	12-1-01	Kroonstad.	,,
4399	,, -	E. Brocks -. -	19-1-01	Heilbron.	Dysentery.
5867	,, -	F. Cooper -	16-1-01	,,	Enteric.
3912	,, -	C. Wooldridge -	30-1-01	Kroonstad.	,,
3693	,, -	W. Baughan -	5-2-01	,,	,,
6014	,, -	E. Avery - -	6-2-01	,,	,,
6118	,, -	E. Marshall -	8-2-01	Heilbron.	,,
5971	,, -	F. Puddifoot- -	8-2-01	Kroonstad.	,,
3775	,, -	J. Tyson - -	7-3-01	,,	Valvular dis. of heart.
5886	,, -	R. Baker - -	3-3-01	Johannesburg.	Enteric.
4284	,, -	W. Sheerman, -	30-3-01	Kroonstad.	Tubercle lung.
2747	,, -	C. Tilbury - -	6-4-01	Heilbron.	Enteric.
3586	,, -	A. Goodenough -	8-4-01	Pretoria.	,,
4912	,, -	H. George - -	17-4-01	Germiston.	Peritonitis.
4516	,, -	L. Vincent - -	20-4-01	Kroonstad.	Enteric.
6005	,, -	W. Baldwin - -	27-4-01	Heilbron.	,,

II.—WOUNDED.

Regimental Number.	Rank.	Name.	Particulars of wound.			Remarks.
			Date.	Place.	Degree.	
	Lieut. -	J. A. Ballard -	18-3-01	Gredgedacht -	Slightly -	Returned to duty.
5150	Private	W. Douglas -	2-2-01	Near Heilbron	,,	
4733	,,	C. Harvey -	,,	,,	Severely.	
1727	,,	G. Gilder -	,,	,,	,,	
5456	,,	J. E. White -	8-2-01	Uitkijk - -	Slightly.	
2442	,,	F. Caudrey -	21-2-01	Houtkop -	,,	
3925	,,	J. Dean - -	,,	Potchefstroom	,,	
5689	,,	G. Batchelor	18-3-01	Gredgedacht -	,,	
4685	,,	A. Stove -	,,	,,	Severely.	

SUMMARY OF CASUALTIES, 1ST OXFORDSHIRE LIGHT INFANTRY, 1st January, 1900, to 1st May, 1901.

	Officers.	Colour-Sergeants.	Sergeants.	Corporals.	Lance-Corporals.	Buglers.	Privates.	Total.
Killed in action or died of wounds - -	3	1	1	—	2	—	22	29
Died from other causes - - -	—	1	4	4	4	2	69	84
Wounded - - - -	8	1	8	2	6	2	68	95
Missing (believed dead) - - -	—	—	—	—	—	—	2	2
Total - - -	11	3	13	6	12	4	161	210

OFFICERS OF THE REGIMENT WHO SERVED IN SOUTH AFRICA IN 1900–1901.

NAMES.	REMARKS.
Lieut.-Col. Hon. A. E. Dalzell - -	Commanding 1st Battalion. Despatches. C.B.
Lieut.-Col. F. J. Evelegh - - -	Commanding M. I. Detachments; in charge of convoy; prisoner of war; civil employment, Pretoria. Invalided.
Major R. W. Porter - - -	2nd in Command 1st Battalion.
Major J. Hanbury-Williams, C.M.G. -	Staff. Despatches. Promoted Lieut.-Colonel.
Major G. F. Mockler - - -	With 1st Battalion.
Major C. R. Day - - - -	With 1st Battalion. Died of wounds received at Paardeberg.
Major R. Fanshawe (2nd Batt.) -	Staff, Special Service; severely wounded; recovered and continued to serve in S. Africa with M. I. Despatches. D.S.O.
Major F. G. L. Lamotte - - -	With 1st Battalion.
Capt. H. R. Davies - - -	With M. I., 1901.
Capt. E. A. E. Lethbridge - -	With 1st Battalion. Despatches.
Capt. E. M. Childers (2nd Batt.) -	Attached 1st Battalion.
Capt. G. N. Colvile - - -	Commanding M. I. Company. Severely wounded at Bothaville; recovered and continued to serve in S. Africa. Invalided in 1901. [D.S.O.
Capt. H. L. Ruck Keene - -	Adjutant of M. I. Battalion; invalided. Despatches.
Capt. C. H. Cobb - - -	Adjutant, 1st Battalion.
Capt. R. E. Watt - - -	With 1st Battalion; wounded at Paardeberg; recovered and continued to serve in S. Africa. [patches.
Capt. F. J. Henley - - -	With 1st Battalion, and A.D.C. to Sir A. Milner. Despatches.
Capt. W. C. Hunter (2nd Batt.) -	Staff; Special Service; escorted Boer prisoners to Ceylon.
Capt. R. M. Feilden - - -	With 1st Battalion, 1901.
Capt. K. R. Hamilton (2nd Batt.)	Attached 1st Battalion, and Adjt. M. I. Bn.; severely wounded; recovered, and continued to serve in S. Africa. Despatches. S.A. Constabulary, 1901.
Capt. L. F. Scott - - -	Special Service, and with 1st Battalion.
Lieut. S. F. Hammick - -	With 1st Battalion; wounded at Paardeberg.
Lieut. A. R. Bright - -	In charge of Maxim, Durham Light Infantry; with 1st Battalion; killed at Paardeberg.
Lieut. F. H. Stapleton - - -	In charge of Maxim of 1st Battalion; severely wounded at Klip Kraal; recovered; Staff, Intelligence Department.
Lieut. C. E. Forrest - - -	With M. I. Company; wounded at Elandsfontein. Invalided. Returned to S. Africa, 1901. [1901.
Lieut. J. A. Ballard - - -	With 1st Battalion, and with M. I. Company; wounded,
Lieut. Hon. G. W. F. S. Foljambe	Do.
Lieut. C. F. Henley - - -	Do.
Lieut. A. G. Bayley - - -	Do.
Lieut. H. L. Wood - - -	Do.; invalided.
Lieut. J. F. C. Fuller - -	Do.; invalided; returned to S. Africa.
2nd Lieut. V. A. Ball-Acton - -	Do.; killed at Paardeberg.
2nd Lieut. G. A. Sullivan - -	Do.
2nd Lieut. R. R. M. Brooke -	With M. I. Company.
2nd Lieut. H. F. Ward - -	With 1st Battalion. Transferred to Irish Guards, 1901.
2nd Lieut. R. V. Simpson - -	Do.
2nd Lieut. E. H. Kirkpatrick -	Do.; invalided.
2nd Lieut. R. M. Logan - -	Do.
2nd Lieut. S. G. R. White - -	Do.; invalided. Retired, 1901.
2nd Lieut. F. J. Scott-Murray -	Do.
2nd Lieut. C. G. Higgins - -	Do.
Lieut. and Qr.-Master W. Ross -	Do.

Officers of Militia attached to the 1st Battalion in South Africa:—

Capt. G. F. Paske (3rd Batt.) -	Invalided.
Lieut. S. R. Christie-Miller (3rd Batt.)	
2nd Lieut. J. A. Pollock (3rd Batt. R. W. Surrey Regt.).	Gazetted to 1st Oxfordshire Light Infantry, 1901.

Capt. M. F. Lathy (University Volunteers).	
Lieut. L. C. Hawkins (1st Bucks Volunteers).	*Officers of Volunteers attached (with Volunteer Company) to the 1st Battalion in South Africa.*
Lieut. C. A. Barron (1st Bucks Volunteers).	

STATE OF THE 1st OXFORDSHIRE LIGHT INFANTRY, 1st JANUARY, 1900.

Distribution.	Officers.	Warrant Officers.	N.C.O.'s and Men.	Remarks.
1st Battalion on passage to South Africa	21	1	637	On SS. *Gaika.*
M. I. Company, awaiting embarkation	4	—	132	—
Already employed in South Africa -	5	—	2	—
Depôt (Oxford) and Details (Ireland) -	2	1	396	—
Total - - -	32	2	1167	

THE 1st CLASS ARMY RESERVE, 1900.

Strength of D Section on 1st January -   -   -   124
Strength of other Sections on 1st January   -   -   49

Total -   -   -   173

Rejoined the Colours during 1900   -   -   -   141
Failed to report   -   -   -   -   -   1
Rejected on medical grounds   -   -   -   31

Total -   -   -   173

STATEMENT SHOWING HOW THE STRENGTH OF THE BATTALION IN SOUTH AFRICA WAS KEPT UP DURING 1900.

(Exclusive of the M.I. and Volunteer Companies.)

INCREASE.

	Officers.	N.C.O.'s and Men.
Strength of the Battalion on landing in South Africa -	23	638
Draft of 5th February	5	300
Draft of 19th March -	2	100
Draft of 29th April -	1	100
Draft of 28th June -	2	70
Draft of 21st September -	—	142
Total landed in South Africa -	33	1350

DECREASE.

	Officers.	N.C.O.'s and Men.
Deaths from all causes	3	89
Invalided to England	6	261
Sent home prisoner -	—	1
Time expired -	—	14
Promoted to Commissions -	—	2
Transferred to the Staff -	3	—
Total decrease -	12	367

PARTICULARS OF DRAFTS SENT TO THE BATTALION IN SOUTH AFRICA IN 1900.[1]

5th February.—Captain E. M. Childers (2nd Battalion), Captain G. F. Paske (3rd Battalion), Lieuts. Christie-Miller and R. M. Logan (3rd Battalion), Lieut. S. G. R. White (4th Battalion), 85 Details, 43 Section D Reserve, 59 Militia Reserve (4th Battalion), and 113 3rd Battalion.

19th March.—2nd Lieuts. H. F. Ward and R. V. Simpson, 62 Details, 12 Militia Reserve (3rd Battalion), and 26 Militia Reserve (4th Battalion).

29th April.—2nd Lieut. Kirkpatrick, 30 Details, and 70 Transfers from 7th Battalion Rifle Brigade.

28th June.—2nd Lieuts. Scott-Murray and Higgins, 30 Details, 15 3rd Battalion, and 25 Transfers from the Border Regiment.

21st September.—101 Details and 41 3rd Battalion.

THE VOLUNTEER SERVICE COMPANY.

This Company left England on the 10th March to join the 1st Battalion in South Africa, and consisted of—Captain M. F. Lathy (1st Oxford University), Lieuts. L. C. Hawkins and C. A. Barron (1st Bucks). and 111 N.C.O.'s and men. During the year two men died of disease and seven men were invalided home, their places being supplied by others sent out from England. Strength of the Company in South Africa on 31st December 1900, three officers and 106 N.C.O.'s and men. The Company (3 officers and 89 N.C.O.'s and men) left Cape Town, in S S. *Lake Erie*, for

---

[1] The only draft sent out in 1901 (up to 1st May) was a Volunteer Section of 25 men, with 1 officer and 2 N.C.O.'s.

England, 23rd April, 1901, and arrived at Southampton on 17th May. The following is from the *Times* of 18th May, 1901 :—

The return from South Africa yesterday of the Volunteer Company of the 1st Oxfordshire Light Infantry was the occasion of a great patriotic demonstration at Oxford. The special train arrived from Southampton a few minutes before one o'clock, and the men were met at the station by the Mayor and the members of the Corporation in their robes, the Regimental band of the County Battalion, the University Corps, the City Companies of Volunteers, the members of the Volunteer Fire Brigade, and Church Lads' Brigade. Large crowds assembled in the streets, and as the procession proceeded to the Cathedral, where a thanksgiving service was held, there were deafening cheers. Many of the men were carried on the shoulders of undergraduates and others. The Cathedral was crowded. The service was conducted by the Bishop Designate of Oxford, Dr. Paget, the other members of the Chapter present being Canons Ince, Moberly, and Driver. Later, the Mayor gave a luncheon in the municipal buildings. The toast of " Our Guests " was very heartily drunk, and Captain Lathy, in reply, referred to the praise bestowed upon the Company by every Commanding Officer under whom they had served, and added that the proudest recollection of his life would be the year in which he commanded in South Africa the Company of the Oxford and Bucks Volunteers.

THE VOLUNTEER SERVICE COMPANY.
Before embarkation for South Africa.

SERVICES AND AGES OF THE N.C.O.'s AND MEN OF THE 1st OXFORDSHIRE LIGHT INFANTRY.

ON the 1st December 1900, the strength of the Battalion in South Africa[1] was 1,308 N.C.O.'s and men, viz. :—Regulars and Army Reservists, 886; Militia Reservists and Volunteers, 422.

	Years of Service.			Years of Age.	
	Under 5.	Over 5.	Over 10.	Between 20 and 24.	Over 24.
Regulars and Army Reservists -	350	197	339	348	538
Militia Reservists - - -	—	—	—	132	185
Volunteers - - - - -	—	—	—	61	44
Total - -	—	—	—	541	767

[1] Including M.I. and Volunteer Companies.

ITINERARY OF THE 1st OXFORDSHIRE LIGHT INFANTRY IN SOUTH AFRICA DURING 1900.

Date.	Place.	Distance in Miles.	
	CAPE TOWN to—		
January 16th	Naauwport	570	By rail.
„ 25th	Thebus	130	„
February 1st	Modder River	240	„
„ 10th	Enslin	22	„
„ 12th	Ramdam	11	March.
„ 13th	Waterval Drift	10	„
„ 14th	Wegdrai and Klip Drift	27	„
„ 16th	Brandvallei	11	„
„ 17th	Paardeberg	5	„
„ 18th	Boer Laager	2	„
„ 19th	Kitchener's Kop and back	6	„
March 1st	Osfontein	4	„
„ 7th	Poplar Grove	22	„
„ 8th	Roodepoort	7	„
„ 10th	Driefontein	10	„
„ 11th	Kaals Spruit	14	„
„ 12th	Venter's Vallei	13	„
„ 13th	Brand Kop	14	„
„ 14th	Bloemfontein	6	„
	BLOEMFONTEIN to—		
„ 31st	Roodeval	12	„
April 1st	Mokesberg	9	„
„ 2nd	Springfield	17	„
„ 3rd	Bloemfontein	10	„
„ 4th	Tempey Farm and back	6	„
June 7th	Kroonstad	175	By rail.
„ 9th	America Siding and back	20	„
„ 14th	Ventersberg Road, &c.	25	„
„ 15th	Riet Spruit and back	15	„
„ 16th	Kroonstad	20	„
August 1st	Doorn Spruit	10	March.
„ 2nd	Belmont	9	„
„ 3rd	Boschkopjes	8	„
„ 4th	Rhebokfontein	11	„
„ 7th	Doornhoek	12	„
„ 8th	Rietzburg	8	„
„ 9th	Venterskroon	14	„
„ 10th	Rensburg Drift	7	„
„ 11th	Across the Vaal and back	4	„
„ 13th	Vredefort	7	„
„ 14th	Vlackfontein	14	„
„ 15th	Scandinavia	10	„
„ 20th	Kerr's Drift	16	„
„ 21st	Wet Kop	14	„
„ 22nd	Gansvlei	10	„
„ 23rd	Kopjes Station	12	„
„ 27th	Vredefort Station	9	„
„ 28th	Shepstone's Farm	10	„
„ 29th	Vredefort Station (and *détour*)	13	„
„ 31st	Springbokvlaagte	8	„
September 2nd	Gansvlei	16	„
„ 3rd	Kristal Kopje	5	„
„ 4th	Roodeval Vlei	6	„
„ 5th	Rhenoster Kop	5	„
„ 6th	Driekopjes	16	„
„ 7th	Blesbokvlaagte	8	„
„ 8th	Tweekuil	15	„
	Carried forward	1,710	

X

Date.	Place.	Distance in Miles.	—
	Brought forward - -	1,710	
	TWEEKUIL to—		
September 9th -	Rhenoster Kop - - - -	13	March.
,, 10th -	Honing Spruit - - - - -	*18	,,
,, 11th -	Boschpoort - - - - -	9	,,
,, 12th -	Paardekraal - - - - -	11	,,
,, 13th -	Hout Kop - - - - -	15	,,
,, 15th -	Welgevenden - - - -	6	,,
,, 16th -	Kroonstad - - - -	9	,,
,, 17th -	Ranjeslaagte - - - -	15	,,
,, 18th -	Blaauwbosch Bank - - -	10	,,
,, 21st -	Kroonstad - - - -	25	,,
,, 23rd -	Hout Kop - - - -	15	,,
,, 24th -	Paardekraal - - - -	15	,,
,, 25th -	Vaalkrans - - - -	14	,,
,, 26th -	Leeuwfontein - - - -	5	,,
,, 27th -	Uitkijk - - - - -	15	,,
October 2nd -	Hartebeestefontein - - -	15	,,
,, 3rd -	Heilbron - - - - -	3	,,
	Total miles - -	1,923	By Rail, 1,217 ; by road, 706 miles.

LIEUT.-COLONEL THE HON. A. E. DALZELL, C.B.
Commanding 1st Oxfordshire Light Infantry.

Lightning Source UK Ltd.
Milton Keynes UK
UKOW06f0653170114

224795UK00008B/168/P